TO DIE IN THE QUEEN OF CITIES

" ...You see, lad, more than nine of every ten soldiers enlist in the field, serve in the field, muster out in the field, and die in the field without once seeing Rome. Only a precious few are ever promoted to some position in the city herself—the high echelons, if you will.

"To serve in Rome, the Queen of Cities, is to be on the top of the pile. And to still be there when you die is the greatest honor of all.

"Of course, lad, that's just the soldier's viewpoint."

Q. Alerian Primus

en route to Rome A.D. 284

TO DIE IN THE QUEEN OF CITIES

SANDY DENGLER

THOMAS NELSON PUBLISHERS
Nashville • Camden • New York

Published in Nashville, Tennessee, by Thomas Nelson, Inc. and distributed in Canada by Lawson Falle, Ltd., Cambridge, Ontario.

Printed in the United States of America.

Library of Congress Cataloging-in-Publication Data

Dengler, Sandy.
  To die in the queen of cities.

  1. Sebastian, Saint—Fiction. I. Title.
PS3554.E524T6   1986   813'.54   85-31009
ISBN 0-8407-5996-7 (pbk.)

PREFACE

"Alien worlds"—science fiction—arcane cultures built by lizardish sorts of intelligentsia. But even those cultures that are the roots of our own sometimes feel alien. The Roman world of the third century A.D. may have been like our modern day in many ways; still, it takes a little getting used to.

In A.D. 287 and on, the people of Milan and Rome felt right at home with a sophisticated system of slavery, a conspicuous military presence, licensed prostitution, and extremes of opulence and poverty. On the streets of Rome, freight traffic was banned in daytime, creating a night-long cacophony of rumbling and clip-clop. Foot traffic crowded the streets by day, though not the feet of the wealthy; persons of importance routinely rode in litters, carried by slaves.

I invite you to enter this intriguing world, to feel as right at home as did the people of that day. The glossary at the rear of this book may help you become more comfortable.

1

Orlestes, surnamed Draco by the seamen under him, was not a timid man. He approached the sea as he approached life—squarely. His Greek fathers behind him for eleven generations, sailors all, knew the sea in her many moods. Their ships had improved immensely in the last few hundred years. The men had little need to.

The sea, albeit sullen, was with him now. One might call this stormy, even dangerously heavy. But with the mainsail furled and the bowsail out he was making way in his intended direction. Therefore the sea was with him.

Neither was Orlestes an incautious man. He looked with pride on the fact that he had never lost a man overboard no matter what the weather. He knew that the sea, regardless of her mood, is unforgiving of carelessness. A safety line stretched the length of the ship. Secured to the neck of the ornately carved goose sternpost, it wrapped around the mast amidships and snugged firmly about the bow mast. Another wave broke over the stern and washed nearly the length of the hundred-foot deck. Orlestes grasped his safety line and made his way hand-over-hand toward the stern, his mind on things other than the pitching deck.

Her width nearly half her length, *Star in Orion* plowed water with a bloated belly heaving, lurching, lunging. A full normal cargo—nearly three hundred tons of wheat—would have kept her running fairly steady. But today she carried rosebushes, onions, and leeks from Spain and her hold half empty at that.

Her flanks, two feet above normal waterline, wallowed keel up to port, keel up to starboard, keel up to port.

"Helmsmen! Bring her in half a league closer to shore. The coast will fall away shortly and we shouldn't lose it."

"Aye, sir." The starboard helmsman nodded forward. "Y've company comin' there."

Orlestes' only passenger was attached to the safety line as a leech locks on between your toes. Slipping and staggering he came, a span at a time. Orlestes noted that both the young man's knees were scuffed.

The grinning helmsman shouted above the wind, "Perhaps y'should string him a line of his own, along the rail!"

Orlestes wagged his head. "Hopeless. Tens of thousands of Gauls and Romans and not a sailor in the whole lot. Ho, Sebastian?"

"Orlestes, friend of my father—"

"I'm considering giving your father a partial refund on your fare. You've spent more time on the rail than you have in your quarters."

"Keep the fare!" Sebastian yelled. "Just put me ashore."

"It's all right, lad. We'll be in Genoa before you know it."

"This wallowing...," the passenger gasped.

"Just a spring squall. It'll spend itself within the hour."

"That's what you said about the last one!"

"And was I not right?" the captain asked.

"Aye! But you failed to mention this squall that followed hard on its heels. No more, Orlestes. I've had enough."

"Sorry, lad, but we've passed Massilia..."

"I don't want to go to Massilia," Sebastian protested. "I want to go ashore!"

"You'll get your sea legs straightway; then you'll—"

Above the snap and clatter of the bowsail, above the halyard thumping the mast, above the creaking groans of rope and wood, above the shrieking wind, rose Sebastian's distraught cry. "I *want off!*"

Orlestes sighed and nodded. "As you will, lad. Fetch your bundle aft."

Sebastian turned away in too great a haste to catch the bemused helmsman's smirk. The captain followed him forward roaring orders. Clion the mate lowered the sail as two hands dropped anchor. Like a languid whale, *Star in Orion* hove to and came about.

Two experienced oarsmen followed the dory over the side astern and steadied it against the port steering oar. With the first trace of eagerness he'd displayed since shipping aboard, Sebastian tossed his bag into the dory and clambered over the side. Haggard far beyond his years, he gripped the dory gunwales with white knuckles. He forced a parting smile to Orlestes, but he did not wave.

Orlestes watched the dory dip and soar shoreward. The Ligurian coast is one long, comfortable sand beach, but the captain knew his dory would not touch sand. Sure enough, the plunging dory was yards offshore when the young Gaul abandoned ship. Now the boy was wading waist deep, holding his bundle high.

Obviously, solid land called to Sebastian even louder than the sea called to Orlestes. And the father was no more a sailor than the son. Orlestes had carried the father on several occasions and every time: "This is the last. No more, Orlestes. I've had enough."

No more. I've had enough. But then, father and son shared redeeming features even if their abhorrence of the sea were strikes against them. Like his father the boy was quick and shrewd. He seemed always to know exactly what he wanted and would spare no sweat to achieve it. And like his father he was loyal—he would give his very life for a friend.

Now the dory was returning, bobbing, prow-up, prow-down, prow-up, prow-down. Orlestes could barely discern his young friend scrambling across the sandy beach. As soon as he raised Nicia, he would post a letter to Sebastian's father. Perhaps if winds and trade were favorable he would return to Narbonne in a month or so and explain in person why Sebastian never reached Genoa. The father would understand.

Orlestes smiled to himself. "May the gods of the land show

you better favor than did Poseidon, lad."

The starboard helmsman tugged his sleeve. "I wager he'll be afloat again within a year, just like his father."

"I take your wager. The father, maybe, but not he. You're standing on the last deck his feet will ever touch."

The dory was nearly here. Orlestes lurched out and grabbed his safety line. "Clion! Put two slaves to the bowsail sheets. She'll be sluggish coming about. Stand by to weigh anchor. We can still raise Ostia three before Ides. The sea is with us!"

"Post coming! Stand aside! Move aside! Post!"

When the post wagon rolled through, it stopped for no one. Leap aside or be run down.

Sebastian leaped aside. The post wagon clattered past him in a cloud of strange and marvelous noises. Had he stayed aboard *Star in Orion* he would doubtless be in Genoa by now, sampling the luxuries that quiet seaside town offered. How glad he was to be walking instead. After three days on solid land—good, hard ground—he still had little stomach and no appetite.

Besides, this was new country. Always before between Milan and Narbonne he had traveled the same route. Whether by sea as far as Genoa or by land along the coast, the same roads took him inland. The Roman highways plunged through from here to there with a single-minded, grim determination. But not this road. This road was built by Gauls. It snaked and slithered through the maritime Alps and now was pouring out into the broad valley, in no distinct hurry to get elsewhere.

The pleasant land was a study in the value of laying farms out by jugerum, square on square. Arrow-straight fencerows traced a satisfying sense of order that mountains could never match. And even though a heavy overcast muted colors and greyed the hills beyond, the country was green—a perky leaf green, not sea green. Apple trees splashed white here and there. They were just blooming up here. Back home in Narbonne their white snowstorm of petals had ended when he left.

Milan beckoned louder, since it was less than three days' travel. He yearned to be back again in the city where he had spent so much of his childhood. As soon as he had greeted his uncle properly he would begin looking up old friends. He could start with the Carullius brothers. No, the Carullii would both be in the army following their father's footsteps. And old buddy Crassius would be spending his days at the Comitia hearing law. Sylvanus—no, he'd gone to Rome. And the girls would surely all be married by now. Sebastian had heard Melita was married.

Melita. She had pressed so close with her tearful good-byes, so warm and close— And foolish little Sebastian, too young and callow to know that he might...Ah well. He certainly knew now. The well-bred girls of Narbonne were not content to live the quiet existence of the province forever. They'd heard those stories about life in Rome—the delicious stories of opulence and intrigue, of excess and thrills. The opulence was difficult to imagine, the intrigues impossible to keep straight. But excesses and thrills—now there was fertile ground for exploration. And the well-bred young men were only too happy to explore with them the ramifications of "thrill and excess." Sebastian could not recall that same attitude in Milan. But then, he had been so young. No doubt he simply hadn't noticed.

The overcast hung murkier. Two bearded travelers passed, walking toward the mountains and Nicia. A farmer ambled by with an unwieldy rucksack of cheese, followed by a litter borne by six weather-browned slaves. The curtains were drawn— probably one of the local landowners.

Sebastian noted that he was overtaking a lone woman. She walked with a slight limp, prodding the road ahead with a staff. He had never seen a walking stick quite so heavy, and carried by a lady at that. She seemed a lady—she did not wear the dress of a prostitute. In fact, she was quite elegantly attired. Her white stola brushed the road at her feet. Her burden, a bulky bundle of kindling, she balanced artfully on her left shoulder, that she might handle her staff with her right hand.

As he drew alongside, Sebastian shortened his stride a bit. The lady's face matched the elegance of her dress. And even better her face was clean, unspoiled by the pounds of cosmetics

11

Narbonne girls seemed to think enhanced their beauty.

The realization hit him like a fist. Of course! No wonder she wielded her staff so, her eyes closed, her head bowed slightly forward. She was blind. In so lovely a face, eyes forever darkened. What tragedy!

Sebastian quelled his initial impulse to walk on quickly and moved closer. "Many pardons, lady. Since we are bound in the same direction I would be pleased to share your burden a while. My name is Sebastian."

Without altering her pace she raised her head toward him. Her eyes were blue, a lovely cornflower blue, and they missed "looking" at him by only a foot or so. She surely had been sighted once.

"You're going to Milan, Sebastian?"

"To my uncle's, aye. I'm from Narbonne."

"I knew I detected the province in your speech. Tell me about your uncle."

"Well, uh...he's a lanky man, but solid; taller than I. Trims his grey hair close. A merchant by trade, a philosopher by preference. The last he wrote he said he was undertaking a detailed study of the sect called Christians. He's forever looking into something new."

"I hear a slight ring of annoyance," the woman discerned. "You don't approve of his intellectual pursuits."

"I admire his inquiring mind very much, but the quicker his interest passes to some other sect, the better. He's too wise and witty a man to be soiling his philosophies thus. But here. I have asked to carry your bundle a while and you haven't replied."

She smiled. "I wanted to hear your voice first. It's the only means I have to measure a man. I am defenseless. More than one traveler would take my bundle and fly. But I discern that you are trustworthy. I would be greatly relieved. Thank you."

"My honor." He scooped the kindling off her shoulder. She straightened perceptibly. He felt immensely warm and pleased with himself.

They walked on quietly. Her staff gritched on the pavingstones. Suddenly she asked, "What are you thinking?"

"The pity that you have no sight."

"I see you better than you realize. May I have your hand a moment?"

Sebastian hastily rearranged his double burden as she extended her arm. He laid his hand upon hers. She ran her fingers lightly across his knuckles, his wrist, his forearms, and withdrew.

"You are young, barely in your twenties at most. And strong. You keep yourself in excellent trim. You are about this tall and your hair is brown. Probably light brown. You wear it a little longer than is the usual style these days. And I will take a wild guess and say your eyes are blue."

Sebastian gaped. "How can you tell?"

"You are accustomed to seeing with your eyes alone. Your voice and the angle of your arm told the height. The texture of the hair on your hand and arm is the key to the hair on your head. It is uncommonly fine, and fine hair flies about and thrusts itself in all directions if it is cut too short. Thus you wear it longer to make it behave. There is no fat, no looseness about the sinews of your hand; hence, the physique. And as I said, the eyes were a guess to go with the hair."

"So you did have sight once."

"Vesta turned her back on me. I fell on the hearth when I was twelve. The infection from the burns spread into my eyes."

"And now you see with your other senses."

"As well you should do, even if your eyes are good."

"Your wisdom is heeded. Thank you, lady."

She smiled. "Have we passed Milestone 38 yet?"

"A few paces ago."

"Oh, dear!" She swung her staff to the left. It thunked against a small tree. "Is this an oak? No. Apple. I smell the blossoms."

"What are you looking for?"

"An oak with two limbs head high. The one facing the road is cut off."

13

"Up ahead forty paces or so."

"Then we haven't missed it." She hurried on, clunking her staff cheerfully.

"Why are you so enthralled by an oak tree?"

"It marks a path. A shortcut. You see how the road arches up to the right over the hill? This little path to the left is steep, but it cuts straight over. Takes nearly three miles off the journey and picks this road up again. However...uh...I can't take the shortcut unless I have a companion. I can't manage my staff and a bundle and a rockslide just beyond the crest—not all at once."

"I'm ready to make my journey three miles shorter if you are."

"I hoped you'd say that. Wonderful! Watch for the path now. It's easy to miss."

There it was, faint but findable. Sebastian led the lady through thick brush. *Why do grass and bushes grow especially lush along roadsides?* he wondered. The way opened. She moved cautiously at first, then with confidence. She followed the track, tapping, as if she were sighted. Amazing!

The way was steep, all right. Carrying both bundles, he was soon breathing heavily and trying to pretend he wasn't. Fortunately, she paused to rest now and then. Suddenly they were standing on the crest. It was a small hill for the road to detour so far around. A Roman road would have plunged straight through. Behind them, farmland and the distant haze of blue mountains shimmered. Before them stretched the level plain and, barely visible in the distant mists, Milan.

"A beautiful view, isn't it." She was facing exactly wrong—toward a rocky knob beyond a tree.

"Aye." He was looking at her, not the haze. She was even more attractive with her face flushed and moist. Tanned skin and rosy cheeks looked so much lovelier than the chalky complexion favored by "fashionable" girls. He felt himself stirring.

She sighed. "Down we go. The track passes between two waist-high boulders."

"Right here. Take my arm."

In courtly manner she laid her arm upon his, pressing her palm against the back of his hand. He calculated briefly and rotated his hand palm upward. She laced her fingers into his and smiled. He hoped she couldn't hear his heart beating. He could.

Now they stood amid an imposing jumble of boulders. Torrents of rainwater probably poured through here during storms. Insects whined around the dank little puddles here and there.

Sebastian mentally picked their route. "All right. Sit down here," he said. He dropped his bundle and her kindling over the side and hopped to a flattop rock below. "Extend your staff to me."

"I don't want to poke you..."

The tip waved near his face. He grabbed it.

"Ah! There you are," she said. "Now what?"

"Scoot forward and slide down. I have you."

She gathered her stola about her legs. With as much decorum as possible under the circumstances she scooted, scooted, gasped, and slid—and she was down. He caught her, held her firmly, steadying her. She stood erect. "Shall we negotiate that next step and then rest a while?"

"Great idea!" He threw the bundles on ahead and hopped down again. This time the drop was not so far.

The lady perched herself as before, on the rim of the flattop rock. Her head suddenly snapped up. "What's that off to your left?"

Sebastian wheeled to look. Her staff jabbed him solidly in the neck, bowling him backwards. The pain buckled his knees and robbed his speech. *Oh, no!* he thought, *She's accidentally hit me, and now she's going to jump and I won't be there to catch her!*

Instead, she came off the boulder at him, straight at him, staring straight at him. Her staff slammed butt-end into his left side. His ribs cracked—he could hear them go. It was no accident. *She's no more blind than I am!* He struggled for his knees but the solid rock, once his friend, turned on him. It attacked him from behind, thumping him on the spine, clunking the back of his head. He vaguely discerned the whistling staff come at his face but he didn't feel it hit.

2

Rain. Gentle, persistent, penetrating rain—the very best rain for the new-planted seed—whispered against the bricks. It whispered louder down the curved-tile gutters on its way to the cistern. It pittered louder still in the puddle at Lavinia's feet. She stood in the farmhouse doorway compassed in gloom, for none of the light from the kitchen could leak through the tight door behind her.

The rain had replaced crickets, nightjars, and all the other welcome sounds of night without really contributing anything pleasant of its own. The rain was nothing more than a noisy sort of silence.

Half a mile distant in the field pond a chorus of frogs tuned up. This was their season. They loved cold and wet. Lavinia despised it. She disliked planting season. She disliked mud, especially when everyone constantly trod it into the house. She disliked milking on chilly mornings when her fingers were half numb anyway. She disliked the clammy feel of her clothes as she worked at chores in the drizzle.

When you came right down to it, she despised everything about farming. She was definitely not her father's daughter. He gloried in the dirt under his fingernails. He spent days repairing aged tools and then boasted of their venerable sturdiness. He sang while he hoed weeds. He complained at staying up all night during farrowing, then lavished the attentions of a grandfather upon the piglets.

Lavinia was trapped. Living on a farm in farm country with none but farmers for friends, she held precious little hope of ever meeting someone with more urbane interests. Farming was the life the Lord had set before her and she would just have to live with it.

The darkness was now too deep for eyes to penetrate. Lavinia' watched with her ears. How could it take her father so long to sell a cartload of fence rails? On the other hand, in all her seventeen years she had never once heard of her father's returning early from such an excursion. Dawdling must be a male family trait. Uncle Taurus was even worse.

At last, cartwheels came critching. Donkey feet tripped smartly. Father usually kept the donkey at a slow walk coming in. *Why the hurry?* she wondered. A bulbous gray donkey head loomed in the blackness. Now she could see her father's massive bulk.

"Vinia. Lyssa. Come out here! I need some help."

Lavinia pushed the door open, shouted to her sister, and stepped out into the rain.

Septus Pollonius gave his daughter a fatherly peck, knocking the hood of her cloak askew. "A good day, Vinia. Sold them all, and for a welcome price."

"How welcome? Enough to buy that boar?"

"Maybe. Is Flumma a mother?"

"Not yet. And where is your cloak, Father? You surely didn't lose your cloak!"

Thirteen-year-old Alyssa came bounding out, the door slamming after her. She carried a lamp but the winds of haste nearly blew it out.

Septus kissed her and she hugged him with her free arm. "Did you happen to bring anything, Father?"

"Oh, Lyssa," sighed Lavinia.

Septus took the lamp, chuckling. "It happens I did. Go tell Galba to drag a pallet over by the fire. And leave the door ajar."

The sparkle in her eyes faded to puzzlement. But one never argued with Father. She yelped the order to her little brother as she arranged the door.

Lavinia followed her father and the tiny circle of lamplight to the back of the donkey cart. Her veneer of sophistication dis-

17

solved instantly in the rain. She hiked her skirts and clambered into the cart.

There was Father's cloak all wet, and wrapped in it a boy. Not a boy, a young man—a full-grown man all curled up. His hand gripping the cloak was icy. *Freezing. Wet and freezing and just look at his poor head!* She tipped his face gently toward the light.

Alyssa hung over the side. "Is he real? I mean, is he alive?"

Septus shrugged. "He was once."

"Where'd you find him?" Alyssa stretched a hand out timidly and touched his cheek.

"Castrella Road, over by the hill. He was wandering out across this field without a stitch on. Dazed. I called to him. He didn't answer. I walked toward him and he dropped like a sack of stones. So I've brought him home to you, Vinia, not because I think you need a husband, but because everyone in this whole district brings you every sick and injured animal they happen to find in some ditch."

Lavinia ignored the barb. She hated to see any animal hurt, and a person even more so. Her father called it an overload of mother-love. Uncle Taurus claimed it was Jesus within her, for Jesus is compassion. She herself had no interest in analyzing her feelings. The compassion was there, and now it boiled up strong inside her.

"Galba? Where's Galba?" Lavinia glanced over her shoulder. "There you are. You run up into the loft and fetch down those extra blankets. Start warming them. Spread one across a chair by the fire and hold the other one yourself, as close as you can without scorching it. Lyssa, draw off some dry-berry cider and heat it for him. Use the iron pot, not the clay one. And put plenty of honey in it."

She glanced up. Alyssa stood motionless by the cartwheel, staring at their guest. Lavinia jabbed her. "Cider, iron pot, honey. Go!"

Alyssa stuck her tongue out. "Bossy!" she called out as she ran inside.

Lavinia wagged her head. *Exasperating little imp,* she thought. *How much pleasanter the world will be when she grows up!* She grabbed the soggy cloak and hauled the young man to a sitting position. He was bigger and heavier than she had guessed. No matter. She was strong, her father herculean. They would manage. Whatever the challenge, they managed. When her mother was stoned for her faith and her older brother torn asunder for his, they managed. They always did.

It was one of the Lord's more practical gifts to them.

His ear itched.

But he was too tired to scratch it. Sebastian wiggled a bit deeper into his cocoon of warm blankets. Even that slight effort made his whole body hurt. Better to just lie quite still and let the Fates direct his course unaided. Behind him the voices of two men discussed the price of hogs in broad Cis-Alpine accents. How could he be so close to his beloved Milan and still feel so remote, so much the stranger? One of the voices moved across the room toward him, talking, laughing. He opened his eyes. A murky ceiling was all he saw, although he detected the dull glow of a fire to his left. He closed them again, intensely weary.

A young woman's voice, sweet and lilting and self-possessed: "Poor Galba. Look. Asleep in the chair. Our busy night finally caught up with him."

"I'll carry him up to bed." The deeper man's voice. "I think our guest is awake there."

Rustles; heavy stomps; Sebastian's pallet bobbed. Perhaps he'd better force himself closer to wakefulness.

She looked much better than any sooty ceiling. Hers was not the cruel and classic beauty of the woman who had bludgeoned him. In fact she was, viewed objectively, a bit plain. But the tranquil face, the lovely brown eyes—his feeling of remoteness fled. He no longer felt like a stranger.

She held out a cup and a perky little girl poured dull brown fluid from an iron pot. Sebastian was going to object that he was not thirsty at the moment, thank you (although indeed he was), but it was too late. The young woman had already temperature-tested it to her own lips and was helping him to a drink. Fortunately, whatever it was tasted much much better than it looked.

There was a comfortable warmth to this place that Sebastian had never experienced before. His parents' home, spacious as it was, felt cold by comparison. His uncle's house was cheerful, orderly, urbane; but not restful, like this. A hulking farmer came stomping down from the loft, anything but silent, and still the place was peaceful. In the midst of teasing and laughter, sedateness ruled. Hundreds of miles from Narbonne and who-knows-how-far from his uncle's villa, Sebastian felt at home. He slept in peace.

It must be morning, Sebastian thought. The ceiling was lighter. He would have turned his head, but his neck was too stiff and sore. *This must be why eyes have corners.* Two windows at the far end of the room glowed with the gray light of an overcast day. The door between them stood open to the morning air. This one room, the familiar plan of a Gallic farmhouse, was, essentially, the whole house. A ladder led to the sleeping loft. A table set about with chairs (no lounges—these people were practically barbarians) marked the dining area near the windows. A sideboard and shelves made the walk-in fireplace to his left seem even more massive. A few embers remained on the huge hearth. They were well banked, ready to ignite the wood that would cook the afternoon meal.

Every pot and utensil hung in its place, each spotless. Even the hearth was perfectly swept. Sebastian envied these people their slaves. His mother longed for service like this from her own house slaves.

There in the far corner was what he was really looking for—the slop jar. Nature was calling persistently, not to be denied. Stiff and sore as he was, he would have to traverse the room to that jar. He started to push the blanket aside when he realized his robber had taken all. Modesty required that he find a covering, perhaps one of the blankets.

Someone rustled. The young girl—the little one—stood beside him, her basket heaped with brown eggs.

"Good morning, sir."

"Good morning. My name is Sebastian."

"I'm Alyssa."

"Pretty name."

"Father says it means a smelly little flower." Her eyes twinkled like Pan's. "Can I get you something?"

"Aye. A man, if there's one about."

She scowled, confused. At last it dawned. "I'll send Uncle Taurus in. He's right outside."

"Taurus. He's the huge bull of a man I saw last night?"

Her eyes twinkled again. "Nope!" She left the eggs on the table and skipped outside laughing.

Sebastian waited long, agonizing moments. Was she pulling a cruel trick on him? She certainly acted like mischief on the hoof. He was about to give up hope when Taurus came scuffing through the door.

Here was a tangled little knot of a man, brown from sun and gray from age. He operated on a tripod system—two T-shaped crutches and his none-to-good right leg. The left leg sickled in a *C* to the right knee.

The gentleman dripped genuine warmth and good cheer. *Why should he be so happy?* Sebastian wondered. "Good morning!" He galumphed over to the slop jar, wedged it into the crook of his disfigured leg, and came bounding *bup-clunk-bup-clunk* across the room.

"Alyssa says you are Sebastian. I am Caius Pollonius Taurus. Here you go. Take your time; you'll not be disturbed."

Taurus cast the blankets aside and Sebastian began the painful process of rearranging his body. "If you are Taurus, who is the massive gentleman I saw last night?"

"Your host, the girls' father, Septus Pollonius Bos."

"Bos! You the bull and he the cow?"

Taurus reached out with a crutch and dragged a chair over. He plunked down, his back to Sebastian, and stretched his leg out. "When we were small, Septus and I, he was much the weaker. Sickly. Always a runny nose. As you know—or perhaps you don't—a cow's nose is constantly wet. She's forever slapping her big tongue up to wipe it. That was Septus. He was Bos, I was Taurus.

"But then illness overcame the bull and left me thus, while he overcame his weakness and grew to...well, as you see. The roles reversed, the names remained. I don't believe his nose has been wet in twenty years."

No bitterness. No envy.

Sebastian nodded. "Alyssa and...who?"

"Lavinia. She and her father are weeding the new cabbage and dusting it. They'll be in shortly."

"Dusting it?" His pallet creaked.

Taurus lurched to his feet. "To kill cabbage worms. Take a jar of lime this tall. Put a double handful of wood ashes in it. Mix it up, of course. And dust your cabbages after it has rained. No worms." He tugged Sebastian's blanket back in place. "Lyssa has been as edgy as a rat in a cat cage, waiting for you to wake up so she can serve you. Put some more of that vile cider down you, I suspect. I warned her not to destroy your ears with prattle, but I best mention it to her again. Can I serve you further?"

"Uh, no...I...fine."

"You want to say something and feel constrained not to. Speak."

"If my father were crippled like you, he would own slaves to carry him about. Your home here is spotless, but I have yet to see a servant anywhere. Do you hide them?"

Taurus smiled. "No, we freed them, soon after we ourselves became servants of Jesus, the Christ. Anything more?"

Sebastian gathered his wits enough to mutter some negative.

Taurus waved cheerfully. "Good day, then." He returned the slop jar to its corner on his way out.

You stupid goat! You supreme fool! To be taken in by that witch yesterday; to walk right into her trap like an ox to slaughter. And then allow yourself to be taken in again; by the Christian cult yet! How could he possibly have felt comfortable in this nest of murdering atheists? How could he enjoy the company of that hideous cripple? For that matter, how could he see anything attractive in that plain, skinny girl?

That is what he had missed in his first perusal of the room—the lararium. He examined every dark corner of the room again, forcing his screaming neck to turn. No lararium. No altar of any sort. You might as well build a house without a roof as without an altar to the lars, for those household spirits protected as much as the roof did, or more. Even northern barbarians kept a little altar to the household gods. But not these people—atheists, to neglect the lars.

He slept most of the afternoon. Taurus came in before dinner and again placed himself at his service. Sebastian made no attempt at conversation.

As before, Taurus settled into his chair, his back to Sebastian, and stared out the door. "You were on your way to Milan, I assume. Do you intend to remain there?"

"No. Not really."

"But you're not going back to the province," Taurus presumed.

"What makes you think I'm from the province?"

"Your speech, lad. Now I also assume you're bound eventually for Rome."

"You assume a great deal."

"Right or wrong?"

"Right."

Taurus nodded. "Thought so. If you wish to appear Roman quickly—that is, not just one more boy from the outlands—you'll speak less through your nose and more from the chest. Like this: lah lah lah lah, as opposed to this: laa laa laa laa. Remember that and you'll shed the province from your speech in short order.

"Now, the styles," the old man continued. "Your hair is right. It's worn longer now in Rome, though not in Milan. The ladies' stolas have gone up a bit, the men's togas down quite a bit. When you have your toga made, have it made long—down to here—at least—and don't let some canny merchant sell you otherwise."

"How do you know so much about all this?"

"Bos is a farmer, skin to core, as a green apple is tart, skin to core. I am not. In the first place, a farmer must be strong—at all ends, to walk. I physically cannot farm. Therefore, what is open to me? I could be a mendicant, but who wants that? So, until a few years ago, I made a business—and a very good business—writing and delivering messages."

"I thought you couldn't walk."

"We had slaves then, remember. A man in a litter doesn't need legs. I carried court orders, death messages, birth and wedding announcements—things of that sort—between private parties."

"The post does that."

"But not with finesse. I specialized in messages requiring great tact. Got to know every corner of Rome, Palatine to the Subura. I advise you to also."

"Why did you quit? You could hire porters if you don't own slaves."

"The nature of the messages, for the most part. For instance. The vice-consul of Milan wants to tell Caesar his superior deserves death. You don't write that in a letter. So I carried his plaint and reasons privately in my own bosom."

"You know the vice-consul?" Sebastian asked.

"Knew. He lost his position—also his head—in that very intrigue. I was lucky to escape with mine. That close call convinced me to seek other employment, so here I am."

"The vice-consul. Was that Cistertius?"

"Aye. He was succeeded by a half-Gaul named Desmontes, who recently retired in order to... You wouldn't catch your breath like that if Desmontes were not a relative. Or at least a close personal friend."

"It may not be my uncle. He never mentioned being vice-consul."

"Caiuses and Septuses are a quadrans for a cartload. How many Desmonteses do you know?"

"True." This time Sebastian tucked himself in.

Taurus hauled himself up on his crutches and pivoted to Sebastian. "As I started to say. The first three days you are in Rome spend on the streets. Prowl the alleys. Learn every inch, every corner; not just the gaudy, but the bawdy and the hidden. Do not mistake my advice for an offer to partake. But know your way around everywhere, from the very first. That knowledge will serve you well. Until later, my delightful friend." He pivoted again and thumped out the door. Sebastian was forced to like the curt and courtly old man in spite of himself.

Lavinia came through a bit later with a handful of something for the stew.

Alyssa bounced in with an armload of firewood. "May we eat out under the trees? It's perfect weather now it's cleared."

"Fine with me. Ask Father."

Alyssa bounced back out. Her strident little soprano vibrated across the countryside. A moment later she bounced back in. "He says yes!" she shouted excitedly as she gathered up bowls and spoons and skipped out the door.

Lavinia stepped back from the hearth, stood erect, and stretched her back. She pulled two large dippers off their pegs, drew water in both, and plumped herself down at the foot of Sebastian's pallet. She handed him one and drained the other herself.

"Lyssa missed her calling. With a voice like that she should be a fishwife."

Sebastian smiled. "Didn't know fish had them."

She chuckled almost soundlessly. "You sound so much better. Now if you feel that much better, you may wish to join us under the trees. It's a short walk. If you prefer to eat here, that's fine. And if you wish one of us to keep you company in here, we would be happy to do that too."

"Why do you people treat me like I'm some kind of a king?"

"Jesus calls us to hospitality. Besides, if He loves you so much He died for you, the least we can do is make you comfortable until you feel like continuing your travel."

"I'm not sure I understand all that, though I certainly appreciate the fruit of it."

"Fruit of it. That's very much the word of God, you know. The Word calls our behavior and attitudes fruits. Fruits of the spirit: love, joy, patience, self-control. Of the flesh: immorality, selfishness, envy, drunkenness, carousing—that sort of thing. Have you had much contact with the Way?"

25

"The *way?* The Christian cult?"

She shrugged. "As you will."

"Only by reputation. And frankly, lady, that's all the contact I care to have."

She smiled. "I thought you seemed too wise to believe everything you hear, especially regarding reputations."

The room darkened suddenly. Bos filled the doorway. As he crossed to the pallet Sebastian felt an uneasy twinge. Here was a very large man, and his daughter was sitting on the foot of Sebastian's bed.

"How's this?" Bos unrolled a tunic and held it up before Lavinia.

"Looks perfect," she assured him. "Ignatio's?"

"Aye. And I gave Claudia those two that Galba outgrew. Her Marcus is nearly the size for them."

Lavinia stood up. "Then I leave you men to your pursuits." She took Sebastian's empty dipper and disappeared out the door with the water jar.

"Here, lad. Try it on."

Sebastian had far less difficulty swinging his legs to the floor this time. Come to think of it, his headache was fading too. The tunic dropped over his head. This hulking Bos was a gentle man. Sebastian couldn't raise his left arm nor tilt his neck back. They struggled together in silence. Then an arm popped through. A few patient squirms, and he was decent before the world.

"Many thanks, Bos. I will return this as soon as I reach my uncle's villa."

"No need, lad. It's a gift."

"But I don't even know this—this Ignatio."

"Nor he you. But he did hear that you needed a tunic. Taurus's would be too short. And truth, lad, you and Taurus both can fit together in one of mine. Now, Alyssa has this grand design to eat dinner outside. Would you care to join us?"

"Aye, thank you."

"Can you make it on your own, or shall I?..."

"I'll do fine. You go ahead."

"Good enough. Oh, here." Bos pulled out a cord tucked in his belt and handed it to Sebastian. The giant scooped the iron pot off the hearth as though it were Alyssa's egg basket. The room darkened again briefly as he strode out the door.

Sebastian belted the cord around his tunic without thinking. He was too muddled to think. The abortive voyage, the abortive walk to Milan, this insane and unfathomable household all churned around inside. His headache was kicking up again. Life had been so simple just a few short days ago. He was up and leaning in the doorway before he realized what he was doing.

Puffy white clouds hung near the horizon. Swallows were dipping about high in the air; their tails snipped open and shut. Blue vaulted sky, distant hills, and squared fields, the smell of damp green grass...Nothing marine—nothing in Narbonne, or the province, or probably even in Rome—nothing at all could match the beauty of this farmland around Milan.

In the middle distance beyond the garden a wood lot came sprawling down off a tiny knoll. Its treetops rustled in the damp breeze. From the sheepcote beyond the house floated a fluttery baaa. A soothing place, this. Bucolic.

Alyssa had spread a cloth by a row of windbreak poplars across the yard, but she herself was nowhere around. Lavinia was setting out bread and a fruitbowl. Septus chunked the iron pot down at the base of a tree. Taurus came galumphing up from the garden with a round-bottom basket wedged in his crook-leg.

Lavinia glanced toward Sebastian. *Coming?* her eyes asked.

He pushed away from the doorframe. His legs worked properly, even if his neck and ribs did not. He chose the corner of the cloth opposite Lavinia and carefully, slowly folded himself to a sitting position.

From nowhere little Galba appeared. To Sebastian's consternation the strange child sat down at his left hand. The boy irritated him. All day Galba had been whisking in and out of the house. Boys are noise machines, but this one was silent: no laugh, no speech, no yelling. When others teased he smiled soundlessly. At least with the boy sitting right beside him Sebastian wouldn't be stared at. The big brown eyes looked up at him once or twice and fell away.

Bos hunkered down beside Lavinia. "Where's Lyssa? This was her idea."

"Checking on Flumma. We'd best not wait."

Bos nodded and extended his arms. Taurus took his right hand and Lavinia his left. *Custom, apparently*, Sebastian mused as he stretched to take Lavinia's left hand. Galba's hand in his was warm and dry. It gripped tightly.

Bos raised his eyes to clouds and swallows. "Lord in heaven, hear our gratitude—for food, for friends, and for life in Your service. In that name above all, Jesus, the Christ."

"Amen!" chorused around—all save Galba.

Lavinia released Sebastian's hand promptly, primly—no flirtatious little squeeze, no casual stroke of the fingers across his palm, no lingering. It was Galba who clung and looked almost ashamed of the clinging, eyes downcast.

"It's here! It's here!" Alyssa's soprano pealed across the yard. She came running around the corner of the house with a white bundle in her arms. Behind her a yellowed old ewe waddled, stiff-legged. Lavinia and Galba jumped up and ran to her.

Taurus tore himself off a chunk of bread as Bos ladled stew all around. "That ewe is as old as Lyssa. If her flanks cave in any deeper they'll meet in the middle. And her teeth—the few still in her head—are as flat as this dish. Every year we're certain she'll die over winter. And every year she blesses us with one or two more lambs." He dipped a bread chunk in his stew and popped it into his mouth.

Alyssa dropped the lamb in his lap. "Is it a boy or a girl, Uncle Taurus?"

"What?! You're thirteen and you ask me that? See to it yourself!"

Alyssa glanced at Sebastian. Her ears and cheeks turned an appealing shade of pink. She sat down suddenly by Taurus and settled the lamb across her legs. "We'll attend to that after dinner. I'm hungry. Have you blessed it yet, Father?"

"It's blessed. Put the lamb to his mother. How can you eat when he can't?"

"It's a *he?*" Alyssa turned the wet and bleating baby on its back for a quick check and set it behind her. "I thought so. It's not a he."

Lavinia giggled. The family roared and all of Alyssa turned red. Beside Sebastian, Galba hissed air in a peculiar way. *Was this the child's idea of laughter?* Sebastian thought. *Detestable!* He studied the boy a moment, then happened to glance across at Lavinia. She was watching him calmly. She looked right through him, reading his thoughts. Perhaps she was a witch of some sort, a specialist in that sort of thing.

She smiled, and her eyes shone with love, not sorcery. "Galba. Tip your head up, please. Way up. That's it."

A clean white scar, its edges only slightly puckered, stretched for two inches across the boy's throat, high under the chin.

Lavinia continued quietly, "The soldier who put him to the sword must have been a raw recruit. The thrust was not deep enough to kill. It missed the veins but took his voice."

"The soldier?"

Bos rumbled, "In the raid that took my elder son. Their mother died three days later in a separate incident. I'm sure you understand you are welcome to stay as long as you care to. But understand also there is an element of risk involved in being here."

"An element of risk you call it!" Sebastian stared at the amiable, composed faces. "I don't believe this. You sit here and eat and talk about losing family members as if they were ticks to be pulled from the ear of some dog. Doesn't human life mean any more to you than this?"

Taurus passed his bowl to Bos for a refill. "You sound perplexed, and I'm sure your headache isn't helping any. But pause and listen. Don't hear what you are thinking but rather what I am saying. Do you understand what I mean?"

Sebastian fought back his anger.

"Human life is infinitely precious to us." Taurus told him. "It extends beyond the body. The body is only the house in

29

which the life resides. The house may perish, but the life continues."

"Impossible," Sebastian scoffed.

"Not at all," Taurus assured him. "What awaits you beyond death?"

"Nothing." Sebastian replied sharply. "And the same for you. The house perishes, the tomb takes over."

"Prove it," Taurus challenged.

"I...well...uh, I've seen death."

"That's the house. What about the life?"

"Departed. Fled and gone."

"True!" Taurus tore off another chunk of bread. "Now listen to the words you just used. 'Departed. Gone. Fled.' Words that suggest the life has transferred, gone elsewhere, but not that it is forever snuffed out. Inside every man, including you, is the hope that death is not the end. It comes through in our speech even when we refuse to declare it with our minds."

"I guess I can see that, but..."

"Have you heard the story of Jesus?"

Sebastian's throat tightened. *Here it comes*, he thought. "A criminal condemned and executed by Rome," he said with contempt.

"And then what?" his host prodded.

"You mean that business that He came back to life?"

"Think about that. While His body hung on the cross, a soldier tested it for life. It was dead without doubt. The soldier knew his job. The Romans who guarded his tomb were handpicked, not like the soldier who botched killing this little boy. They were Caesar's best out of the Guard, not the army. Jesus was dead. Dead and buried.

"And yet, all His disciples (save Judas, of course) saw Him and testified that He was alive again. Over five hundred people. And most of them chose to die rather than recant their story. Think how many have died since then rather than deny Him. For three hundred years, nearly, His church has been persecuted; and it's stronger now than ever."

"You're saying that logic demands He rose again and therefore it's logical to adhere to this Christ."

"Logic and solid evidence. But He doesn't want just your logic. He wants your whole being. Your all."

"That's stupidity, not logic!" Sebastian exploded. "What kind of monster calls His followers to destruction? Give your all to some god you can't see so you can die a hideous death. I said you hold no value for human life."

"Ah!" Taurus sat back with a happy grin. "Here we are full circle. Now listen to this: If life ends in the tomb, Christ is the most foolish of ways. But if life extends beyond the body's death, and Jesus claims to be your only hope beyond death, His testimony bears hearing. His testimony is this: He did not stay dead. That hope inside every man—that hope that there is something beyond the grave—takes its form in Him."

"I want more than some vague hope if I am to greet my torturer."

"What is hope?" Taurus shrugged. "I hope it doesn't rain before we finish eating. I hope the wheat yield is high this year. I hope that pretty little girl who just winked at me will consent to follow me home. I'm not talking about that kind of hope. I'm talking about a certainty that has not yet happened."

"A sure promise."

"Precisely. Couldn't have said it better myself."

Sebastian picked at his bread. Taurus was speaking boldly, so would he. "Some self-made prophet learns a few flashy magic tricks two hundred years ago, so you decide He is God. Well, the Roman government thought differently."

"Not really," said Taurus mildly. He did not seem the least bit offended by Sebastian's insolence. "The government officials acquitted Him four times. But they yielded to pressure by a rabble-roused mob. I'm sure you are sophisticated enough to know that justice is shaped by politics."

"But why? If you're God..."

"Ah, my favorite question! Everything has its price, Sebastian. You pay one way or another. According to the supreme God, the price of sin—that is, wrongdoing and wrongthinking—is death. Your very life. Even in the so-called sacred stories of the pantheon, the gods must pay for their mistakes. So must we."

"And we shall. As you say, one way or another."

"True. Unless Someone else pays for us. Let us say I owe you a hundred aurei. I could never in a lifetime pay such a debt. But Bos here is wealthy."

Bos snorted derisively and mopped up the last of his broth.

Taurus continued undaunted. "Bos pays you one hundred aurei. I didn't pay a quadrans, but the debt is canceled all the same."

"Now you owe Bos. Same debt, new debtor."

"I owe Bos indeed—my very life, for I would have been lost without his help," Taurus confirmed. "And it is exactly that with Jesus. He was sinless but—"

"Impossible!"

"For us, yes. But He managed it—in spite of temptation, I might add. Because He committed no wrongdoing, He was exempt from paying with His life. He had nothing to pay for. Yet He died prematurely for us who could not pay. His life instead of ours."

"Sounds foolish," Sebastian said, dubious.

"Agreed, on the surface. Examine it at depth. How profound it is, how perfect. A voluntary system, for all men have free choice—take it or leave it. A complete system with no additional complications, and it satisfies logic in the bargain."

Sebastian stabbed at a wedge of onion. "So now that you've laid all this faultless logic out before me, you expect me to leap right in and join you."

"Not at all," Taurus ensured him. "As I said, Jesus calls you to the faith expecting that every fibre of your existence be yielded to Him. That doesn't happen instantly except in certain rare and unusual cases. But I tell you this," Taurus stuffed the last of his soggy bread in his mouth, making his speech a bit mushy, "Jesus has great plans for you. I feel it. I sense it all through me. You are very special to Him. Wait and see."

What could he say? Sebastian had always felt himself rather special. His mother did, too, of course. But a dead prophet? He ate faster. His stew was getting cold out here in the breeze, but he wanted to know more about these extraordinary people. At length he asked, "Why did you have to free all your slaves?"

Bos brushed the crumbs off his broad, stubby hands and reached for the figs. "Didn't have to. Just did. They knew the Christ before we did. In fact, it was their lives that first called our attention to Him. One master is enough for any man. They have Jesus. They don't need us as well."

"I have a question for you, Sebastian," said Lavinia. "You obviously own slaves. I thought a man of your position would never travel without at least two or three. Why were you alone?"

"Because, lady, my slaves are luckier than I. Both of them fell ill just before I left. Rather than wait for them or take Father's, I chose to come anyway."

"Perhaps, had they been with you, you would not have been set upon," she said sympathetically.

"Perhaps. But probably not. She could have handled the lot of us."

"*She?*" Bos roared.

"Aye, she. A wicked and deceitful and beautiful lady who feigned blindness to—"

His tale was drowned out by Bos's raucous laugh. The farmer laughed until tears rolled down his cheeks. He sniffed and wiped his nose on his sleeve. Sebastian could feel the redness pour down his face.

Taurus pointed at his brother. "Wonderful, Bos! Wonderful! Your nose is back to its original state—wet as an eel! Now tell us—I know you're not laughing at this lad."

"Aye," Bos paused for another spate of giggling. "Aye, I'm not laughing at you, lad. No, but at those men in Castrella."

"What men?" asked Lavinia. From the way she looked at Sebastian, she obviously shared his embarrassment.

Bos waved a fig in the air. "This fellow showed up in Castrella beaten as badly as Sebastian here. And the same way exactly, especially the bruise on the neck. He, too, was picked clean, every thread and sandal thong. He claimed it was three men jumped him. Three! Then another fellow just recovering from the same sort of blows—the same exactly as yours, I swear, lad—he said, 'Oh? Then they lost one, for it was four jumped me.' Sure as I am Septus Pollonius Bos sitting here eating figs, those two fellows fell prey to—how did you call her?—one wicked, deceitful lady. Three indeed. And four? Bah!"

Lavinia smiled sweetly. "I admire your courage, Sebastian—to speak truth when a lie would provide better refuge."

"I've learned a fine lesson here," said Sebastian between bites. "Never trust a blind woman carrying kindling, and never leave the high road."

Bos gaped, "Indeed? Why I've seen her! A proper lady, not a strumpet."

"That's your opinion. However, when I woke up I found she had left me her kindling, so I suppose she's not totally heartless."

"Left her kindling because she could not carry all. This is excellent! Now that we know the true culprit the garrison need not look for parties of three or four." Bos extracted a fig skin from his teeth with his thumbnail. "Where's Flumma? There she is by the well. Galba, take them back to the sheepcote. Lyssa, you clear the meal here. And no whining. Taurus and I had best get to work on that boar pen. And you, Vinia, take our guest for a walk. Show him about."

"But Father..."

"I expected an argument from Lyssa, but not you. Go. You've the afternoon free. Behave yourself, of course, but enjoy a bit of relaxation."

Alyssa moaned, "Why she and not I?"

"Because she's been up since cock-crow working and she deserves it. Get yourself busy."

Taurus grabbed one last fig and struggled to his feet. Sebastian felt a warm body press close to his leg. Galba was looking up with those big brown eyes. Sebastian grinned. The boy's eyes lit up. He didn't need a voice all that much—his eyes spoke clearly enough. He hopped to his feet and ran to Flumma. He brought her lamb to Sebastian to be patted, rubbed, held. Sebastian admired it for what seemed to be an acceptable length of time and handed it back.

"Go, shepherd. Flumma looks like she wants a nap."

Grinning, Galba slung the lamb over the nape of his neck and jogged off toward the sheepcote. The old ewe tagged along behind with a weary disdain.

3

The afternoon had warmed up, but spring warmth is fleeting. As the sun dropped low, so did the temperature. Sebastian lay stretched out on the crest of the wooded copse he had been looking at earlier. In the branches overhead the breeze rattled dry limbs and wiggled the budding leaves. Last year's leaves smelled pleasantly wet and moldy. Sebastian wished there were a drink that tasted the way old leaves smelled.

A few feet away, Lavinia sat propped against a tree. Its trunk sloped at the perfect angle for a comfortable backrest. Her eyes were closed, but she didn't seem to be sleeping.

He sat up with painful difficulty and scooted a little closer. "Sleeping?"

She smiled without moving. "Now how shall I answer that? Yea? Nay? Ah...Maybe."

"You enjoy teasing, don't you? Don't answer that." He scooted closer. "Girls your age are usually married by now. Are there no suitors or did they all run and hide when I showed up?"

"You think quite a bit of yourself. Occasional suitors, but none lately. Christian girls are poor risks for marriage. We tend to die suddenly, you know."

"There you go again, treating death like a joke."

She turned sad eyes to him, suddenly solemn. "It's no joke." She leaned back again and watched the waving branches. "I often wish the faith were—I don't know—respectable, somehow. At least, tolerated enough so that death is not a constant threat. Even the Jews are less persecuted than we."

"Then why stick with it? Why give up everything for some religious theory?"

"What am I giving up?"

"Your life, for starters. You just said so. And other delights of living. Be honest. The fruits of the spirit you listed for me this afternoon weren't anywhere near as appealing as the fruits of the flesh as you call them."

"I shall indeed be honest. The flesh satisfies only temporarily and then not completely. The fruits of the spirit give lasting satisfaction. Since you haven't yet tried our way of life, you'll just have to take my word for it."

" 'I haven't yet.' Which means you expect me to."

"Oh, I agree with Uncle Taurus."

Sebastian snorted and moved in closer. Conjurers, the whole family. Perhaps they cast some spell to make him like them this much. Strange little Galba. Taurus, simultaneously so repulsive and so winsome. Lavinia here, plain and skinny and exceedingly attractive. He noted the swell of her form beneath her stola, the way her body moved as she breathed. He noted also that her arms were all gooseflesh. She was getting cold sitting here. Why did she not suggest they leave?...Unless she had some other idea in mind....But she'd made no move, no gesture to that end. She was complicated and he preferred things simple.

He took her hand and she jumped, startled. He held on. "Your hands are cold. Why are we just sitting here?"

"Because it's too pleasant to move elsewhere. Anyway, my hands will warm up around June or July."

"Why wait?" he asked with a grin.

"Be patient. Good things take time."

Sebastian tried a fresh tack. "I asked you about suitors. You ask me something."

She shrugged. "I assume a man your age would be divorced at least once by now. Your private life, however, is none of my business, so— How's the province this time of year?"

"You're being deliberately frustrating. I can tell."

"Aye, and I'm sorry I frustrate you. But you just don't understand. I know what you're trying to get to. I may turn away suitors, but I'm not that dumb."

Sebastian nodded grimly. "I'm so glad for you."

She laced her fingers through his. "The bond of marriage, Sebastian, is given by God. When we abuse it by breaking it with adultery or divorce—or ignore it with fornication—we lose more than we gain. But that's not the worst of it. Fornication and adultery displease God. That's the worst of it. There is purity in the marriage union. Nowhere else."

"Lavinia, the gods are inventions, all of them. There may be spirits of some sort—the lars, for instance—but the gods we know—the Zeuses, the Minervas, even the Januses—are man's imagination. Don't miss out on the pleasure of living for the sake of a figment of someone's imagination."

"Man didn't make Jesus. He made us. Man's imagination can't invent the kind of Person He proved Himself to be. The gods of Rome are nothing more than magnified human beings with magnified human faults. He is perfect. Zeus can't save you. Minerva didn't die for you. But Jesus did. He is real and I am happy to postpone the 'pleasure of living,' as you call it, for His sake."

"What you are saying is no, right? Before I even ask the question."

"It isn't easy, Sebastian. You are the most charming, the most open and honest...and I only met you last night. Even when you could hardly breathe, and you were so cold you were shaking, and I was wiping the blood off your face and...I mean..."

"No is no." He unlaced her fingers one by one. Her nails were short, the toll of hard labor. "But I tell you this, Lavinia. Yours is the most gentle and philosophical no I've ever been handed. Beautiful in its directness, pure in its form, firm in its resolve. But a no, nonetheless."

"Are you making fun of me?"

"Absolutely not!" he said firmly. "I can see you believe what you say. I think you're wrong. There is a value in pleasure for the moment. It's one of the reasons for living. But I'm not going to change your mind in an instant any more than you could change mine." He studied her deep and liquid eyes. "True?"

"True. I can't change your mind. But God will." She was so happy she glowed, and he hadn't even touched her. She kissed his knuckles and tucked her legs under her to leap up. She was halfway to her feet when he pulled her down against him. He wrapped around her quickly before she could gain the leverage to unbalance him and he kissed her.

He put much effort and expression into the kiss. Into it he put I-am-willing-to-wait and an expression of this-is-my-token-for-the-future. And within moments deep affection was there, too; affection he didn't realize existed when the kiss began.

She twisted free. The wrench wreaked havoc with his cracked ribs, leaving him breathless. He sat weakly and watched her run through dry, cackling leaves down the hill toward the farm. She paused. She turned and looked up at him a moment, curiously, as a fallow deer might turn to watch the huntsman. Then she scrambled over the fence and was lost from sight.

Sebastian lingered a long while on the knoll. The beauty of the place was sufficient in itself. But that beauty was magnified by the fact that Lavinia had been there. Girls had told Sebastian no before. But always they refused him out of fear or petulance, or perhaps a desire to curry the favor of some third party. Lavinia said no for a remarkable reason—purity itself. She was an unspoiled lily, undefiled. Sebastian would not have thought he could find one.

He wondered how deeply farming was ingrained in her. Was she born to it like her father or as eager to avoid it as Taurus was? Perhaps he could come courting frequently. He couldn't be that far from Milan. Rome could wait awhile. He was strictly a city person. If she didn't mind city living too much...

He decided he had better start back. The sun was nearly down, and he felt unnaturally tired. He could recite the precise location of every lump and bruise on him. A spiteful woman, that, to continue pounding on him after he'd lost his senses. What had he ever done to her? He thought of the stories about the gods. Lavinia was right. They, too, were constantly acting out of spite for some fancied wrong—magnified human faults. How different were Lavinia and her God!

He paused to lean against a thick and charry oak. For one thing, his knees felt wobbly. For another, by parting the head-high bush in front of him he could just see the whole charming farm spread out like a stage setting.

Lavinia should be down there somewhere. There she was, sitting on the edge of the well, drinking a ladle of water. Taurus was crossing to her from the garden, his basket squeezed as usual into his leg. He must have hailed her, for she turned and raised her hand. Beyond the corner of the house came Bos with Galba at his side and a load of rails on his shoulder.

Was that horses Sebastian heard? Surely not. And yet, there they were, out beyond the windbreak by the road. Now what would a dozen horsemen be doing here? He'd better hurry down and tell Bos. Too late. Lances leveled, the Romans were charging forward at full gallop, down into the farmyard. Horror nailed him against the tree, helpless, to watch the unimaginable scene play out.

Taurus realized immediately what was happening. He pivoted to face his murderers and cast aside his crutches. He would not need them anymore. He balanced on his sickle leg and raised his arms shoulder high, waiting. He had to balance a moment only. A horseman's lance lifted him up and dumped him to the ground, a truncated pile of rags. The lance, vertical, swayed back and forth in a lazy arc.

Lavinia! Two horsemen were converging on the well, thrusting their lances where she had been sitting. Their horses blocked his view. The ends of the lances balanced briefly and disappeared down the well. When the horses wheeled and galloped off, the place was empty. It was as if she had never been.

Bos and Galba were parts of a tangle of rails and rags and blood.

Already they had set the house afire. A black crescendo of smoke poured out the windows. Alyssa appeared in the doorway, her skirt over her face. She ran out into the yard and was immediately swept back against the wall by two horsemen. They were jostling each other, competing for the kill.

Now the barn began to crackle. A lick of flame brightened its doorway. Horsemen churned everywhere, chaotic and yet efficient in their chaos. There was no escape. They jabbed their lances into the hay ricks, into sacks of grain. They drove the animals out into the yard, herding them into a tight knot. Flumma and her lamb were lost in swirling dust and legs. Four horsemen moved the animals out to the road. Flumma tried to turn back and they prodded her forward. Her tiny one had disappeared.

The remaining horsemen patrolled back and forth, torching the outbuildings, toasting each other with wineflasks saved, no doubt, for this occasion.

The sun slipped out of sight just as the fire broke through the roof of the house. Sparks and flame burst up through the smoke—bloody, gaudy red.

Sebastian's wobbly knees collapsed. He oozed down the rough bark, grasping for something solid. But not even the oak tree was solid now. It wavered, undulated, and casually stepped aside, leaving him all alone. He sank to the brown and bitter duff, to dank dead leaves from yesterday.

The whole world was out of control. He could not control his violent shaking or his racking sobs. They ripped his ribs apart, and he could not control his mind enough to feel the pain. Destiny was beyond control of the gods. The Christ could not control the suffering and death of His own.

Because gods are ineffectual, the world was gone in a blaze that howled to heaven, gone down a blood-poisoned well.

It was all gone.

Desmontes stretched his lanky body out on his pallet. He felt weary from mind to bone. He drew a deep breath and closed his eyes. They burned. It had been a hard morning, arguing and haggling. He hated haggling, but it was, after all, the most important part of merchandising. Tomorrow perhaps he would take it easy. No, tomorrow he must meet with Melitus. Melitus was not a relaxing person to meet with. Perhaps the next day, then. His mind drifted into that soothing suspension that immediately precedes sleep.

"Master. Sebastian is here."

"Not now...what? Sebastian?"

"Aye, master."

"See to his needs. I'll be there shortly."

"Forgive me, master, it would be wise for you come to him directly."

Desmontes opened his eyes and studied Dexter's black face. He had told this slave no intrusions, none at all. And yet, if Dexter said—the little African possessed a wisdom beyond his years, a trustworthiness.

Desmontes sighed. "Very well. See him into the peristyle."

Five years. When Sebastian left he had been training daily at the baths, trying to make his laggard little body grow faster. Had he gotten his growth yet, or would he be forever short and dumpy like his mother? Desmontes picked up his toga and dropped it again. Why dress up to meet a boy more your son than your nephew? Because he may have someone with him, that's why. Desmontes should have asked if he was alone, but he had been too nearly asleep to think. He flipped the toga corner over his shoulder and stepped out into the peristyle.

The boy had indeed gotten his growth. He filled the doorway on the far side of the peristyle. He filled the doorway as tall as Desmontes and, yes, a bit wider. He was even more strongly muscled than his father. And yet he looked so forlorn there. No cloak, no sandals...and his face carried all the sweat and dirt and sorrow in the world.

"My boy!" Desmontes extended his arms and started across the tiled floor. Sebastian took a few halting steps toward him, stumbled, and started running. The strong young man-body wrapped around Desmontes, but a little boy's sobs shook him. The tears put gray watermarks on his toga. What manner of greeting was this? Desmontes felt his own eyes brimming in spite of himself. He glanced at Dexter. The black boy turned away, his cheeks wet.

Desmontes could think of nothing to do save hang on. So he clutched the lad and waited. He remembered when Sebastian was seven and his puppy died. And the boy's first real fist fight when he was nine—the only one he ever lost. The sobbing ran its course. The passion slowed.

"Dexter, prepare the bath straightway. Then run over to Claudius and tell him I wish the use of his masseur. Straightway now."

"Warm, master?"

"Tepid. He's a bit feverish. Tepid is best. Bella is to have dinner waiting immediately thereafter." Desmontes stepped back, his hands on the boy's shoulders, to study him at better length. "Lad, you look like forty miles of abandoned siegeworks. I rejoice to see you even thus. Welcome home, son."

"Thank you, Uncle. I'm sorry I...I'm afraid you just have to take my word; I'm happy to be here."

"Not as happy as I that you're here. They've been a long five years without you. Come! Let's begin at once the arduous task of pasting you back together. Look at your feet. And your face is a mess. What happened to your neck there? Given the chance, I'll sink Orlestes' boat for letting you be used so shabbily. I'll wager much has happened to you in a brief time, and most of it disastrous."

Sebastian drew a shuddering breath. "I have always admired your gift for understatement, Uncle."

Desmontes ushered his nephew into the bathing room and paused to draw the curtain. Dexter knelt at the edge of the pool swishing water as his twin poured from the hot water jar. It was a simple matter to tell the two boys apart. Dexter carried a white brand on his right hand, Sinister on his left. The two boys nodded in a jerky little bow and disappeared out the curtain.

Sebastian sat a moment on a bench, his elbows on his knees; just sitting, staring at the jiggling water. He loosed the cord around his waist and cast it aside. "You bathed, Uncle?"

"Shortly before you arrived." Desmontes sat down on the

other bench and pulled his toga off. *Ghastly garment. Why can't the rulers of the earth invent some decent clothing?* he thought in passing.

"Uncle. I hear you were vice-consul after Cistertius."

"True."

"And that you retired."

"Also true. For a half-grown pup you have good sources. The vice-consulship is common knowledge. The retirement is not."

"Why?"

"I'll explain in good time. We have five years of conversation to catch up. This is a major adjustment for me, you know. You left a boy and return a man, my equal. More than equal in some respects, I judge."

Sinister re-entered with a tray of oils and lotions. He tugged and pushed and otherwise attempted to help Sebastian disrobe. The job took awhile. Desmontes stood up and circled to the other side to see why Sebastian could not raise his left arm. *Grief!* He'd seen healthier ribcages on sides of raw beef. Sebastian slid carefully, gratefully into the water, letting it cover his body.

A frightening thought struck Desmontes. "Sebastian. Orlestes didn't hang his boat up on some rock, did he?"

"Not as I know. I abandoned ship just beyond Massilia when the deck refused to stand still. I am no sailor, Uncle, nor will I ever be."

"Nor I, but your father gets foolish every year or two. If God wanted man to take to sea He would have provided us with fins."

Sebastian sat upright, staring. "One God, Uncle?"

"I wrote you that I was making a study of a certain religion. I'll have to show you what I learned. But later. Did you sleep at all last night?"

"A little, I think, around third watch. Most of the night I traveled. Walked a while, rested a while, walked. I wanted to get here."

"And I assume you haven't eaten."

"No."

"Then you'll eat first, sleep second, and talk third. Tomorrow we will get you out and moving so you don't freeze up like a rusty axle. I have a lunch appointment with Melitus. Come along with me and marvel at how little the old curmudgeon has changed in five years."

"I doubt time stood still for his daughter."

Desmontes snorted. "Hardly."

Dexter appeared. "The masseur is here, master."

Sebastian stood up dripping and stepped out. Both Africans were on him instantly with towels, rubbing him down briskly, but patting carefully where there were bruises. Desmontes took care to keep his own body tight and trim, but his nephew's excelled.

Desmontes sighed in a sudden surge of contentment. Tonight he would hear the news from his brother's house. He would learn all about Sebastian's adventures and misadventures. Then he would explain to his nephew about this religion of one God and one savior. Sebastian would not accept it at first. Like his father, he was conservative. But he'd come around.

Sebastian stretched out prone on the massage table, closed his eyes, and said with a sigh of contentment, "It's so good to be here."

4

He had just stepped into the past. Sebastian remembered every tile, every detail of the garish frescoes that graced Melitus's villa. Nothing had changed. Like everything else that belonged to Melitus, the atrium was just a bit larger than anyone else's. The same female houseslave, now graying and pudgy, led them out into the peristyle. It was just a bit greener than anyone else's. In the center the fountain danced just a bit higher.

In the shade at the far end sat two women, a baby playing at their feet. Melitus rose from his chair by the fountain and turned in greeting.

"My friend and benefactor, Desmontes. Welcome to our home. You, ah, didn't mention bringing guests. Your friend here...who is this? Not Sebastian!"

"Greetings, Melitus, and greetings from my father. I'm glad to see you again. Except that you look more distinguished, you haven't changed a bit. And except for those new cast-tile rain-spouts, neither has your house."

"Remarkable that you should notice them! Imported, you know. Delightful surprise! Come!" Melitus still had his old phony air, tart one moment and unctuous the next. His sharply pointed nose still contrasted grotesquely with his rotund body.

Like a helmsman Melitus grabbed Sebastian's elbow (fortunately, the right one) and steered him to the fountain. "I trust you are in business with your father now. How is the good man?"

"Well, thank you. I was with him, but I've left Narbonne for good."

"Fine. Nothing worthwhile out in the province."

"My father's out in the province."

"Well, of course...I didn't mean...Desmontes, let us complete our business straightway and save lunch for conversation untrammeled by finance. Sebastian, hie yourself over there and greet the women. Good lad." Melitus weighed anchor and launched Sebastian off in the right direction. No, Melitus had not changed a minuscule bit.

The women. Very well. Sebastian recognized one of them, Melita's mother. He was shocked to see how much she resembled that dastardly woman on the Castrella road. Same classic features, same blue eyes, but a face older by twenty years. She rose as he approached. She'd settled a bit in the hips, but not much. Sebastian extended his hands.

She took them and pressed her cheek to his. "Ah, Sebastian, you're magnificent. I always said you would grow up to be Adonis."

"And you, lady, resemble Juno just as much as ever. How is Melita?"

"Ask her yourself." The woman nodded toward her companion.

If Sebastian had changed as much as Melita had, it was a marvel that Desmontes recognized him at all. She was gorgeous. The pimples were gone, that pockmark on her cheek buried beneath make-up generously applied. Gone, too, was her flat, beanpole shape. Long gone.

"Juno has a serious rival." Sebastian dropped to one knee, took Melita's hand, and kissed it. He had watched his father do that occasionally, and had been impressed with the courtliness of it.

Melita appeared equally impressed. Her eyes danced. She tipped his face up and shook her head sadly. "Sebastian, Sebastian, fighting again. Look at your face. And your neck. Will you never learn?"

He stood up. "Believe me, lady, I have learned. I won't even tell you who my opposer was."

"Or who won?"

"And bruise my reputation even more than my body? Let the local swains think I can still beat them."

Her mother rose regally. "I believe I should keep a closer eye on lunch preparations. Will you excuse me?"

Sebastian nodded toward her. She graced him with a cold smile and flowed off into the back somewhere. A slave set a chair close beside Melita; Sebastian sat down.

"If you fear for your reputation, you must be intending to remain in Milan," Melita said.

"No plans yet. I just got here." Sebastian casually picked up her hand again. Her nails were long—grotesquely long like eagle talons—with a delicate red flower painted on each. Her soft skin looked unnaturally white. The comparison was obvious and Sebastian decided he liked tanned, work-worn hands better. But then again...

"Desmontes has filled you in on all the news, no doubt."

"Actually, no. I arrived late yesterday, bathed, ate, and fell promptly asleep. Tiring journey. We talked a bit this morning on the way over, but nothing consequential." He shifted position to accommodate his ribs better. "So what's new, Melita?"

"In five years, a great deal, m'love." She laughed. "M'love. Remember when we used to sneak about and call each other 'M'love'? And we didn't even know what it meant. I was true to you, you know. You were the only boy I permitted to explore me. I am very proud of my fidelity."

"Obviously. And except for Celia and some girl whose name I can't remember, I was true to you."

"Celia! Why, you lecher!"

"We're discussing the news."

Melita smiled graciously. "I forgive your indiscretions, all of them. Generous, am I not? The news. Remember Marcus Cannius?"

"Painfully. I used to fight him weekly, on the average. Twice on holidays."

"He is the father of little Marcus there."

Sebastian realized he was gaping and hastily rearranged his expression. "I heard you were married, but not to whom."

"Then you haven't heard the latest. I am also divorced. Little Marcus here goes to his father as soon as he's weaned." She shrugged. "Then, I suppose, I start over. And you? Surely some girl has captured your heart by now." She paused. "And recently. You know, I've often heard of a cloud passing across someone's face, but I never saw it until just now. What's her name?"

"Lavinia, and she's gone, and she was not the least like you. Not the least. Tell me more news."

The gray houseslave announced sonorously, "Lunch is served."

Melita stood up. "Henna, the baby. Come, Sebastian. It's just as quick, and much cooler, to go to the dining room the back way." She led the way into a dark corridor. She turned so suddenly she nearly tripped him. She wrapped her arms around him as naturally as if the five years were five hours. Her body pressed against him just as warmly as he remembered it at their parting. But her kiss had matured immeasurably. This curious mix of the familiar and the new intrigued him.

She relaxed against him. Her hands slipped casually down his back. Strictly by way of experiment he let his own right hand slide down to the swell of her hip. She pressed closer. So she was starting over.

He had often contemplated what his return to Milan would be like, and Melita had been a part of those contemplations. But the reality was nothing at all like his anticipation. Life was unfolding surprises more rapidly than he was prepared for.

Sebastian reached out, hesitated, and chose. He would taste the creamy yellow cheese this time. This was the first meal in three days where he and Desmontes were able to recline together and just talk, the two of them. It had been a delightful three days, though—lounging in the baths, greeting old friends and acquaintances, catching up on the news, entertaining and being entertained. The wounds were healing under the balm of old memories. Just to ensure that the wounds were not ripped open, Sebastian neglected to mention the Pollonius farm at all.

"...Of course, Cestertius had it coming. He'd earned his execution ten times over. Still, it was unfortunate that it should occur as it did." Desmontes paused for a sip of *mulsum* before continuing. Sinister refilled his goblet. "Have some more of that Geneva. Excellent this year.... That left a gap, you see, that neither party could fill without revealing their hand in the whole grisly business. Since I belong to neither faction, they prevailed upon me."

"You were the only disinterested person in the whole city of Milan." Sebastian smiled.

"Give or take a few. Miletus would have loved the job—and botched it miserably. But he's a red winger by association if not conviction. Sertius Cannius remains aloof of both factions simply so he can play one against the other to his own advantage. You can imagine how...."

"Melita's father-in-law, you mean. Sertius Cannius."

"Ex-father-in-law. Messy affair. Both parties very careless in

48

their choice of paramours and assignations."

"I thought an adulteress is unable to remarry legally."

Desmontes waved a hand. "Oh, I suppose that's the law. But it only operates on the indigent, who usually don't bother with legal marriage anyway. When you have as much money as Melitus, you adjust the law to fit. She'll find some influential sucker. How old is the girl, anyway?"

Sebastian calculated briefly. "Seventeen, now. You still haven't explained why you retired."

"Ah, that. Well, you see..."

Dexter appeared in the doorway. "A guest, master. Marcus Cannius."

"Show him in." Desmontes scowled. "Perhaps he's calling on us for his father—business of some sort. But Marcus?"

Sebastian shrugged. "He's the only citizen left in Milan that I haven't bumped into yet, deliberately or otherwise. Perhaps..."

The curtain parted. Marcus Cannius had always been a little larger than Sebastian, though not quicker. He was now immensely larger. Only his face remained as ever—tiny, snapping black eyes close-set beneath heavy brows. He had not lost his perpetually sullen scowl.

"Greetings to you, Desmontes, and greetings from my father. Sebastian."

"Marcus." Sebastian crossed and extended his arm. Marcus gripped it hard. *He must work out for hours daily,* Sebastian judged quickly.

Desmontes waved toward the lounge Sinister had moved in. "Greetings to your father and welcome. Join us."

Marcus reclined cautiously, as if expecting a dagger to leap out of the cushion. He received a goblet of *mulsum* and raised it. "To the host."

Sebastian raised his own goblet simply to be mannerly. He realized immediately he hadn't missed a thing in not seeing Cannius until now; he disliked the fellow as much as ever. He wondered if Cannius still had his penchant for picking fights for no reason.

Cannius was speaking. "...You must have heard, then, that there is a move afoot to unhorse Numerian."

"If I ever heard such a rumor I have forgotten it," Desmontes replied. "I have retired from intrigues of that sort, young Cannius."

The beetle brows pushed closer together. "As I said, a move to depose Numerian. The army, of course. But a successor is unclear. Various *legati* have been mentioned, and I'm sure each legion has its favorite. But certain of us feel it is time to install a civilian Caesar, a leader from the people. I realize this is hasty, but we are gathering a petition of names in the next day or so—all prominent citizens, of course—of which I have a copy here," he said, indicating the parchment he was holding.

"The army is from the people, essentially. Your plan sounds politically naive already. Go home and study the structure of power in the empire," Desmontes advised.

"As I was saying. This petition, on which we seek your signature, will show that the real power is still in the people. The real power behind the army, and—"

"And I am no longer in the power game. I am immersed in other pursuits which leave no time for the sort of political finagling you're talking about. I am—how would you say it, Sebastian?—I am politically inactive."

"Blood of Zeus you are! You may have gone underground with your machinations, but you're still—"

He stopped as Sebastian tapped his arm. "Excuse me, Marcus. Don't do that again."

"What?"

"Call my uncle a liar where I can hear you. It's dangerous to your well-being. Where I can't hear you, either, as that goes. Should word trickle back to me—"

Desmontes raised his hand. "Ho, boys. None of that, both of you. The matter is closed. Let us open another."

Cannius waved his rolled parchment. "You refuse, then, to add your name to those seeking responsible government?"

"If you choose to create a Caesar, more power to you. But you must do it without the name of Desmontes Theosus."

Cannius stood. "Then invoke the blessings of the gods upon our efforts."

"That I will not do either. You must petition the gods on your own behalf."

Cannius's face twisted into his version of a smile. "Perhaps I should pay better attention to rumors of your new religion. I hear you are making dangerous affiliations."

Sebastian stood because his uncle did. Desmontes locked Cannius eye to eye. "Dangerous? Let me explain danger to you, young Cannius. I am not politically active. That means I am neither ally nor antagonist. Count yourself fortunate that you have no opponent in this house, for on any ground I am a formidable adversary."

Cannius lost the stare-down almost immediately. He wheeled to Sebastian. "What about you?"

"What about me?"

"What are your ties, provincial, if any? Your affiliations?"

Sebastian felt his blood rising. "Marcus, you know we've been squabbling our whole lives, and we both bear the scars to prove it. I don't like you any better than I did five years ago. Or ten. Raise your hand against Desmontes and you'll find me on your throat. But for myself, I will not deliberately oppose you politically—or in any other arena, for that matter."

"A noble speech. But you needn't wear the white for my sake. You see, I know you were on Melita's doorstep within hours of your arrival, so I know just how noble you really are. I also know—"

Desmontes cut in. "His presence in the house of Melitus was my doing, the circumstances dictated by chance. Neither of us knew she was there."

"Of course." The twisted smile came back. "As you say, Desmontes, you have no time for intrigues, no desire to set up either caesars—or nephews. A noble pair."

"Sebastian, sit down! Now!" Desmontes shouted as Sebastian moved toward Cannius.

He didn't sit, but he stepped back half a foot.

Desmontes continued, firm and even, to Cannius, "Like

you, the lad is young and rises to bait more readily than I. You are leaving my house today still under the aegis of my friendship. My advice to you is to take care that things stay that way. Go in peace, young Cannius, and greet Servius for me."

Cannius stood a long moment, his burly hands opening and closing. He paused at the curtain on his way out, then turned. "Don't get the idea I'm jealous, Sebastian. Not at all. You two deserve each other." He disappeared beyond the curtain. Sebastian glimpsed Dexter following Cannius to the door.

When he was sure Cannius was gone, Sebastian said, "I trust, Uncle, you don't mean that 'aegis of friendship' business literally. That is your enemy as surely as I am your nephew."

"Aye, I meant it. I have been lately constrained to love my enemies. What better place to start than the bottom of the barrel?"

"Love your enemies indeed. Your philosophies occasionally take a whimsical turn. But this turn is deadly."

Desmontes stretched out on his lounge and drained his goblet. "Sebastian, you're an ass."

Sebastian reclined across from him. "Thank you. I have always trusted you to see me as I am."

"You needn't be sarcastic. I mean it in all affection. I refer to the fact that you were ready to defend my honor by taking on that muscle-mind right here and now. A stupid presumption. Until those ribs knit, Sinister here could best you in a fair fight. And Cannius doesn't fight fair."

"Neither do I. How do you think I won all those years?"

Desmontes' laughter rolled like thunder. He reached out to Sebastian. For lack of knowing what to do, Sebastian extended his hand.

Desmontes grasped it warmly, lovingly. "My boy, my son, you will never know how rich you make my life, nor how deeply you gladden my heart." Desmontes leaned back and chose a date from the fruitbowl. "And now let me explain what I have learned in my studies of theology—of gods and the One God and a savior, the Christ."

The following evening, damp and overcast, promised still more rain. Desmontes and Sebastian rode reclining on a litter borne by eight slaves. Sebastian disliked bobbing litters almost as much as Orlestes' boat. He rode with his uncle because it pleased his uncle.

He had hoped life would slow down a bit until he could sort it out, but it kept rushing faster. Last night his uncle had spent hours explaining about the Christ. With his usual thoroughness, Desmontes was reading every scrap of literature he could lay hands on. He owned two of the four accepted biographies of the Christ ("But I'll find the other two—I want Tatian's *Diatessaron* too"). He spread the writings of the Hebrew prophet Isaiah out in front of Sebastian and explained in detail how the Messiah's credentials had been established a thousand years ago. "Now this is Paul's writing. Remarkable man. You'll like him..."

Sebastian had seen this sort of enthusiasm in Desmontes before. But always in the past, the enthusiasm waned as the lanky philosopher analyzed the heart of whatever he was studying. This time the enthusiasm waxed brighter and brighter. That meant a great deal. He had found what he was seeking.

Lavinia knew the Christ emotionally. Personally. And here was Desmontes, equally enthusiastic about Jesus on an intellectual plane. It was a telling commentary on both persons, but even more so on the Christ. If this Jesus really did meet the greatest needs of each person's temperament, how would He appear to Sebastian, were he to embrace the religion?

Sebastian had remained carefully noncommittal during Desmontes' discourses. He must have time to consider. He would not yet admit that his uncle's scholarly demonstrations filled in the second half of a picture, the first half of which had been painted in fire and blood.

Desmontes poked him. "You haven't heard a word I said."

"You're right. My mind was wandering. Sorry."

"I was just saying that I can't wait for you to read these books Demetrius owns. They will reinforce what I was showing you last night—that the Messiah proved Himself in many ways—

the Jewish writings, the testimonies of the faithful, the writings that have come out since His death and resurrection, the...Ah, here we are! There, I summarized in two sentences what I was babbling on about for half the trip. I must be more careful and edit my speech. Save all manner of time and energy."

The house looked like all the others. The iron gate stood open. Demetrius must be expecting them. A slave appeared, backlighted by torches beyond. Sebastian could not see his face but he felt a chill. Fear?

"Desmontes and Sebastian to see your master," the uncle announced.

The slave turned, and they followed him into the atrium.

Sebastian's feet and mind stopped cold simultaneously. Without thinking, he and Desmontes swung around back-to-back in defense against the forest of drawn swords around them. Soldiers! How many? A dozen? The farmhouse, the blazing house and wagging lances, came back with full force.

He felt strangely safe backed up to Desmontes. The tall philosopher was a splendid fighter when the need arose; as he had said, a formidable adversary at any time.

His uncle's voice rolled like oil across the room. "I am Desmontes Theosus. My nephew Sebastian is from Narbonne. Why have you drawn swords against us who are citizens of Rome?"

"Why did you come here?" The voice came from beyond Desmontes—Sebastian couldn't see him.

"It's poor rhetoric and even worse logic to answer a question with a question."

"Answer!"

Sebastian loosened his cloak and let it slip from one shoulder. Desmontes' voice hesitated. "I came to see Petronius."

"Petronius who?"

"Tullus Petronius Pincus, the master of this house. Who else?"

"The master of this house is Demetrius Antipater, and I think you know that."

Desmontes cocked his head toward his nephew and said, "Sebastian? We followed directions correctly, did we not?"

"Don't ask me. I just got here. Your streets look all alike to me." Sebastian ran his vowels out through his nose as Taurus had discussed, the better to sound provincial.

The centurion stepped around to get a look at Sebastian. The voice now had a form. He was a head shorter than Sebastian and three spans broader—a square box of a man, solid and every inch a fighter. Sandy red hair crept out from under his helmet. Apparently he hadn't shaved today; his chin stubble was pinkish red and almost silky. "Narbonne. The cult is strong there, I hear."

"Depends. Which one?" Sebastian said evenly.

"You tell me."

"You're talking riddles. There're a thousand cults in Narbonne."

The centurion raised a hand, a hand as square as the rest of him, with stubby fingers all nearly the same size. It was not a threatening move. He simply tilted Sebastian's head a bit to get a better look at his neck.

The centurion smiled, amused. "Less than a fortnight ago, I judge. Must have been an interesting fight. What other marks do you carry from that fight?"

"None I care to display."

Desmontes' voice over his shoulder suggested, "Show him your ribs, lad. They're a sight worth seeing."

Sebastian scowled. Desmontes must have had some purpose in saying that. "Very well, Uncle. But because you asked, not he." It took a moment to drop the corner of his toga, to loose the belt, to raise the hem of his tunic.

A quick glance seemed to satisfy the square little man. "I'll be polite and refrain from asking who won."

Another, apparently second in command, was barking at Desmontes. "Where does your group meet?"

"My group? Soldier, I have heard nothing but silly questions since I walked in here. Ask a proper question couched in proper Latin and I will be happy to answer it to your satisfaction."

"Don't play word games with me, sly-mouth!"

Out of the corner of his eye Sebastian saw the soldier's arm swing upward. He heard Desmontes grunt—had he been struck or was he striking back? Sebastian gripped his loose cloak and swung it wide. It caught the man in the face and entangled his arm. Sebastian followed behind it and struck the soldier down backhanded. He yanked the toga off his shoulder into the sword arm of a second. The man fell backward in a tangle of white wool.

Sebastian kept moving, smashed into a third, but something caught his shoulder and the side of his head. He was hurtling. A splintering crash by his ear sounded like a small table shedding legs. He slammed into a cushioned seat. The seat tipped backward gently and rolled him out onto the floor.

He lay with his eyes closed a moment, listening, waiting for his muddled wits to reassemble, hoping his uncle was not injured.

Above the confusion rose his uncle's voice, reassuring and firm. "...not acting in his own defense but mine! You know as well as I the illegality of raising a hand against a citizen before charges have been declared."

The centurion's voice cut off Desmontes' argument. More noise and confusion, then hands grasped Sebastian's tunic and hauled him to his feet. He expected his uncle's face before him but it was the centurion's. He studied Sebastian eye to eye, steadying him until he recovered his balance. Very well. Marcus Cannius lost such matches quickly, but Sebastian could stare back with the best of them.

Without breaking his gaze the centurion extended a hand toward a subordinate. "The censor," he commanded.

A soldier plunked a brass censor into his hands. Its acrid smoke nearly brought tears to their eyes.

"Let's see you burn incense to Caesar, lad," the centurion ordered.

Sebastian recognized the request—one of the two tests to reveal a Christian. Christians refused to worship gods other than their own. Sebastian had worshiped Caesar a thousand times. There was nothing to it. You didn't even think about it. And suddenly, now he could not. And yet, he must. If he didn't...His ears were still ringing, drowning out his thoughts.

Sebastian took the warm censor in his hands. "Gladly. At what altar?"

"An altar. Aye. Ah, here. The lararium will do." The centurion crossed to the niche and stood waiting.

Sebastian realized for the first time that most of the room's light came not from torches but from a pile of burning books and scrolls beside the impluvium. His head finally started to clear as he walked over to the lararium. He studied the niche a moment, then turned and held the censor out to the centurion. He must choose his words very carefully now.

"If a man came into your home and made love to your wife simply because she happened to be the nearest woman around, you would not think kindly of that man. Let him go to the woman who is his own or not at all.

"This altar belongs to the spirits of this hearth and home, the gods of this house. Not Caesar. I will be happy to honor the lars here any time, and I will burn incense to Caesar on an altar dedicated to that purpose. But I will not offend these lars by borrowing their niche on behalf of other gods. If indeed this household is of the cult of Christians, these poor lars are offended enough already."

The centurion's mouth arranged itself into an unreadable smirk. Silently he took his censor and crossed to Desmontes.

"You, sir. Deny before me the name of Jesus the Christ."

The other test.

Desmontes showed no hint of fear or worry. In fact, he looked bemused. He shrugged and spread his hands. "Whatever you wish, Centurion. Uh, I don't remember hearing it. What did you say that name was again?"

"I said, deny the na—" The centurion stopped, drowned out by guffaws. He laughed himself. "You are masters of words, both of you. I envy your gifts of speech. Your manners, your attitudes—the fact that neither of you is afraid to jump right into a fight—young Sebastian. That is your name? Aye. Sebastian. You must learn to restrain yourself when the numbers are so hopelessly against you. No wonder your side looks like an accident in a slaughterhouse. Incidentally, it will heal faster if you bind it—immobilize it—so the bone ends can't work on each other." He waved a square hand. "You may go, both of you."

Sebastian hesitated because Desmontes was not moving. His uncle smiled. "Thank you. May I ask two questions first?"

"Say."

"First, you handled the situation with authority and good humor. I appreciate that in a soldier. So often the sword brings with it a dour sense of duty that dulls all the sparkle. I go to Rome after ides next and I wish to commend you before Lucinus, who is a friend. What is your name?"

"Quintus Alerian Primus, Third Cohort. You know Lucinus. You were in the army?"

"Until I took ill on the Rhine. They mustered me out so I wouldn't die on the payroll. But then I disappointed everyone concerned, except me, by recovering. May life reward you well, Quintus Alerian Primus." Desmontes extended his arm and Primus took it smiling. "My second question. Can you direct me to the house of Tullus Petronius?"

The centurion grinned. "Not I." He glanced about. "Anyone here know the house of Petronius? You, Demetrius. If he lives in this district you should know him."

From the corner of the room a bass voice mumbled, "I know no such name."

A voice from the ranks volunteered, "There's a Petronius on the hill by the river."

Desmontes wagged his head. "No. This Petronius has too much money to fill his nostrils with the stench from the river district. Thank you, anyway. Come, Sebastian."

Sebastian paused by Primus. "Since you're in a mood to answer questions..."

"Say."

"I've been thinking of fighting for pay—entering the military. Praetorian Guard by preference, of course. Have you any suggestions about when and where I should enlist?"

"The way to earn a spot in the Guard is to acquit yourself

well in the standing army. Do you know their main camp at the edge of the plains district?"

"I'll find it."

"Before lunch is best. And good luck to you."

"Thank you. Good evening." Sebastian nodded and followed Desmontes out the door. The cold night air washed his face and told him he had been perspiring. He stretched out on the litter beside Desmontes. It lurched and they were headed home, safely home.

In the privacy of the litter, Desmontes could at last lower his defenses. He was shaking. "Sebastian, do you realize what a godsend that battered body of yours was tonight? You see, Christians refuse to fight, as a general rule. Your eagerness to wade into the whole Praetorian Guard—plus those spectacular bruises from past skirmishes—were the only proofs Primus really accepted that we aren't of the cult. I invoke a blessing on that lovely, deceitful woman who cudgeled you."

"I liked your little touch at the end there. About finding Petronius."

"And you! You played your part perfectly. But I do think that business about joining the army was a bit much."

"I was serious."

"Come, lad! Life has much more to show you than a sword and a few sestertii a month."

"Who can save Demetrius?"

"I don't know. I'll try, but I don't know," Desmontes replied pensively.

"A soldier could. At least, a soldier would have a better chance at it."

"My boy, by the time you get through basic training and earn a spot in the guard—if you ever do—Demetrius will either be saved or long gone."

"I know that. Not just Demetrius. Christians. The army and the guard are the primary instruments of their capture and execution. So the military is as good a position as any from which to save at least some of them."

"I don't understand. What are Christians to you?"

Sebastian flopped down on his back. He watched the sunsheet catch the torchlight, bobbing in rhythm with the slaves' strides. He had no time to think, no lengthy processes of reasoning. And yet his scrambled life was somehow fitting itself together.

"I'm not certain. I don't... I believe I am one."

5

Once upon a time God decided He would put on earth a tiny touch of Hell, in hopes that seeing a bare suggestion of the netherworld, His people would turn in horror from the error of their ways, never to sin again. And so He invented the army.

It wasn't the martial aspect, not even the drill. Sebastian was in good shape; he could take the miles of running, the hours of sword practice in stride. The camp surgeon strapped his ribs and they healed with a minimum of fuss.

It wasn't the food, which was pretty much cook-it-yourself.

It wasn't his fellow recruits, jovial boys every one.

It was the chain of command, the whole irksome chain. Soldier vied with soldier for position, for rank, for favor. Officers vied with officers and tried in any petty way they could to manipulate each other. They even squabbled over whose tent was to be pitched next to whose on maneuvers. Sebastian detested pettiness, and this miserable army was riddled with it.

There were legitimate ways one could advance oneself, even from the beginning. You could, for example, earn an extra sestertius each month by exceeding a certain score as an archer. Sebastian tested and scored high immediately. All those goat-hunting forays with his friends into the hills behind Narbonne paid off.

Another sestertius accrued if you could handle a horse according to a certain set of specifications. That, too, was no problem. After all, how does one reach the hills to hunt goats if not on horseback?

At wrestling and hand-to-hand he excelled. At swordwork he did not. And he broke into a cold sweat the first time a lance was dropped into his hands.

The first flush of enthusiasm in the new recruits quickly faded under the pall of drudgery and hard work. When the monotony got heavy, Sebastian set his mind to thoughts of Bos and Taurus. By freeing their slaves they denied their own comfort and sentenced themselves to a life of hard labor just like this—Taurus especially. For a principle. For their Jesus. Sebastian would do the same.

Near the end of training Sebastian prepared a letter to the commanding officer. He phrased his letter carefully, clearly, simply in Julian Latin. He pointed out as modestly as possible his fine record and his desire to serve well. He closed with his formal request for assignment to the Praetorian Guard. While he was at it, he sent through the military post a letter to Quintus Alerian Primus of the Third Cohort, Praetorian Guard.

After a millenium or two—perhaps three—the recruits were lined up before the barracks one fine morning and officially labeled "soldiers." After addresses from every ranking officer in the training camp, the commander whipped out a scroll and commenced calling assignments. Sebastian's spine tingled.

"Sentorius, Cestus, Marcus Veridian—Ninth Cohort, Third Legion. You sail from Ostia kalends next."

"May we ask where the Third Legion is, sir?"

"Numidia. Celsis, Sebastian, Quintus Spasus, and Quintus Commocius—Fifth Cohort, Fifth Legion, Moesia. You have sixty days to get there any way you can. Septus Romanus, Vestus..."

Moesia! The last place in the world Sebastian wanted to go was Moesia. He had not joined the army to be stuck in the hinterlands. Rome called, Milan called, even the province called. Moesia thumbed its distant nose. And there was nothing he could do. Neither Desmontes nor his uncle's friends could help. The only persons he knew with decent connections were the

Cannii. Ask Marcus to intercede for him and he'd spend the rest of his life mucking stables in a frontier garrison on the Black Sea—which was what he was assigned to anyway, it seemed.

For the first time since he arrived in Milan he felt truly, irredeemably, totally lost. Without resource. He finished out the day under a black cloud, stood for half an hour in the paymaster's line, and walked into town to the house he knew best.

The gate was locked when he arrived. He clanged the bell. Long moments later Sinister appeared, the white scar on his hand distinguishable even in the darkness. "Sebastian, master!" The boy's small fingers fumbled the lock. The gate parted.

Sebastian helped him lock it again.

Desmontes and five others were sitting around the low table in the tablinum, togas cast aside for the summer heat. On the table, *mulsum* cups sat among a tangled disarray of open books and scrolls.

"Sebastian! Well, praise be! My nephew, gentlemen. Join us, lad."

Dexter set a chair for him.

Five faces watched him with foreboding.

"Thank you, Uncle, but I just stopped by a moment to greet you. I'm obviously intruding. I'll return in the morning."

"Nonsense! Sit! Sepio, show him that one there."

One of those seated passed a scroll across the table. Sebastian twisted it to the light and ran his eyes down the column that happened to be open. He hadn't read a written word in months, other than work assignments, and they were not in Greek.

His mind stumbled at first, but the words smoothed out. "This is one of those biographies you were looking for."

"Indeed. My supplier in Alexandria came through."

"The one by Johannan?"

"Lucanus. Luke." The lanky man's eyes glowed.

"I rejoice with you, Uncle."

"Thank you, son. Have you eaten?"

"Not lately."

Dexter's bare feet pittered off behind him into the kitchen.

Sepio cleared his throat. "The, ah, the tunic is army issue, is it not?"

Sebastian glanced from face to face. He leaned back. Of course! "Sorry I didn't catch the gist quicker, gentlemen," he said with a smile. "Other things on my mind. You are fellow believers, and because of my army affiliation I represent the enemy. Or at least I'm suspect. I don't know how to assure you of your safety except to say it. You're safe."

The short, aged man to his left extended his arm. "If Desmontes greets you with joy, so do I. I am Felician."

The rest followed, but Sebastian couldn't keep the names straight. Dexter placed a small table at his elbow and Sinister set out cold lamb, seasoned oil dip, and bread. Sebastian sat back and listened while he ate.

The men were in the midst of a discussion comparing this gospel of Luke and one of Paul's letters. Sebastian could see now a part of the satisfaction his uncle found in the intellectual aspects of this religion. Desmontes was in his glory.

After a while the discussion began to fade. Sebastian was fading too. He'd worked hard all day, under a cloud of gloom that was more wearying than any work. The dark, stuffy air was starting to put him to sleep in spite of the stimulating company.

Two of the men stood and begged their leave. Desmontes saw them to the gate. Sepio and his companion rolled their scrolls and excused themselves. Felician rose to go.

Desmontes laid a hand on the elderly gentleman's shoulder. "Felician, can you not remain a few moments? I'd like you and Sebastian to get to know each other better. One last goblet of *mulsum,* perhaps?"

"Very well, a moment. But I'm sure you and your nephew want to talk."

Usually at the word *mulsum* either Sinister or Dexter was at the guest's elbow with the jar. Where were they now? Sebastian looked over the side of his chair. A black head lay against it, and Sebastian tapped the wool. Dexter snapped up to sitting, wide-eyed. "*Mulsum,*" whispered Sebastian, and Dexter hurried off.

Desmontes grinned and flopped out on his chair. "I'm considering educating the boys, both of them. Dexter especially—despite the fact he fell asleep just now—is very interested in the finer details of the faith."

"Educate them and then free them?" Sebastian asked.

"First things first."

Felician turned to Sebastian. "Are you stationed in Milan?"

"Not anymore."

"Ah!" Desmontes rubbed his hands. "Where to?"

"Ready for this, Uncle? Moesia."

Desmontes gaped at Felician. "Moesia! The armpit of the world."

"Four and a half weeks of summer—in the hot years," Felician added. "Nine months of winter and rain in between."

"Mud you wouldn't believe. Sucks whole horses under."

"Butter instead of olive oil."

"Incredibly dumpy women. Homely," Desmontes added, a grin spreading across his face.

Felician leaned forward as Dexter handed him a goblet. "Do you look forward to going?" he asked Sebastian with mock seriousness.

"What an insane question! Even if I had when I walked in here, you two jesters would have killed my enthusiasm."

Felician chuckled from deep inside. "Have you made supplication to your Lord?"

"About what?"

"About going. Tell Him you don't want to. If it doesn't matter one way or another to Him, He'll change your orders."

"He *who?*" Sebastian asked in frustration.

"God, of course," Felician replied.

Desmontes sipped at his goblet. "Sebastian, have you been talking to anyone in the faith since your induction?"

Sebastian shrugged. "Frankly, I haven't thought much about Jesus at all. I never told you, Uncle, about a family I met west of Milan. They took me in after my, ah, encounter with that person with the staff—remember? They were wonderful. Committed to the Christ. And I watched them die. Dacian Lancers; I checked with the quaestor."

"Ah, I see," nodded Desmontes. "That explains a great deal."

"I think about that family a lot, but that's all. You know why I entered the army. Now it looks as though..." He shrugged again, helplessly. "You see what things have come to."

Desmontes turned to Felician. "Sebastian wants to help Christian army victims from the inside. I think it was Demetrius's arrest that set him down that road."

Felician sat forward and took Sebastian's hands in his own. His eyes bored into him. Sebastian was certain he ought to feel uncomfortable, but he didn't.

"Sebastian, where do you feel you can function best?" Felician inquired.

"Praetorian Guard. Second choice, Dacian Lancers."

"We'll try for the guard. When must you leave Milan?"

"I'm supposed to be in Moesia in sixty days. I figure it will take me forty days to walk there, spend ten here with Desmontes, keep ten for a cushion."

"Then we've not much time." Felician explained, "Tomorrow morning I will start it through the prayer chain. We must not mention names, of course, or your specific situation. If you are labeled a Christian your work is lost before it begins. You must not appear to be of the Way."

"That's not hard. Not the way my life has been these last few months."

Felician studied harder. "Tell me. Have you ever made a full spoken commitment to Jesus the Christ as your Lord and savior?"

"Well, uh, not exactly in those words."

"Have you been baptized?" Felician asked. "Instructed in the faith?"

"I was listening to you men tonight."

"Good! Keep listening." Felician leaned closer and counted across Sebastian's knuckles: "First, you must give your life over to the Christ. Totally, sincerely. Recognize that you have no purpose or power apart from Him. Second, be baptized. This is an outward sign of your inner rebirth. Third, learn all you can about the faith. Desmontes here is accumulating a superb library of writings. Read them all. Study them. Fourth, meet with your brethren regularly to build each other up and worship God. Sit at the feet of the elders—the bishops and leaders. They, too, will teach."

"For ten days?" Sebastian questioned wryly.

"No, no! Don't bother leaving for Moesia. You'll not be going there. Your work is here, I feel it very strongly. You attend to these other matters, these things of God. Let Him take care of Moesia."

"Felician, that's desertion!"

"Trust God!" Felician patted his arm and stood up. "Desmontes, I beg your leave. The evening was marvelous. Thank you for opening your home to us, especially to this withered old servant. Go in peace, young Sebastian!"

Sebastian stood and honored the gentleman, watched vaguely as Desmontes saw him to the gate. *How do you talk to God? Where is the altar where He will hear you?* he wondered. Desmontes would know.

Life had been settling down comfortably, in some respects at least. Suddenly, between Moesia and this startling old man, it was all churned up again.

Tell God you don't want to. After a lifetime of giving lip service to a variety of gods and spirits, Sebastian found prayer as Felician described it an impossibility. Waving a censor before an altar or a statue was definite. You did something, a simple something, and either the desired effect resulted or it didn't.

The moment he started prayer to an unseen God his mind wandered. His thoughts were not spiritual thoughts, either. Frequently they embraced girls in general, Melita in particular. He tried various attitudes—kneeling, standing, palms pressed together, arms outstretched...no, arms outstretched would never do. That position reminded him too sharply of Taurus, of the final moments of that saintly man's life.

Four days into his regimen of study he hit on it. He was sitting on a bench in the peristyle, the late sun just dropping behind the roof. Desmontes' small fish pond had no fountain to disturb its surface. Some sort of fly—just a small one—touched the water, and the surface burst from below. The fly disappeared. Familiar rings of ripples marched out, tight and orderly. He was looking at the rippling surface, but what he really saw was the evening sky and yellow-orange clouds. Reflections. He might have been able to imagine sky and clouds, but his imagination could not have envisioned exactly the way those ripples bent the reflection and tossed it about. Now the surface was smooth again. He touched his finger to the water, tapping it sharply. The same concentric rings rippled out—his drill instructor would have loved their precision.

Some disturbances were random, some deliberate. He saw water and heaven both at the same time. He might not be able to concentrate on God directly, perhaps not even to discern Him; but he could see the reflection of God in his own mind even as he discerned his own mind.

He began a conversation with God as reflected within the pool of his mind. It seemed one-sided at first. He finally realized with delight that it was not. *First, this business about Moesia. If You want me to disobey orders and stay, You'll have to give me some sort of sign, please. I need guidance, an assurance. And then there's Melita. Need I say more? And Cannius. To be worth anything, faith must be able to bear heavy demands. I realize that. But to love Cannius as—for instance, as I love Desmontes—that's impossible. Sorry. And God, if You expect me to love You with all my heart like Lavinia did, or with all my mind like Desmontes does, You're going to have to change me.*

The answer to that last came to him immediately. He was not to love God as Lavinia did or Desmontes or Taurus or Felician, but as Sebastian.

Felician called the next morning and stayed most of the day. Desmontes broke several appointments in order to sit with Sebastian and talk literature. The day before kalends Sebastian put aside his army tunic in favor of one of Desmontes' to attend a gathering with Felician and others. After the meeting he and nine others were baptized. There was no turning back now. He was in it.

67

That evening Felician came by again. He was working on a translation of the Greek writings into Latin, but Sebastian couldn't see the use of it. Anyone who could read could read both languages. Why bother?

After he left, Sebastian sat on the rim of the fish pond and counted again on his knuckles. He had made his commitment to the Son of God, privately in prayer and to his mentors. One knuckle. He had been baptized, essentially telling the world. Second knuckle. He was studying, heaven knows. Third. And fourth, he was meeting with the brethren.

The ten days' grace is up, God. Where is that sign, please?

Moments later, it seemed, the ten days' cushion was gone as well. *God, the sign, please. Remember?* Sebastian wrote again to Primus, wherever he might be.

His thoughts turned to Melita. He sorely missed female companionship. Melita. It was not the same as Lavinia's case. Lavinia had been pure and undefiled; Melita was not only defiled but eager. Sebastian himself was certainly not untarnished. He didn't even mind sharing Melita's affections with others, if it came to that. It wasn't the same as Lavinia's case at all. His body stirred, tightened, just thinking about Melita.

There was no sign. Tomorrow he should be leaving. Did God's silence mean acquiescence? No sign is no sign. Sebastian put aside the Moesia problem for the moment in favor of more immediate concerns. In Narbonne he had enjoyed several delicious months of simply saying good-byes. Might Melita wish him good-bye as well? No sign is no sign. He borrowed Desmontes' toga with the modest yellow band and went out, as it were, to test the wind.

He rang Melitus's bell. It tinkled just a bit more musically than anyone else's. Henna answered. Normally stodgy and dispassionate, her face fell in disappointment. He was surprised by that faint display of emotion, however restrained it might be, though not by the nature of it. Beyond in the peristyle raged violent argument. The slave at Henna's side ran ahead of them, and the quarrel ceased abruptly.

Sebastian stepped out into the peristyle, paused, and sighed. He knew a sign when he saw one. This was a sign like a slap in the face. He crossed to Melita, took her hand, and kissed it. But he didn't drop to one knee. "My greetings to your father and to Juno." He turned and extended his arm to Marcus Cannius. "Greetings, Marcus, and greetings to your father."

Cannius crossed his arms. "Amazing whom you meet when you just drop in."

Sebastian smiled. "I was thinking that very thing."

Marcus waved toward his ex-wife. "Melita and I have said everything we intended to say to one another and then some. Since I wasn't invited here, and obviously you were, I should be taking my leave now." He plopped down into a chair. "How's the army, Sebastian?"

Melita's eyes were all red and puffy. "I heard you enlisted. Why did you do it?"

He shrugged. "Oh, to see the world. To serve the empire. To learn enough fighting tricks to become invincible."

Cannius smirked, "No one's invincible. I suppose now, Melita, you are considering becoming a camp follower."

She was blocking Sebastian. She was pressed against him, but it was not a pleasant pressure. She held both his hands in hers, gripping them so tightly her knuckles were white. *No!* her teary eyes said. *Don't!*

On the inside he was crestfallen—not the least of his disappointment was that God would use Cannius to signify His no. Cannius! On the outside, he kept it chipper. "Marcus, my friend, I'm sorry. This is going to ruin your whole day, I realize, but you're not interrupting a tryst. Even worse, we're not lovers—never have been. Drop by anytime, you won't be messing up a thing. I came as an old friend to wish her good-bye because I'm leaving."

Melita gasped, "Where?"

"Fifth Cohort, Fifth Legion, Moesia. I look forward to occasional letters from my old friends, Melita. Feel free to write also, Marcus. I'll read mail from anybody."

Cannius stood up laughing. "Moesia. Wonderful! You couldn't deserve it more. As for the tryst—" His voice went cold. "You're a liar."

Rigid, Melita screamed, "Stop it! Get out!"

Sebastian carefully moved her aside. It was difficult keeping the smile on his face from hardening. "That's two, Cannius. A few moments ago Melita made an unspoken request that I not tear you apart. I honor her request. Besides, I promised myself I'd give Desmontes first crack at you, since he received the first insult. As with him, you rest under the aegis of my friendship. Unlike him, I can't guarantee its permanence. Good-bye, Melita."

He peeled loose from her, turned on the polished tile, and walked unescorted to the gate. He half expected Cannius to come roaring up behind him. Henna's stout form jogged ahead, her breath coming in short gasps, and she was holding the gate for him when he got there.

He kept walking, past other villas almost as sumptuous, past vending stands and girls in scarlet who stood in the alleyways. *Melita.* He was hurting. He wanted her so much he was hurting. He might even consider one of those girls, but he hadn't brought a purse. He had never backed down from a fight before, either. Never. And particularly not a fight with Cannius.

God had saved him from his sins, but He was wrecking his life.

6

No sign, no omen, no hint, nothing. To arrive in Moesia late could mean death if the garrison were sufficiently manned at the moment and the commanding officer sufficiently petulant. Death might even be preferable to some of the tasks assigned those who had fallen from favor. And late arrival was hardly a good way to curry favor.

Thirty days gone. He need only have averaged twelve miles a day or so to get there, had he started promptly—see the country, enjoy a leisurely journey. Now he could ride two horses to death and still not get there in time. Why, oh why had he listened to Felician? What did Felician know about army orders? Sebastian sprawled across his comfortable old chair in Desmontes' tablinum. Desmontes had obtained a signature containing the two letters Paul wrote to Corinth. He and Felician had their heads together over it, punctuating their reading with comments and an occasional outburst of "Now-listen-to-this!"

Sebastian wasn't listening. He suddenly wanted to go to Moesia. He wanted to soak in a warm bath. Most of all, he wanted a woman. And according to Paul's letters here, not even harlots were permitted him.

A light dawned. That's it! Marry Melita in a quick ceremony and take her along to Moesia! Explain to his superiors that his bride slowed his journey—not by design, of course, but she was frail. So long as they didn't see her sleek and full-blown figure, they might believe that. He would beg their forgiveness and swear to live up to the promise he had shown in training camp. Top of the class, remember?

Desmontes glanced up. "Sebastian, you haven't said a word. I don't think you even know who's here."

"Why, Uncle! I thought you'd gone to bed hours ago."

Felician chuckled. "Don't tease the lad, Desmontes. Can't you see the boy is in contemplation? Right, Sebastian?"

"Absolutely. Deep contemplation."

Desmontes snorted. "I have yet to see the day you actually think something through. What are you contemplating?"

"Getting married."

Desmontes waved a hand. "Ah. I assume you're going to skip completely that boring, thankless task of courtship and plunge right in."

"Who needs it?" Sebastian said flatly.

"That depends upon whom you are marrying," his uncle contended.

"Melita. I suspect she's been courted sufficiently by now."

Desmontes' face fell. He relaxed and leaned back. "You're serious, aren't you? Ignore that line in Paul's second letter about being unequally yoked with an unbeliever. Since it doesn't fit your plans, delete it."

"Why not? You're deleting that line where it says it's better to marry than to burn. I'm burning, Uncle. You can live like a hermit if you wish. I don't care to."

"Then find a girl in the faith!"

"I did. And she died the same hour I kissed her. Melita will do. She'll even come into the faith, given the opportunity to see what it's really like."

"You don't know that. Paul says—"

"Master!" Dexter's voice, choking, broke between them. He was the color of yesterday's ashes. "Soldiers are here."

Felician sighed and closed his eyes.

Sebastian grabbed the old man's toga and threw it across the table, covering the offensive literature. "Soldiers are my department. I'll go."

Dexter jogged ahead with the lamp. Sebastian grabbed the boy's shoulder. "Keep the lamp well behind me. They're not to see my face."

Beyond the pale a horse snorted. Hooves scraped the cobbles. Sebastian knew them at once for Dacian Lancers. He left the gate locked. "Aye?"

"Desmontes Theosus?"

"Aye."

"Your name is on the record as being your nephew's next of kin, to be notified in the event of his death."

"Which nephew?"

"Sebastian."

"Well, has he died?"

"No sir. We need information. He is traveling to his new duty station in Moesia. We want to know when he left and by what route."

"Wait here." Sebastian shooed Dexter back through the atrium. "Uncle, they want me, not you. I'll try to send word once I learn what's happening. Felician, may we trade togas? Yours is handy here." He grabbed it and threw it over his shoulder as he jogged back out to the gate. "Dexter, lock it behind me quickly."

Sebastian stepped out through the gate, heard it clank shut, heard the chain rattle. "I am Sebastian," he said casually.

"Come with us," a soldier ordered.

They flanked him on each side, before and behind, the two lead riders carrying the torches. They rattled briskly through the streets, creating a clattering racket on the cobbles and bricks. The sudden hard exercise after the long evening in a chair winded him quickly. He was sweatier than the horses by the time they reached the training camp.

For the first time in a long time Sebastian was truly afraid. They entered by the south gate, clattered beside the cold, bland wall of the quaestorium, and passed the ominous stone wall of the praetorium. Three soldiers dismounted and stood beside him while a fourth entered the commander's quarters. He wanted to rest, to lean on something. The altar was the only something close by. *Don't offend further by leaning there,* he said to himself.

He heard snatches of the talk inside, "...the man himself." He ran his fingers through his hair, wiped his face on the inside of the toga, and arranged its folds. *Miserable toga.* It was all wool—too hot for tonight. On top of that, it was much too short for Sebastian. Felician was a small man.

A voice from the doorway beckoned gruffly. He squared his shoulders and walked inside.

In the middle of the room the camp commander sat at his table, a lamp burning by each side. As he saluted, Sebastian discerned others in the background, but he could not make out their faces.

The commander looked weary. "You should be halfway to Moesia by now."

"I walk fast, sir. I'll make it."

"No, you won't." The commander pushed a letter across the table. Sebastian picked it up cautiously. Apparently, he was to read it. He tipped it toward a lamp and scowled at the semiliterate scrawl. Sebastian had now become accustomed to reading in Greek, and he had to switch languages mentally. It took a bit. He was picking out maybe half of the scribbled words.

"You do read, don't you, soldier?" growled the commander.

"Every chance I get, sir. Sir, I don't know this Castulus."

"Well, he obviously knows you. And as you see, he wants you specifically," the commander said briskly.

When in doubt, bluff. Sebastian smiled. "What can I say?"

"Nothing. You shut up and take orders, same as I do. Castulus tells us to stand on our heads and stack shinny-balls, we stand on our heads and stack shinny-balls." The commander snatched his letter back and rolled it. "Since we don't have to crawl all over Illyricum searching for you, you might as well leave right now with Primus here."

"Pri—" Sebastian checked himself. "Aye, sir."

The commander stood up so suddenly Sebastian took a step back. "Never heard of putting a rank amateur in the Guard. But if there has to be a first time, you're as good a first as any. Congratulations, soldier." He extended his arm.

Sebastian took it. "The Guard...uh, er...aye, sir! Thank you, sir!"

He stepped back and saluted as smartly as his spinning brain permitted. *The Guard.* Four soldiers stepped out of the gloom. The square little centurion, their leader, spoke thanks and well-wishes, took his leave, saluted and was saluted, in return. *The Guard.* Sebastian followed them out into the fresh night air in a swirling, giddy cloud of joy.

The Guard! He fell into step with the four other soldiers, marched proudly down the principal way and out the east gate, saluting the sentry in passing. He could contain himself no longer. The centurion must have shared his elation in part. They turned as one, wheeling to pump each other's arm.

Sebastian was so happy he stammered. "You don't know how I rejoice to see you, Quintus Alerian Primus! You can't imagine how...how I've been stewing for...what this means!"

Primus was laughing. "I almost missed you, lad. I couldn't pull you straight out of the training camp. But we were out on maneuvers when you got your orders. Moesia! Blood of bulls! I was sure I'd missed you by a month. Providential that you hadn't left yet."

"Providential." Providential. Sebastian rolled the word over in his mouth. Sweet flavor. Providential. "But tell me who this Castulus is. What's going on?"

74

"On the way. We heard of some little tavern in the river district called The Donkey's Tail. You wouldn't happen to know where it is?"

"Aye, it happens I do," Sebastian assured him.

"You see, boys? Talk about your providence. Here's our simple native guide to lead us straight to the door."

Sebastian started west on the Imperial Way. "We'll go the back way. The streets are safe enough for five of Caesar's finest."

"Listen to him now, and he not yet in the Guard an hour! Sebastian, this is Quintillian. And this hairy giant is Prometheus. Make a joke about his name and he'll floor you; I know....And Castor here—Castor's Greek, an ex-slave. Best swordsman in the legion. Any legion."

Prometheus mumbled in the blackness behind, Castor grunted, and everyone exchanged greetings.

"You've still not said who Castulus is, or why he asked for me specifically," Sebastian prodded.

"He's second in command to the caesars themselves, lad. Treats the Guard like brothers and lords it over the army. Your C.O. was a bit wrong. Castulus doesn't know you, except for what I told him. I ran down to Rome as soon as we came off maneuvers, told him I had to have you."

"But why? You went to all that trouble to get me and you don't even know me, except for that one night."

"Oh, I know enough. My outfit's the best, lad. Handpicked. The best of the best. And you floored three of them bop bop bop. Then you bounce right back up with enough wits in your head to deliver a treatise on lararia. I know enough."

"You must stop by and visit my uncle sometime. He'd be delighted to see you again," Sebastian said with his tongue in his cheek.

"I shall. Tell me now. What's his political affiliation?"

"None. He calls himself politically inactive."

"And you?" Primus probed.

"Same," Sebastian said blandly.

"Good," Primus approved. "What's your opinion of Numerian?"

"Never met the man."

"Ah, now. I almost forgot your way of not answering a question with anything useful. Tell me truly. If that had been an altar dedicated to Caesar, would you have burned incense to him?"

"Primus," Sebastian said, laughing, "I've been worshiping Caesar since I was this high. Of course, it helps to know who Caesar is at any given moment. Out in Narbonne we sometimes didn't hear for two months who was the latest leader, and by then the names had changed again. How many caesars have we worshiped in the last hundred years? Do you know exactly?"

"Depends how you count." Primus scratched his pink stubble. "Count only the most enduring, twenty-five or so. Include all those who ruled for a week or less, forty."

A bass voice rumbled from the rear, "Make that forty-one."

Sebastian laughed. "A born scorekeeper."

"Prometheus refers to the latest. Rumor has it that Numerian's days are numbered."

"And Carinus?"

"A bit more firmly entrenched. But don't bet heavily on him."

"I never bet on emperors. I have yet to see one that can outrun a horse," Sebastian said as they turned into a narrow street. "Here we are. The Donkey's Tail."

Castor sneered, "This is it?"

"I didn't promise you opulence, I promised to bring you here. Enjoy."

"You're not coming in?" Primus asked in surprise.

"Left home too quickly to bring a purse."

"Ah." Primus pressed coins into his hand. "You now owe me two sestertii. Join us."

Sebastian sighed. "I shall, with thanks. But Primus— Primus...You'll never know how much I owe you."

Sebastian stood shoulder to shoulder with Castor, but all he could see were the Greek's eyeballs. Somewhere in the blackness beyond the door beside them, Quintillian and Prometheus waited. Two steps away, a cricket started chirping. Its strident kee-deet startled them both.

Their job was to guard the rear of this villa lest anyone try to sneak out the back way. Primus and the others were entering the front gate to seize those inside. The charge: encouraging and perpetuating the Christian cult.

Castor snickered and whispered, "You're as nervous as a twelve-year-old bridegroom."

"How can you tell?" Sebastian's voice was on edge. "You can't see me."

"I was, the first couple times."

Sebastian took a deep breath. "Well, you're right."

Silence. Then Castor whispered, "Guess it's my Greek heritage. Free-thinker. It bothers me to slaughter people just because they believe something. Or don't believe it."

Sebastian whispered back, "You know all those stories about them."

"Aye. But I never saw it. Orgies, murder, sedition? I've been in on a hundred raids like this. Never saw anything but modesty. Pure modesty. And I don't mind saying I know what an orgy looks like from the inside."

The portico door opened slightly and a fist inside thumped it three times. Castor and Prometheus darted inside; Sebastian and Quintillian followed. Sulla, the squad leader, handed each of them a torch. Sebastian and Castor were to search the southside rooms, all sleeping rooms save one. Castor paused in the doorway of the first as Sebastian entered. He flared his torch in the corners. He dropped to his knees and raised the bedcovers.

Down under the bed, hard against the wall, a pair of round eyes gleamed in the torchlight. The boy was probably nine or ten—reminded him a little of Galba. Sebastian dropped the cover and stood up. "Nothing here."

He pressed his hand to his mouth to keep his heady elation from forcing a grin. His very first raid and already one saved! He was disappointed when he found no one else under beds.

The soldiers gathering their captives into a tight knot reminded Sebastian briefly of the animals being herded from that farmyard. They came so meekly, these captives. The patrol eventually marched out into the night, over the cobbles. Four torches led the way.

These people must be from another meeting, Sebastian thought. He recognized none of the faces. What would he do on the day he did?

The group strung out as the streets grew narrow. Sebastian knew this end of town well, every inch. The torches were twenty feet ahead, he and Castor at the rear. He could see the prisoner ahead of him, a barefoot boy of twelve or so, only because the lad's tunic was white. Castor probably could not see the boy— an overweight man obscured his view. Who else might be watching? No one.

They passed an alley Sebastian knew was a dead end. The next one was not. He moved up closer behind the boy. Wait. Not yet...not yet...past this shuttered shop...Now!

He grabbed the boy's arm and yanked hard to the left—threw all his weight into it. The boy disappeared—literally—swallowed up into the black alleyway. No sound, no noticeable motion. Sebastian had not broken stride. He kept marching, eyes front. Did the fat man see? No matter. The man faced dead ahead now. Two in one night!

The torchlit parade marched in through the ponderous front doors of Besentine prison. Primus put heads together with the keeper of the roll, listing names and ages. Sebastian had never been inside these heavy walls. He tried, not very successfully, to avoid gawking.

Primus's voice brought his mind to heel. "I'm sure we had a half-grown cub in the pack. About this high. Prometheus? Did you see him?"

The hirsute giant mumbled, "Don't remember one that high. You thinking of the fellow over there?"

"Nay, smaller." Primus turned back, confused. "Couldn't have escaped. We had them packed too tight."

Sebastian kept his face grim.

"Down they go. Step out, now." The knot of prisoners milled about and reassembled itself into a ragged line. The fat man was over there in the bunch, now over here. Then he was inches away from Sebastian. Looking elsewhere he whispered softly, "The boy is my son. God bless you." There were tears on his cheeks.

Encouraged by the passing equinox, winter came early and heavy. Cold rain, mud, dismal nights, cold rain, the solstice and Saturnalia, still more rain.

On one occasion Sebastian took time to stop by Melitus's. Melita was not there. So sorry you missed her, she's visiting a sick friend. Sebastian stayed a polite length of time making small talk with her mother and left. He had not come to visit her mother.

Saturnalia, he discovered, was no fun for soldiers. The whole cohort was kept on full-time duty to keep peace during the riotous celebrations. Besentine prison overflowed with drunks and looters. Sebastian's squad drew extra guard duty at the prison twice in three days. Saturnalia was getting worse every year; everyone said so.

January boasted sparkling winter sun half the time. Sebastian made several more attempts to visit Melita. She apparently had very sickly friends and relations.

February kalends brought more rain. Half the garrison developed some sort of ague that left the chest tight, the throat voiceless. Sentries barked "Who goes?" like harbor seals and received barks in reply. The standard joke became: to prove you're in the Praetorian Guard, cough.

No one was elated, therefore, on the day before nones when the cohorts were called out for inspection by the *legatus*. In the drizzling rain Primus flustered over his maniple as a hen clucks over her chicks—every thong tied correctly, every square inch of metal polished.

Primus himself sounded like the death of the Medusa. He doubled up coughing, straightened, and barked, "Now listen, lads. I don't want to see an eye twitch, a finger flick. And no coughing, you hear? You turn purple, you cease breathing and die, but you stand there. This is a big one—bigger than you know. Hah *hot!*"

Eyes rigidly front, Sebastian could not see the *legatus* well, but the brief view he got of the top man in the Guard was sufficient. He didn't like him. For one thing, the man reminded him of Marcus Cannius; he had the same beetling brows. For another he strutted just like the peacocks in Miletus's garden—cold and prideful.

Apparently this *legatus* felt it beneath his dignity to address only two cohorts. He offered no praise, no blasphemies, no comments, and certainly no mundane announcements. Having done his duty in reviewing his troops he retired promptly to the praetorium—the warm, dry praetorium.

The Fourth Cohort was dismissed. Wet soldiers disappeared quickly into barracks. The Third remained at attention. Oh, come on, commander! The camp commander stepped up on the dais. Sebastian had to strain to hear him above the rainpitter.

"There are some small shake-ups inside. Your centurions have the new command assignments. Now for the big shake-ups. The Fifth Cohort, serving in Dalmatia, is moving into Rome. The Ninth, now in Rome, will be coming up to Milan." After a pregnant pause he added, "And since there is no need for three full cohorts in Milan, you the Third are going to Rome."

Tension like imprisoned lightning flashed across the compound. It gripped Sebastian and vibrated his breast. The commander grinned and shouted, "Dismissed!"

The cheers, the celebration, reached to heaven. The noise so deafened Sebastian he couldn't hear his own lung-ripping contribution.

Rome! Milan was the second grandest city in the empire. Every quadrans of trade from Britain through Moesia filtered through Milan. Her business district was second to none. Not even Rome could match the grandeur of her wealthy homes. But Rome...! Sprawling and gaudy and wealthy as she might be, Milan was the plain sister to the queen of cities.

It was near midnight before Primus managed to get his whole maniple together to read off the new command assignments. He stood on a box at the barracks door, his two hundred men packed into the bunkhouse like wheat in a sheaf. His voice broke and rattled, much the worse for rain and shouting.

"Quiet, lads, or I'll bring you to full attention. Quit your squirming. Manlius and Basil. You two are transferred over to Sulla's squad. You know which one that is? Aye. Sulla, you're promoted from squad leader to centurion of your century. Congratulations! Bass—Sebastian, you're the new squad leader behind Sulla..."

Sebastian didn't hear the rest. Fortunately, it pertained to the other century. Squad leader, and he in the Guard only a few months. Felician surely knew what he was saying! You devote yourself to God and let God handle the details. Rome, a promotion...what next did God have for him?

The next night Sebastian joined Primus, Prometheus, Castor, and Quintillian for an evening at The Donkey's Tail—the old four, as on that first night. They took a table in the corner, well away from the main bar and the prying ears of the tavernkeeper.

Primus leaned forward over his tankard. "Old Victor didn't say the half of it. The reason the Ninth is coming up here is because they supported Numerian and Numerian is out."

"So it finally happened," Castor murmured.

"Aye. And that's why the Fifth is going to Rome. It's their commander who will be our new caesar instead of Numerian. Diocletian."

"But why are *we* going?" Quintillian asked.

"Because our commander is sympathetic to Diocletian," explained Primus. "Had a hand in bringing him to the chair. In fact, I hear that instead of entering Rome from the east, Diocletian is bringing his cohort over to join us. We'll march into Rome from the northeast or north—two full cohorts—and the best two in the legion. It'll be glorious!"

Sebastian wagged his head. "Then who's the *legatus* who reviewed us yesterday?"

"Now look." Primus counted off fingers. "Top are Carinus and Diocletian, the two caesars. Under them, Castulus is in charge of military—army and Guard both. He signed your papers, you'll remember—I went right to him. Now the *legatus* here yesterday, Pavo—"

"Pavo!" Sebastian interrupted. "Then it wasn't just me."

"What?"

"I took one look at him and thought of a couple of peacocks I know."

"You've a fine eye for birds. Pavo is in charge of all cohorts in the Praetorian Guard, in the same way I-forget-who is responsible for all legions of the standing army. Incidentally, don't call him Pavo to his face. It's a good way to become a carpenter in the auxiliaries. And the rest of the chain in our cohort you know."

The next question came naturally and Sebastian had to bite his lip to keep from asking it.

Primus wet his raspy throat with a draft from the tankard. "And now you want to know how you got to be squad leader, I'll bet."

"Since you mention it, how?"

"Popular vote. Sulla was moving up, so I asked Prometheus to take over. He has seniority. He refused. Said he can't think fast enough in an emergency and I should ask you. So I asked Castor. He said you. And right down the line."

Sebastian glanced over at the dark and wiry Greek. Castor was miles away, his face blank, joyless. Sebastian poked him. "Listen, sword-slinger. I'm the least deserving—the junior of the bunch. You take the job, will you?"

Castor smiled soberly. "No, you'll do just fine. I was thinking about something else. Really."

"What?"

"I wonder what Diocletian's attitude toward Christians will be."

Primus wiped his arm across his mouth. "That's always bothered you, hasn't it?"

"Enough that I've considered more than once just getting out of the Guard. You laugh at being a carpenter. Why not be a carpenter? Carpenters don't round up innocents for torture and death."

"Innocents you call them!" Primus fumed.

"Look at them objectively." Castor spoke with slow deliberation. "What do you see?"

Primus sat back and sighed. "Innocents."

Sebastian's throat tightened. He wanted to speak and knew he dare not. His mouth opened in spite of himself. "Primus? What do you see in the Christian cult?"

"Atheists. No lars, no gods, no protecting influences at all. That's why they're dangerous, why they cripple the empire. They offend the gods that be."

Sebastian nodded. "And you believe in these offended gods with all your heart, from Zeus right down to the lars."

"Does anybody really?" Primus wagged his head. "The only one of the pack that comes close to being a proper god is Mithras. The others are...I don't know what they are."

"Mithras belongs to the army. What about the civilians?"

"Mithras is not just army. He's for anyone. Mostly army, true, but not all army."

"I said, what do the rest of the people have to believe in?" Sebastian persisted.

"Other than Caesar, that's their problem," Primus snorted.

"No, it's the empire's." Sebastian counted. "You just said failure to believe in the gods weakens the empire. What does the empire as a whole have to call on, since we all know Caesar at least starts out mortal?"

"Mithras."

"But the empire as a whole does not call on Mithras. Why should Mithras be offended by one cult who ignores him when half the empire does the same?"

"By all the gods, I wish you would talk straight, lad," Primus said with annoyance. "Given the chance, you'd convince Cerberus he has only one head."

"Am I wrong?"

"How should I know?" Primus muttered. "I can't keep track of all that."

"You can and did. Now I put this to you," Sebastian pressed. "What if there is one God, a supreme God? Not a flock of petty gods who are magnified human beings with human faults. One all-knowing, all-powerful God without weaknesses."

"Without weaknesses?" Primus shrugged. "You couldn't prove such a god exists, but we'd all be better off if he did."

"More than you know. Let's say that possibly this God cares enough about mortals to want to remove the barriers between them and Himself."

"Barriers?" Primus said, confused.

"If He's all-good and we are faulty, we aren't in the same class," Sebastian explained. "We don't have anything in common. In fact, if He is all-good He hates evil and we're evil, at least in part."

"All fantasy. No proof."

"More proof than Mithras by a goodly bit," Sebastian assured him. "Let's say this supreme God sets up a system of His own for erasing men's faults. He doesn't just drop it out of the sky, like Diana's stone. He doesn't say 'Take it or leave it,' or men would have no real reason to believe Him instead of some other god or man.

"So a thousand years ago He puts His plan into action. He sets it up first. He sets prophets to writing about it, predicting it—a whole body of writings all pointing to His system.

"The system comes to pass. A pure and undefiled, faultless Person who is actually man and God together suffers torture and dies when He doesn't deserve it. He uses His death as payment, then, for the faults of everyone else. First He proves who He is by His genealogy, His miracles, His teaching. Then He rises from the dead, with hundreds of witnesses ready to die rather than deny what He did. The ultimate proof."

"Fantasy!" Primus scoffed.

"Proved!" Sebastian said with intensity. "Proved by the writings, the teaching, the people who saw Him before and after His death, by the way His believers grow the more they get cut down."

Primus sat transfixed, his mouth agape. He exploded, "Blood of bulls! You're one of them!"

It was done. Why had he said what he said? It was all over,

almost before it started. He regretted only that now he would never see Rome.

Primus was trembling. "No, you wouldn't have burned incense to Caesar that night. And that first raid you were on. We had a lad in the bunch but he wasn't there when we...You let him escape somehow. That's why you're in the Guard, to spring prisoners! To spring Christians!"

Sebastian kept his voice quiet. "That's right."

"Blood of bulls! My best man. One of *them*. How could you—? One of them!"

Castor's pall of gloom had fled. "Two of your best men. I wasn't a Christian when we sat down here, but I am now. For years I've wondered why I don't hate them. Now I know. This one faultless God. You can see it in them. In the way they live, the way they die, in the way they bless you while you're killing them."

Quintillian nodded. "I always wondered why they hung onto that Jesus so tightly. I never guessed they might have solid reasons. I thought it was just like—like Jupiter. You grow up worshiping Jupiter because everyone else does. No reason to. Never hear of anyone ready to die for him. No proof he ever existed, let alone that he exists now. I never thought about that until this very hour."

"And I suppose you're a Christian now too," Primus rumbled.

"No, but I want to see those writings Sebastian talks about. I can tell he's read them."

"Some of them," Sebastian corrected. "That's why we went to the house of Demetrius that night—to borrow the very books you were burning in the atrium."

Primus turned to Prometheus. "You, you hairy giant. What do you have to say?"

"I'm still thinking."

Castor was chuckling now. "Sebastian, you should have seen Peaches after he met you that ni—"

"Who?"

"Castor, shut up," Primus growled.

Castor waved a hand. "Why not Peaches, Primus, when no one is listening? You see how he always needs a shave. He shaves more often than any three of us put together. And he still has that pink fuzz constantly sprouting. Peaches. When it's only us, of course.

"Anyway, you should have heard him raving. 'Smart boy.' 'Quick boy.' 'Good fighter.' Two days he talked about you. He checked to make sure you really had enlisted, then double-checked. He walked clear to Rome and back just to get you signed into the Guard. So your confession comes as a particular shock to him."

Primus, weary, succumbed to another wild spate of coughing. "Now what do I do?" he grumbled aloud to himself. "I don't know what to do."

Castor shrugged, "You can turn us in. You can ignore what you know. Or you can be one with us. Simple as that. Christians talk about eternal life in a paradise—even when this earth becomes a Hades in the meantime. I'll accept that. Earth is often Hades whether you're a Christian or not. Mithras gives you life, maybe, if you earn it. Jesus gives you life. Period."

"You've been talking to Christians before, Castor," Sebastian said.

"I have. In Besentine Prison when we were on guard duty over Saturnalia. They were so cheerful; I asked why."

Prometheus dragged himself more or less out of his slouch. "If you don't want the decision, Peaches, we'll take it. Those in favor of turning these two louts in, speak aye."

Silence.

"Those in favor of joining them at the peril of our lives, speak aye. Aye."

Quintillian shook his head. "I want to read those books first. I abstain. But I'll keep my mouth shut."

Primus took another swill from his tankard. "No double-talk, lad. If need be, would you die this night rather than deny your Jesus?"

"I would die tonight rather than deny my Jesus, if need be. But then, Primus, I would die tonight defending you, if need be; simply because you're my friend."

As Sebastian watched, the corners of the hard, square little man softened. Primus looked from one friendly face to another. "I've been in the army for twenty-two years and an initiate of Mithras for twenty-one. I'm not sure..." He sighed. "I don't know what I'm getting into. But aye."

"I think," bubbled Castor cheerfully, "what we are getting into is eternal life following a grisly and painful death. Do you realize how casually we are sitting here discussing our date with the torturer?" He waved his arm high. "Even you, Quinn. Guilt by association."

The barmaid pushed her way through a dice game and paused by Castor's elbow.

"Five of those raisin-studded honey cakes and another round for my friends," he ordered. As she left he turned back to the others and said, "This is a night of celebration, gentlemen. I for one have never been to Rome, and we all know what an honor it is to die there. Let us pray, therefore, that we at least reach the queen of cities before the ax falls."

7

He had only one free evening left before they marched out. Should he spend it with Melita or Desmontes? His uncle was as dear to him as ever. On the other hand...

He arrived at the villa of Melitus two hours before dark. Melita was not there, but Melitus was. For an hour Melitus filled Sebastian's sails with much wind, guiding him through the narrow and treacherous channels of life to financial success. He steered Sebastian clear of the folly of abandoning valuable business contacts and opportunities for a mere soldier's pay. Sebastian felt no real need to mention that he was no longer in the army and that he enjoyed a relatively handsome salary in the Praetorian Guard.

Melitus addressed him as he had been addressing him for the

last twenty years, extracted the assurance that Sebastian would attend his sterling advice, and steered him out the gate. No, Melitus had not changed.

On the way to Desmontes' house, Sebastian reflected on the changes just this last year had made—the little decisions: never to set foot aboard a boat again, and the big ones: Jesus, the Christ. A year ago less a month or two he hung sobbing on his uncle's arms. Bos and Taurus were as sharply etched as yesterday. Lavinia, strangely enough, had faded somewhat.

Dexter opened the gate for him. "Your uncle is out, master. He is due to return shortly."

"I'll wait." Sebastian settled into his favorite chair in the tablinum. Dexter set *mulsum* and apples before him.

"Dexter?"

"Master."

"My uncle mentioned he was thinking of educating you two. Has he commenced?"

A big smile lighted up Dexter's face. "He has, master. We are reading Latin."

"Read for me."

"Thank you, master!" The boy left at a dead run and returned almost instantly with a huge scroll. He settled at Sebastian's feet and started through the first familiar passage of the Gallic Wars, reading flawlessly in singsong.

"Hold it," Sebastian interrupted. "What is the case of the *German* there?"

"The dative, master."

"Why?"

"To agree with *proximi* which requires the dative."

"Continue."

The boy did continue, with an enthusiasm Sebastian had never known in his own youth. He was good, very good.

Dexter was nearly hoarse, Sebastian nearly asleep, and the night nearly spent when Desmontes finally returned. They talked a few hours, embraced and parted. The day was dissatisfying—the whole day—and Sebastian could not put his finger on why.

The next morning at dawn he was marching south.

The Third Cohort with its baggage and auxiliaries struck a truly imposing picture. It tracked down the road like a disjointed caterpillar, undulating, half a mile long and six men wide. To it were attached the Mauretanian Archers and the Dacian Lancers with their colorful accoutrement.

Solid wooden wheels on the ox wagons made a sound separate and distinguishable from the lighter wheels of the horse carts. The oxen contributed the most interesting noises—the pad of huge feet interspersed with gentle ticks as the cloven hooves clicked together. Men's voices spoke occasionally. Someone might drop something. A skinner would whistle to his horses, crack a whip. The oxbows creaked. Caligae whispered on the pavingstones. The whole cacophony blended together in a joy-filled orchestration of movement. Rome!

Sebastian's maniple marched just ahead of the supply wagons. Essentially, this meant he got the most noise and saw least of what was happening. On the other hand, he didn't have to be concerned about deposits made by the baggage animals.

They joined the Fifth at the close of the sixth day. The Third, weary as it was, was paraded past the Fifth. Somewhere in the Fifth, probably on some sort of dais, would be the new emperor, Diocletian, watching his strength pass by. Sebastian tried to look for distinguished personages. He noticed none. But then, looking alert with a full pack on your shoulder marching eyes front does not commend itself to sight-seeing.

Primus was trotting up and down among his ranks, speaking privately with this man, then that one. What was happening? Now he was abreast. "Sebastian, fall out."

Sebastian stepped aside and plunked his pack on the ground. "What's up, Peaches?"

"You have no nose for politics."

"So?"

"So you're valuable," Primus told him. "Tongues loosen up around you. Tell me now. Have you heard anything at all about this maniple's response to our new caesar?"

"I don't know what you mean."

"What the men in the ranks think. Any rumors, opinions, comments?"

Sebastian scratched his head. There had to be three pounds of dirt in his scalp. "I don't remember anything. But like you say, I don't notice. What should I be listening for?"

Primus moved closer, dropped his husky voice further. "An assassination attempt. There's a persistent rumor that somebody in the Third doesn't take well to Diocletian—has their own candidate groomed and waiting. Might try to do the man in before he reaches Rome and gets dedicated in the temples and appears before the senate and all that."

"That I would notice. Certainly nothing in our century."

"Hmmm. That's what Sulla says, too."

They walked for a while, each lost in his own thoughts. Sebastian broke the silence. "Hey, wait a minute."

"Aye?" Primus pricked up his ears.

"Something's cooking over in the Fifth—I've heard they're looking for additional recruits. Talk to Manlius. I think he heard it."

Primus rubbed his hands together. "Ah. Well, lad, keep listening."

Sebastian hefted his pack again. "Peaches, how long before we reach Rome?"

"Soon, lad. They're talking about forced marching a couple of days to pick up time. Ides at the very most. Patience, lad. Believe me, marching to Rome is a lot quicker and sprightlier than is marching away from her. Good evening."

"Good evening, Peaches." He had to jog to catch up to his place in formation.

As his century approached the night's camp he noticed the two cohorts would be within a quarter mile of each other, on opposite sides of a cluster of three springs. The terrain was gently rolling—not ideal, but adequate.

The daily miracle happened. In swirling confusion the marchers broke rank and within the hour transformed themselves into a city of a thousand souls, complete with ditch, stockade, streets, and leather tents. Sebastian's squad performed their part in the erection of the stockade. Manlius and Prometheus, the tallest, put up the tent; Sebastian handled fire and drink. Castor permitted no one but himself to cook; he even carried his own herbs. Again he made reference to the pleasure of satisfying his stomach.

Manlius, ever disgruntled, made reference to the pleasures and satisfactions of other parts of the anatomy. And Sebastian thought again of Melita. Perhaps when he was established in Rome he could send for her, invite her to the city. Wife of a member of the Praetorian Guard was a position of honor, and she enjoyed assuming positions of honor. After all, she was the daughter of the wealthiest businessman in a city full of wealthy businessmen.

Sebastian ached. The others joked, talked, complained. He didn't hear. Dinner finished, he decided to use his new clout as squad leader and let the others clean up. He declared Castor leader *pro tempore*, shook out his cloak, and took a walk.

He knew as soon as he left the gate that this was what he needed—well, it was the best substitute available. The air felt chill and refreshing. The quarter moon coasted in and out of broken clouds; utter blackness to dull grey to utter blackness.

He chose a spot at random on the gentle slope and sat. Among men and cities too long, Sebastian had nearly forgotten the soothing panacea of silence. Silence poured balm on the nerves. He passed the time listening to a toad chorus by the springs, a distant owl's hoot, the quiet rustle of homebound cattle a quarter mile away.

Perhaps he would find a girl in Rome. She might be of the faith, or simply ripe for the faith. God was doing fine so far; let Him work out this detail as well.

And if You please...promptly, God.

The moon changed clothes for the hundredth time, from dense wool to thin bridal veil. As that woman on the Castrella Road said, watch with more than just your eyes. Animals of some sort approached less than twenty strides downhill. Goats feeding across the hillside? A dog pack prowling? Not goats this time of night. There, he saw one. He stiffened. A man—a man hunched over, moving with great stealth to some sort of vantage point. Another. And beyond, crouching, stalking...robbers? Then who was the intended victim? They certainly hadn't detected Sebastian yet.

Why had he not worn his armor—or at least brought along his sword? Because you don't escape the army a few moments by wearing all that stuff, that's why.

Silhouetted against the gray-black night a man was approaching, ambling along, wrapped in thought as well as darkness. There was no stealth in his approach; obviously he must be the intended victim. The moon emerged. Sebastian counted six....no, seven. Eight? Or seven and a boulder? Too many at any count. He mustn't pause to think; if he did, he'd know better than to intervene unarmed. He must plunge right in.

Sebastian sprang up and started running. "Hold there!" The victim pivoted toward him. The moon disappeared—frustrating! Why hadn't he paused to check that? From the blackness a voice cried "Now!" Rustling footsteps...Sebastian came down on the back of the nearest, plowing the fellow into the ground. The man wielded a dirk of some sort, a stubby weapon. Sebastian twisted his wrist, trying to break it forward. The man was clawing at his hair, pulling his head back. The dirk dropped. Sebastian grabbed it and stabbed blindly. The hand released his hair and fell away.

He leaped forward, the dirk in hand. He slashed out at a second but the man vaulted aside. He had his cloak off now, draped loosely over his arm to fend off blades. One of the ambushers came at him but the others seemed intent on their original quarry. Sebastian dropped to his knees and rolled toward his attacker. The man tripped over him in midstride. He made a weird gurgling sound when he hit the ground.

Ah! The fellow just ahead was using a sword! Sebastian almost caught him from behind, but the man heard him coming and half turned. Sebastian grasped the sword arm, with one hand and wrapped his cloak around the robber's neck. The man who would be victim ran the fellow through. Now the two of them were back to back. Sebastian felt more comfortable with a sword in his hand and this fellow at his back—a splendid fighter.

Someone's blade caught his cloak, nearly pulled him down. He yanked his arm free. Another plunged in so close his stinking breath was hot on Sebastian's cheek. They struggled hand to hand. Sebastian's sword arm was pinned down straight. He twisted his wrist and brought the sword up between the man's legs. In dull half-light the man's eyes went wide, horrified. Sebastian swung one arm free and slammed the fellow back.

The man at his back was still struggling with someone, but Sebastian's only remaining opponent was turning tail.

"Get him alive!" the intended victim cried. Sebastian took off. He followed more with ears than with eyes. The fickle moonlight never emerged at the right moment. He discerned the fellow just ahead and swiped his sword across the back of the man's knees. The ambusher dropped, hamstrung.

Gulping air the man rolled to his back, arms out. "Kill me! Kill me!"

Sebastian was too winded to reply. He hooked a caliga in the man's armpit and rolled him over. He locked around the fellow's neck and shoulder and dragged him back across the hill, the legs dangling loose and useless. Clumsily, Sebastian dropped the erstwhile murderer at the feet of his intended victim. The man stepped on the fellow's hair, tilted his head back, set his sword at the man's throat.

"I guarantee your life if you speak. Who sent you?"

"Guaranteed?" the ambusher groaned.

"On my word."

A long silence.

Sebastian turned his back on them and listened carefully to the blackness around them, watching. The moon came and went again.

"Quintullius Octans. Your word, M'lord."

The cloaked man stepped back. "I'll send someone out for you." He sheathed his sword and joined Sebastian. They started ambling back toward camp at the same leisurely pace with which this man had first approached.

"I'm indebted to you," the stranger said.

"I'm ashamed," Sebastian replied. "We're only three hundred paces from camp. You should think a lion can walk in safety this close to the pride."

"I doubt there's a safe square foot in the empire," the stranger observed. "You're in the Guard, too, I take it."

"Third Cohort. My name is Sebastian." He extended his arm.

"Fifth Cohort. Diocletian." The man gripped warmly.

Sebastian felt himself freeze, felt his mouth drop open. An eternity later he gathered his wits enough to drop to one knee and bow his head. "Your Clemency."

"Stand up, man. I may be Caesar, but I'm a soldier first, and therefore your colleague. Actually, I'm delighted, Sebastian. The look on your face just now quelled any suspicions I had that this whole business was an elaborate set-up. But didn't you think four-to-one a little tight?"

"Better than seven-to-one, sir."

"You enjoy fighting."

"Depending on the cause, aye, sir."

The moon graced the scene a moment, long enough for Sebastian to at last get a look at this man. He was built along the same general lines as Primus, but he was more powerful. His complexion was Castor's, his hair Desmontes'. Now that the fight had ended Sebastian was in a cold, shaky sweat. This man walked along in complete composure, perfectly self-disciplined. And he had been the intended victim. The empire needed a good, solid disciplinarian guided by reason. At last they had one.

"How long in the Guard?" Diocletian asked.

"Oh, a few months, sir," Sebastian replied.

"And before that?"

"Training camp in Milan, sir."

Diocletian paused a moment. "Rank?"

"Squad leader, sir."

"Assignments?"

"Guard duty, routing out a few nests of the Christian cult. Otherwise, Milan's pretty quiet, sir."

The man nodded. They were nearly at the gate of the Fifth's camp. "Rome is proud of her tolerance," Diocletian told him. "Does it bother you to be stamping out one cult among so many?"

Sebastian shrugged. "Orders are orders, sir. When I'm making the decisions, then I'll analyze the facts."

Diocletian turned and offered his arm. Sebastian took it. "Who's over you?"

"Quintus Alerian Primus, sir."

"Good man?" the emperor probed.

"The best, sir," Sebastian answered truthfully.

"No doubt. Again I express my gratitude. Good evening."

"Good evening, sir."

Caesar saluted his sentry, gave the password just like anybody else, and disappeared. Would he really send help out to the hamstrung assassin and preserve the hapless ambusher's life? Yes. From the few moments Sebastian spent with him he was certain. He had given his word. He would.

Rome, at last. This had been Sebastian's ultimate goal when he stood on the dock at Narbonne and bade farewell to his parents. Never in Narbonne had he imagined he might be marching into the city with two thousand companions and the new caesar. Even if some sybyl had foretold it, he could not have imagined the pomp and glory, the supreme thrill as his unit marched from the shadow of Salaria Gate into the brilliant splendor of the sunlit city.

Whatever he envisioned Rome to be, she was far less and yet far more. Compared with the hills behind Narbonne, the fabled seven hills were mounds. Building crowded upon building. Massive temples squeezed shoulder to shoulder with their secular fellows. And hidden behind these glorious edifices, the squalor of the Subura remained to remind him who would elevate Rome to eternity: she is very, very human.

Taurus recommended three days of prowling to learn the city. It would take him a month. In fact, it was nearly a week before he had enough free time to go out and purchase a sheet of parchment, an inkpot, and quills to draw up a map.

He grabbed half a day here, an evening there. On the center of his sheet he sketched in the old forum, Trajan's, and the forum of Augustus. He drew in both walls—Aurelian's, although it was not quite complete and old Servian's. He noted the gates and low spots, and wondered where the walls might be scaled.

He prowled the warehouse district below Aventine; the base of Janiculum with its water mills; the cattle, fish, and vegetable markets. He sketched in all the major thoroughfares and as many of the alleys as he could figure out. The city who built the world's finest highway system could not lay a sidestreet out in a straight line. They tumbled off the hills to meet in confusing angles and tangles between the slopes.

The major duty of the Praetorian Guard was to guard. They guarded the Palatine; they guarded the forums and policed the markets. They manned the walls. They made conspicuous displays at public functions.

The splashiest function, of course, was Diocletian's inauguration. Accompanied by carefully arrayed lines of guards, Caesar visited each of the temples of Jupiter in its turn, from Heliopolitan's across the river to the temple on Aventine, with the procession ending at the largest of them all, Capitolinus. There amid elaborate ritual, Diocletian received from Jupiter himself such special powers that even the very sun might serve him.

The sun might serve Diocletian, but it was not Sebastian's friend. A minuscule bit of those carefully arrayed lines, he stood in the sun for days while his helmet heated up and baked his brain. He wore an extra tunic to protect his shoulders from his scorching pauldrons. He stood at attention for hours and envied the centuries who took part in the processions (all Fifth Cohort). At least they got to move a little.

Finally the emperor was sufficiently inaugurated and a routine settled—guard duty, patrol, and wall-walking on a rotating schedule. While this was not Sebastian's motivation for joining the Guard, persecution was minimal for the moment, and it was certainly an enjoyable way to earn a living.

From the Fifth came rumors that insurrection still brewed in the Third. Sebastian in the Third heard that the trouble was in the Fifth. The Guard could get just as petty as the army, apparently.

He wrote to his parents and received a short note of approval from his mother. He wrote to Desmontes and received a booklength scroll in answer. By private post. He also wrote to Melita, but got no reply.

Three before nones in June, Primus's maniple drew palace guard. The stocky veteran was his usual armorful of nerves. Sebastian was now accustomed to his ways; it amused him, where once it had made him nervous too.

Sebastian's squad was assigned the main hallway leading to the auditorium, the throne room (which Diocletian refused to call a throne room) in which citizens made petition to Caesar. Hall guard was boring. No enemy could penetrate that deeply into the palace. You either stood in the hall all day or stood at the doors. Door detail was best; at least you got to open the ponderous auditorium doors as people entered and left.

When the six cast lots for door duty, Prometheus and Sebastian won. Castor and Manlius pouted. Just before the emperor was due to arrive, Primus came bristling through, checking.

"Prometheus, you ape, your helmet's on crooked."

Sebastian interceded. "Excuse me, sir, but look closely. You'll note the helmet's straight. He keeps his head tilted at that jaunty angle to impress the ladies."

Prometheus chuckled.

Primus fumed. "Forget to be funny, will you, you loafers? This is serious, this hall duty. The assassination business isn't cleared up yet. In fact, a prowler was seen on the palace ground early last evening."

Sebastian licked his lips. "Uh, Peaches. Don't spread it around, but that just might've been me."

"Blood of bulls! What are you talking about?" Primus bellowed.

"It's my basic policy," Sebastian explained. "I like to know all the ins and outs of a place, so I checked out the grounds yesterday when I got off duty."

"Do you realize what would happen if you got cau—"

The doors at the far end swung open. Primus pivoted and snapped to attention, cold as a statue and twice as rigid. Diocletian entered with two aides and traversed the hall with his easy, unmistakable stride. Sebastian and Prometheus grabbed the door handles as they had rehearsed and swung them open, snapping a quick salute.

The emperor fired a casual salute in return. Without breaking stride he smiled and said, "Good to see you, Sebastian." Sebastian returned a cheery "Your Clemency" to Caesar's departing back. The doors swung shut.

As one, Sebastian and Prometheus dropped to a parade rest, staring straight ahead toward the doors at the far end. In the periphery of his vision Sebastian discerned Primus move, mumbling to himself. As the centurion strode toward the far doors Sebastian could barely hear his incredulous "Blood of bulls!" Sebastian managed to keep a straight face, but it was one of the more difficult achievements of the last few years.

An hour passed, then two. Prometheus was getting visibly restless; Sebastian felt the same way. The hairy doorman glanced over and rolled his eyes ceilingward.

Sebastian whispered, "At least we're not standing in the sun."

"Aye to that."

The doors at the far end opened for the twentieth time. The man who emerged resembled a weasel, small and slim and gaunt—a nervous, slinky body topped off with a long thin nose. He paused before them, eyeing the doors.

"Well?"

"Your pass, please." Sebastian smiled amiably.

"Do you know who I am?"

"Don't tell me," Sebastian said. "Let me read it off your pass."

"You'll pay dearly for your insolence, soldier. I am vice-consul and I *demand* entry," the man said threateningly.

"No pass, no entry, sir. Now if you'll just step out to the reception room, a clerk there—"

The doors heaved open from the inside. A match for Sebastian in age and build, the man behind the doors must have been a centurion at least. "What's going on here?" he snapped.

"Centurion, these gentlemen seem bent on denying me access. I have an appointment with Caesar," the weasel said.

The young man stared at Sebastian. "Who's in charge here?"

"I am," Sebastian replied.

"Do you know who this man is?" the centurion asked.

"No. That's why I want to see his pass."

"Name and rank, soldier."

"Sebastian, squad leader, second maniple, Third Cohort."

"Third," the centurion snarled. "It figures. Stand aside, soldiers."

Sebastian shot Prometheus a what-can-you-do? look and stepped aside. The weasel marched imperiously through the doors.

As they swung shut Prometheus muttered, "I'd dearly love to teach that squirt not to sneer at the Third."

"That's the least," Sebastian retorted. "Why does a vice-consul need a dagger?"

"I didn't see a—"

"I didn't either," Sebastian cut him off. "Just the suggestion of one under his toga. Castor! You two want to join me in putting my head in a winepress?"

Castor trotted up. "You know how sanguine I am about groundless hunches."

Prometheus nodded. "Lead on."

"Manlius, Quinn—take the doors." Sebastian pulled one door open part way and looked inside. The centurion, another guard, four scribes seated at benches, the chubby little man whose audience was ending, the weasel preparing to approach the dais—nothing looked suspicious. Groundless, like Castor said. *This is foolish,* Sebastian thought as he stepped into the room.

The weasel was halfway to Diocletian when Sebastian started forward. "Hold there!"

The centurion reached out wildly to grab Sebastian, but Prometheus's bulk knocked him aside.

The weasel had reached the dais, his arms hidden in the folds of his toga. He wheeled and looked not at Sebastian but beyond him at the young centurion. His face told Sebastian his mind had changed course. Then it said his mind was set. Sebastian could read it. The fool was going to—

"For the good of the empire!" the weasel screamed. Dagger in hand he was lunging for the dais, for the throne. Sebastian was hurtling, locking around the little man's waist, slamming against the floor on his back. His helmet clanged against the tile. It stunned him, causing him to loosen his grip.

The weasel wrenched free. Prometheus came lumbering up but the assassin slipped past him and disappeared behind a heavy curtain. Sebastian nearly tripped over Prometheus's bulky foot as he scrambled up.

Sebastian slashed across the curtain with his sword. The severed half floated down as the door behind it slammed shut. He hit the door with his armored shoulder, but the latch held. He rolled aside for another attempt, but Prometheus was whomping into the door. The latch held; the hinges gave. At the far end of a dark passageway the weasel was yanking another door open.

They were halfway down the passageway as the far door slammed behind their quarry. They heard a bar fall. Sebastian slowed as Prometheus gathered speed. No door can withstand a juggernaut in full armor. Sebastian leaped the pile that was Prometheus and the splintered door and kept running, out onto a balustrade. Below lay a small formal garden lined with privet hedge. Sebastian had him now! He knew from his prowling about that this garden wall was too high to scale, that the only gate was at this end. And the weasel had just gone over the side.

Sebastian jumped over the balustrade, dropped into a soft flowerbed, and rolled to his feet. He moved forward carefully toward the shrubbery at the far end. He was now between the weasel and the only way out.

But for a small fountain, silence. His helmet hampered both

eyes and ears. He pulled it off and carried it under his left arm. Somewhere in this row of neatly trimmed hedging, at any moment, at any place, that dagger could come slashing out at him. The angle of the sun made him the clearer target. He could try hacking the hedge down foot by foot, but he might break his sword.

Silence. Had the man somehow evaded him?

He tossed his dented helmet high in the air. It dropped down on the far side of the hedge. He heard simultaneously the quiet bonk of his helmet beyond and the rustle of disturbed bushes nearby. He stabbed blindly into the hedge, a wild guess at where the man's legs might be. The man cried out.

Sebastian stepped back quickly. The dagger came piercing through the hedge, stabbing just as blindly. He grabbed the scrawny wrist and held on.

Now Prometheus was at his shoulder. Together they pulled the luckless weasel out through the dense hedge. The clutching branches scratched the man's face and arms and stripped his toga off. They sprawled him out and Prometheus gently laid a gargantuan foot on his neck.

The garden gate burst open and a surfeit of guards swarmed through. They hesitated, looking to Sebastian for instructions. Very well. He could wear the purple.

He kept his voice quiet. "Bind his leg there where I stuck him and deliver him before Caesar." He wiped his sword on the man's tunic and started off toward the gate, Prometheus at his side.

"Prometheus, my gentle friend, I thank you." He was leaving his helmet behind. He didn't care.

Prometheus laid a heavy paw on his arm. "Eyes are on you. Look up."

On the balustrade above them the emperor beckoned briefly with a gesture and disappeared inside.

Prometheus rumbled, "Do you suppose we need a pass?"

"I think we just got one."

The hallway, empty moments before, was now alive with people of all sorts—togas, armor, and everything in between. Sebastian let Prometheus lead and walked comfortably in the giant's wake. Quintillian and Manlius stood at the opened doors with swords drawn, shields up.

Sebastian grinned. "You two look so professional. Shall we just hang up our helmets and retire or take over for you?"

Quinn shook his head. "You can't. You're supposed to go inside."

Primus was one of half a dozen people in the auditorium who had not been there before. He stood by the dais facing the door. Diocletian's back was to them. As they entered he turned and seated himself. A splash of blood on his sleeve was the only hint that he had been marked for death moments before.

"Primus, close the doors. Have your men clear that hall. Don't leave. You, Thaleus. Come forward."

So the young centurion's name was Thaleus.

"Did you recognize the intruder?"

"No, Your Clemency."

"Then why did you bid him enter?" the emperor demanded.

"He, ah...frankly, sir, he seemed to carry authority. I thought I recognized him as an official. He resembled...ah, he just naturally..."

"Naturally. Choros, the new command assignments."

One of the scribes shuffled out a hefty parchment and placed it in the emperor's hand. Diocletian unrolled it slowly. In addition to a soldier he was a good showman. Sebastian made mental note of the psychological value of deliberation.

"As you know, Thaleus, we have a big shake-up in the Fifth. New assignment sheet here. You are slated for the captaincy, did you know that?"

"Well, ah...I...," Thaleus stammered.

"You heard a rumor to that effect perhaps," Diocletian suggested.

"A rumor. Yes, sir."

"Untrue. The rumor, that is. A pen." The same faceless scribe quickly passed a quill to the emperor. "Scratch Thaleus...insert...Sebastian. Hmm. That leaves a hole in Primus's maniple. Squad leader. Thaleus, I perceive that being a squad leader under Primus here teaches the value of following orders to the letter. You don't seem to have learned that lesson yet. Let's put you in that slot."

"Your Clemency!"

Diocletian roared, "I do not hand out promotions as personal favors, Centurion. Sebastian has earned my trust twice over and you have earned my disrespect, if not suspicion. Had you not pulled rank on these two doorkeepers the man would not have entered. The incident would not have occurred. Castor's blood would not be staining my sleeve here n—"

"Castor!" Sebastian and Prometheus blurted it as one.

Diocletian sat back and put himself in better repose. Then he explained, "As you were diving for my assailant, Castor was diving for me. Protecting me with his own body. Now he has a marvelous story to bore his grandchildren with. You, giant. Your name."

"Marcus Gallitinus Prometheus, Your Clemency."

"You, too, have earned a promotion."

"Sir, may I speak?" Prometheus ventured.

"Say."

"I have no desire for promotion, Your Clemency. I am content to serve with men I trust and enjoy. If Your Clemency please, might I transfer to the Fifth also and serve at the side of my friend? We seem to make a good team between us."

"It seems you do." The emperor looked at his new captain. "Sebastian?"

The rumbling hulk had never expressed his thoughts or feelings. Sebastian would not have guessed. "Your Clemency. Uh, I am surprised—and very much honored—that he should value our friendship above his loyalty to the Third. I would be delighted to serve under him or over him—so long as I am with him."

Some color was at last returning to Diocletian's face. His eyes did not look so sunken. "Primus, I remember the old days in the Fifth, when we enjoyed just this sort of comradeship. Then this emperor business started. Influence, jockeying for position. I watched power plays tear our cohort apart from the inside. It's still the best in the Guard, but even it has lost something. Your unit still has that something." The emperor paused and sighed. "Primus. Never aspire to become Caesar. Your men will thank you for it."

8

The promotion to captaincy brought more than just heckling and head-wagging from his friends. Sebastian was now in a position to rent a small apartment outside the camp, to marry, to take a concubine, to buy a slave. He wrote again to his parents, to Desmontes, and to Melita. Desmontes returned his letter fourfold; there were no other replies.

As often as duties permitted, the five old friends got together. They explored the baths, sampled the taverns, roamed the markets and helped fill in the blank spots on Sebastian's map. They might attend meetings of some local group or just sit under a tree outside Nomentana Gate and discuss whatever piece of Scripture one of them happened to dig up.

When he could, Sebastian frequented the slave market, looking over prospects. He noticed nothing inviting. But then, the pretty ones would change hands privately, not on the block.

Over the course of the summer Pavo sent out several sorties against Christian meetings. Sebastian got in on only two of them and was able to salvage seven persons. It was nearly nones in August before he and Primus perfected the best plan yet. The day after an arrest they simply "transferred" some of the prisoners to other prisons. Sebastian soon became adept at forging fictitious initials and seals.

September kalends he received a charming note from Melita inquiring after his general health, well-being, and happiness. The next day Sebastian, Prometheus, two squads, and four Dacian Lancers were gathered at a warehouse near Probi Bridge, prepared to raid a Christian meeting. As always before a raid, Sebastian felt nervous and sick in his stomach.

The plan was by Pavo himself, for the *legatus* had heard that men of high civilian rank were among the criminals. Sebastian as captain would make the formal arrests. The Lancers would aid on foot, taking to horse only if necessary to pursue and cut down escapees. The Lancers did not muck out stables daily for the privilege of operating on foot. Grumbling, they left their mounts outside the warehouse in charge of a recruit.

The raid proceeded smoothly enough, disgruntled Lancers notwithstanding. Sebastian was especially pleased, as they herded their prisoners toward the warehouse doors, to see a blond head duck down behind some bales. They stepped outside, the person safely left behind; but then the blond head panicked.

As Sebastian was lining up the party for the march across the Sublicius Bridge, the blond boy burst out a side door, running for the horses. Expertly he leaped aboard the nearest Lancer horse and clattered off toward the Cestius Bridge. The other three Lancers lunged for their horses.

"Never mind! I'll catch him!" Sebastian reached a long-necked roan twenty feet ahead of the Lancer that should have been riding it. He swung aboard and raced off after their escaping prisoner.

Behind him came the other two horses. He should have known those Lancers would get into the chase. Now he could not simply pull up short and claim the boy got away.

The boy was a good rider. He crossed Cestius and Fabricius Bridges safely, weaving in and out between the carts. Now they were in the vegetable market. Women cursed and shook their fists as the four riders rattled through the narrow streets in the wild and giddy race.

The roan slipped on the cobbles and nearly went down. What if the boy's horse fell? The escapee turned into an alley lined with stalls. An awning prop caught Sebastian in the knee and nearly unhorsed him, but it gave with a loud crack. Glancing back, he saw the awning float to the street, slowing the Lancers.

A chicken squawked and the roan stumbled, then picked up the beat again. Someone would have chicken dinner tonight.

An ox stopped short of crossing the alley as the boy drummed past. It started forward again, belabored by its master's goad, and lurched right in front of Sebastian. Before he could think, Sebastian felt his horse's shoulders bunch between his knees, then they were airborne. His horse cleared the ox handily, avoided going down on the slippery cobbles, and kept running. The Lancer directly behind him cleared. The second fellow did not.

The three crossed the broad Flaminia Way at full gallop. More women cursed as the boy plunged his horse into another sidestreet. Did he know that the Servian Wall blocked his escape to the east? He would not be able to negotiate the Salutaris Gate.

Just ahead of them a pony cart blocked the alley, parked exactly sideways. The boy's horse cleared it easily enough. The ox had been larger. Sebastian dug his heels in, kept his horse coming hard. At the last moment, as his horse gathered itself for the jump, he wrenched its head around. Thrown off stride, the roan plowed into the cart with a piercing squeal.

Sebastian skidded across the pavingstones on his side; on his back, his armor clanking on the cobbles. He must get himself out of the way before that Lancer came over the pile-up, for he would not clear it. Helpless on his back, Sebastian watched the Lancer's black horse loom above the churning wreck, tangle in the roan's legs, and slam into the cobbles beside him. The race was over. The boy had won.

Sebastian stood up and took a deep breath. He was relieved to find that his ribs worked. He pulled his helmet off angrily. *Stupid helmet.* His head rang. Now that it was all over his hands shook.

The cart might as well have been trampled by an elephant. Its shaggy little pony was thrown down, still in the shafts. A young woman tugged at the harness, trying ineffectively to free it. Sebastian drew his sword and crossed to the pony.

The woman leaped up and blocked his way. "No! Please! Don't hurt it! Don't hurt the poor thing, it was my fault!"

Women, he said to himself. *Hopeless bundles of wayward emotion.* He pushed her aside, hooked his blade under the shaft loops and sliced them. He shoved the shaft up and out with his foot. The pony squirmed and rolled to its belly. That gave Sebastian the space he needed to slip his blade under the bottom shaft loops. Freed, the pony lurched to its feet and stood trembling, its nose nearly touching the ground.

Sebastian's roan was still legs-up in the tangle of shattered wood. The right foreleg kicked wildly as the horse struggled, trying to roll, trying to get off its back. Gleaming white bone protruded from red blood just above the knee. Sebastian sighed deeply. Better that this horse die than a child of God. Still... He looped his fingers into the roan's nostrils and twisted its head back. The long neck curved into a graceful arc. One swift stroke finished the job.

"While your sword is drawn, Captain..." The Lancer was kneeling by his black horse, holding its head down. Sebastian stepped across his own dying roan, away from the steamy blood coursing between the cobbles.

The Lancer could not be more than sixteen. His eyes were moist, but otherwise he was doing a good job of being a soldier. "Shame, too, sir. Good horse."

"That all that's wrong, his stifle there?"

The boy sniffed. "Enough, I'd say."

"Ever set a stifle?"

"What?"

"Neither have I, but I saw it done once. Sometimes when a stifle's thrown out it will slip back, sometimes not. Worth a try. But it will take three of us; one to—"

"I'll keep his head down." It was the woman with the pony. Without waiting for by-your-leave she knelt by the horse's head and threw one leg over its neck. She grasped an ear, locked her fingers in its upper lip, and waited.

Sebastian nodded. "Come here," he said to the boy as he pulled the hind leg of the dead horse free. "You pull down in this manner... That's right, like that. While I pull back this way. See what we're trying to do?"

The Lancer's face brightened. "Let's try it!"

The swirling, babbling crowd, the barking dogs were pressing close around. Sebastian had no patience to spare on them. A whole church taken prisoner. And he didn't like to see animals suffer either, especially when he was responsible. And these people smelled. Didn't they know what the public baths were for? He slammed his armored shoulder into two of the tougher looking churls. "Move back! The lot of you!" The crowd fell back a foot or so.

The woman was still on the horse's head, waiting patiently. Cautiously the Lancer grasped his horse's hock and adjusted to a good, tight grip. Sebastian braced his feet on the cobbles, set his hands, and threw his weight into it. The horse squealed, then groaned a throaty moan.

Sebastian stepped back. "Let him up."

The young woman swung her leg off. Her skirt flipped momentarily to the knee, revealing a particularly graceful shin and ankle. Then the leg was modestly shrouded again. Why couldn't Christian girls be this pretty? The only girls Sebastian met at assemblies were plain as fenceposts and every bit as shapely.

The horse lay still as if assessing its situation. It lunged halfway to sitting and paused, breathing heavily. The Lancer watched and gnawed his lip. His eyes were getting wet again. *Come on, boy, stay tough,* Sebastian thought. The horse hauled onto its forelegs, hesitated; the big back end lurched and he was up.

A heartfelt if disorganized cheer rose from the onlookers. Sebastian realized the Lancer was still standing beside him. It was the girl who was urging the horse forward, a step at a time, hands just right on the bridle. She was talking softly, cooing, praising. The horse hobbled and put weight on its bad leg.

Sebastian jabbed the Lancer. "Lead him out before he freezes up. Matter of fact, walk him back out the way we came in and send someone for my horse's gear."

Delighted for the job, the boy threaded his limping horse around the shattered cart and led it off toward Flaminia Way.

Sebastian realized belatedly that he had given the boy the

only job there was to do. He had nothing to do himself save stand there, look authoritative, and wait. The crowd was no less dense, but the content of it changed as people came and went, wagging heads, muttering. Descriptions by second-hand witnesses were already magnifying the spectacular nature of the wreck. In a last-ditch effort to look busy, Sebastian crossed back over to the pony.

Its muzzle was wet. The young woman must have watered it. *Lucky pony,* he thought. Then she was at his side, wiping her mouth and chin on her sleeve. "Drink, soldier?" She offered an unglazed jar.

He took it. The water went down clean and cold.

On the pony's back lay a wet rag, grey and resinous and pinkish with blood. Someone had been washing off the pony's scuffs.

"Came out all right," Sebastian nodded. "Lost a little skin, is all."

"Are you talking about the pony or you?"

Now that she mentioned it, his arm was on fire from elbow to wrist. He twisted it around for a better look. "I'm going to have to speak to the governor about putting down softer cobbles."

"Tile, perhaps."

"Right. Tiled streets. Ever ride a horse across tile?"

She smiled. "As a matter of fact, I have. Come over here in the shade and rest a moment." She snatched the resinous rag in passing and plopped down under a shop awning that was obviously hers.

Sebastian sprawled beside her in the cool shade. He noted now that she was not so young as he had thought—probably his age or a little older.

"When I was ten I got very mad at my father because he suggested that I couldn't ride. Only boys can ride well, he said. So I bridled his favorite horse and rode it through the house, one end to the other. Around the impluvium, around the peristyle half a dozen times. He kept lunging for its head and I would duck the horse away from him—and all the while screaming that I can't ride, so I can't control him. I waited and waited for that horse to lift its tail. It wouldn't. Obviously it was better mannered than I was."

"I could tell you grew up with horses. Gallic or Germanic?"

"Germanic, but my father was in love with Romanesque. Raetia. He was a contract horse breeder for the government post. He sold them in Milan, of course. And if the post wasn't buying, the army was. When he died I decided I didn't want to live up north."

"You don't like snow," Sebastian guessed.

"Exactly." She poured some water onto the rag, tipped his elbow up and slopped gently at the scuff. He dearly wanted her to quit—the water made the fire burn twice as hot—but he couldn't think of any manly way to say so.

She shook her head. "Look at this mess. You can write with it." She stroked her reddened finger across his arm in a smooth arc.

The act was so off-handed Sebastian almost missed it. Almost.

"You're right." He struck an opposing arc to complete the sign of the fish. Grinning brightly she wiped the sign away. He was grinning for a different reason. There was at least one pretty believer left in the world.

"I know that boy you were chasing. And now I know why you spilled your horse deliberately."

"It was an accident," he corrected.

"Right. I compliment your perfect timing. And your courage. You could well have had that horse in your lap for a boy you don't even know."

Impulsively he asked, "Are you married?"

"No," she said quickly.

He heard horses' hooves but no wheels. *Lancers coming,* he thought. He stood up and retrieved his helmet, but he couldn't take his eyes off her.

She smiled a strange, sad smile. "Don't bother to ask my name. I'm tainted. Definitely not marriage material. Do you know why Mary Magdalene is my favorite disciple? She, too, was a prostitute until she met the Master."

For a week Sebastian haunted the Lancers' quarters and training stable, watching. Finally he found just what he wanted—an injured horse. He spoke to the prefect, left his sword and armor at the stable and rode off with the crippled horse in tow.

The sun had just dropped behind Janiculum. The air sparkled clear and cool and golden. She was there at her stand, just closing up for the day. Sebastian noted what he had failed to note previously: she was a vendor of willow baskets and clever little broomstraw toys.

She saw him coming, of course. How do you ride up inconspicuously with not one horse but two? He slid off his mount and waited as she lowered her awning. She seemed a bit discomfited. "Good evening, soldier."

"Good evening, lady."

"Can I, uh, help out with something?" she asked hesitantly.

"As it happens, aye. I know an expert when I see one, and I need an expert opinion here."

As she turned to him he led the crippled gelding forward a few steps. "Right forefoot there. He got cut up a couple weeks ago. It's not healing."

She dropped down and started poking around the injury. *Beautiful face, beautiful figure, beautiful attitude,* Sebastian silently assessed.

"I'm afraid, sir, it's not going to heal, either, until you cut out that proudflesh and pack it."

Sebastian dropped to one knee close beside her and feigned interest in the horse. "How do I go about doing that?" He glanced up at her. She was staring at him.

"How long did it take you to dig this horse out of the dunghill? Since the accident?"

"What?"

"For the excuse to come back here? You're as transparent as a fishpond, soldier."

Sebastian felt his cheeks flush hot. This impudent woman! This prideful, irritating, absolutely correct woman! Since he stood up, she did too.

"All right! All right, since you prefer to deal with directness. My name is Sebastian and as you know I serve our Lord. A year ago I joined the Guard to try to save some of the brethren, and already God has promoted me to captain in the Fifth Cohort. Unheard of, but that's what He did. I asked Him for a wife and now that I have the captaincy I can afford one—a first step, you see. Since you are the most beautiful woman I have ever met in or out of the faith I want to court you. My uncle, who was my favorite person until I met you, claims courtship is painful, boring, thankless and I don't remember what else, and you're not helping matters a bit. But I want to court you nonetheless."

She was gaping, wide-eyed. They were a luminous gray, her eyes.

"Also, lady, I arrived in Rome very recently from Milan. I want to become associated with a group for fellowship and deeper instruction, and I was hoping perhaps you could tell me when and where.

"And, since I'm here, it would be nice if you could do something for this horse's wound which is, as you see, not healing. And also, I'd like to buy you another pony cart to replace the one I deliberately wrecked a week ago. Oh, and incidentally, that black horse is doing all right. It's not limping anymore, just in case you wondered."

"I...I did wonder, now that you mention it. I have never..." She stopped and drew a deep breath. "No! I told you right from the very beginning, I'm not available. Thank you anyway. What I mean is, I am deeply moved—really, much flattered—by your eloquent appeal. But no."

"You certainly have a way of dumping cold water on a courtship."

"You have a way of stubbornly persisting in a barren venture. However, no use the horse should suffer for your stubbornness. Let's see, we may have to tie up a hind leg to keep him halfway quiet for this."

They worked on it by the fountain. Deft as she was in her ministrations, it was still pitch dark by the time they cleaned up.

Sebastian insisted on seeing her home. After all, he reasoned, he would not permit his worst enemy ("Who is, incidentally, a man named Marcus Cannius up in Milan unless a Thaleus down here has taken over the title") to walk the streets alone. Her protests yielded to "safety" and "common sense."

The crippled horse was very sore, so they walked slowly, strolling along the Servian Wall, talking of Milan and horses. He wished it were light so that he could devote his full attention to her instead of minding the ominous, dangerous dark around them.

She stopped at a shabby apartment house just inside the Salutaris Gate. Sebastian was delighted. This was less than a mile from camp and the Nomentana Way would take him nearly straight home.

Now what? Sebastian thought as he lingered at the door, but she seemed determined to go inside. Somewhere out in the blackness a horse whinnied.

"Thank you for seeing me safely home. Good evening."

The crippled horse raised its head and answered the distant whinny.

Sebastian scowled at the horse, then nodded. "Oh, well. All right, if you insist."

He tipped her face up quickly before she could pull away and kissed her lips—a gentle peck. "That was for him, by request. He says thank you, but he can't pucker. Good evening, lady."

She was speechless. He had rendered this arrogant, self-possessed, forward woman speechless. She started to say something. Instead she pulled her palla close around and disappeared into the black hallway.

"Oh." She reappeared. "Three before ides at nightfall. That burned-out villa just south of Collina Gate." She disappeared again.

The villa still smelled of charred wood. The fire must have occurred recently. Sebastian stood in shadow a hundred paces away, watching the front entry, Prometheus at his shoulder. He glanced over at Quinn, Castor, and Primus. Castor nodded.

The three of them moved off into the dark. They were in full armor. Sebastian was beginning to regard helmets with the same loathing Desmontes afforded togas.

Believers were arriving by twos and threes, furtively, silently. Sebastian could see no one he could say absolutely was she. The trickle of believers seemed to end.

Prometheus moved out beside him. Together they stalked soundlessly to the burnt doorway, stepped carefully over the buckled iron gate. Inside, a soft rich voice intoned prayer.

In one of the side rooms little damaged by the fire, perhaps thirty worshipers sat in bunches on the cluttered floor. A white-bearded gentleman at the front had completed prayer and now unrolled a worn scroll. Beside him burned three of the five lamps in the room. Sebastian could not see into the darkness beyond the front of the room, but apparently Prometheus could. The giant nodded. They stepped forward, swords in hand.

From the shadows beyond the front of the room Castor appeared, sword drawn. Primus and Quinn materialized to either side of him. The congregation gasped in unison.

Castor should have been an actor. He stepped forward imperiously. "Those of you who wish to spare your lives by denying this Jesus may do so by leaving now."

A woman sobbed and buried her face in her hands. The man beside her laid his arm around her shoulders.

"Go! Do not play the fools! Spare yourselves!" he implored.

No movement. There she was, on this side of the room. She was staring at Sebastian with tears in her eyes. No anger, no hatred. But that expression of betrayal—he couldn't bring himself to look at her.

Castor melted into a broad grin. "Not a one, Bass!"

Sebastian grinned back. "You expected anything less, my friend?" With the others he carefully laid his sword at the feet of the bearded old man.

"You see, good father," said Castor, "we are members of the Guard whom God has prospered with a fruitful work. We can't risk betrayal, so we determined this would be as good a way as any to weed out the weak in faith who might inform against us. May we join you?"

A long pause. "And if we prefer you not join us?"

"We go our way with no harm or betrayal to you," Castor promised. "With our blessings all the same."

The gentleman bent over. It took him several moments to gather all five hilts into his quivering hands. He stood up with difficulty. "The question was academic, children. We would not refuse the fellowship of any believer." He extended the swords. " 'He who lives by the sword shall die by the sword.' But then, many of us who do not live by the sword seem to die from it all the same. My name is Caius. I welcome you in the name and peace of our Lord, Jesus the Christ."

Sebastian relieved the gentleman of holding out the swords. The man seemed so frail. When only his sword was left in his hand he sheathed it, pulled off his helmet, and sat down on the only piece of floor worth sitting on. She did not look at him. But then, neither did she sidle away from him.

Caius was a brilliant teacher—more magisterial than Felician, less flamboyant. How Desmontes would love to know this fellow! He expounded upon a letter by James, just a short piece. Sebastian had never read it. The message was greatly illuminating, the warm and vibrant body beside him only mildly distracting.

They sang a hymn Sebastian did not know, then Caius spoke the blessing and people got up to mill around. No one seemed anxious to leave. Quintillian engaged Caius immediately in some discussion. White head and dark bent together over the text. *Good!* Sebastian thought; he had suspected Quinn still wasn't certain. Caius was the best thing that could happen to him.

Primus was surrounded by three men, discussing the remarkable similarities between Mithraism and Christianity.

Sebastian smiled warmly. "Good evening, lady."

"Did you have to do that? I mean, that way?" she asked reprovingly.

"It was Castor's idea. He's Greek to the core: suffers from a flair for melodrama, so we humor him."

"Castor. He's that one," she said, pointing in the right direction.

"Right. Primus over there; Prometheus; Quintillian is talking to Caius. I'm Sebastian, remember?"

"I remember," she said softly.

After a long silence Sebastian prodded, "Well? Do you tell me your name or do I ask any one of these believers, who surely know?"

"Irene."

"Just Irene?"

"No matter how much you get, you're still not satisfied. Do you realize that?"

"I'm not greedy. However, I'm always prepared to accept more. You lived in Raetia on your father's horse farm until he died. Since most of his horsetrading was done in Milan you went there, a city familiar to you. And no snow. Since there are no women in the cavalry, you had only one means of supporting yourself. You turned away from that profession when you turned to Jesus Christ. But how did you get from Milan to here? And who was instrumental in your conversion?"

"I will admit you are smarter than I first gave you credit for." She even permitted herself half a smile (he was making progress). "For a while I was the favorite of the vice-consul of Milan. He was beheaded in some sort of political intrigue and I was—oh, you might say I was 'bequeathed'—to his successor.

"The man became involved in the Christian cult, as he called it. Casually at first, but eventually all-consuming. His position as vice-consul was drawing unfavorable attention to the Christians who came to see him—not to mention on he himself, so he arranged his own political defeat. It was beautiful. Helped a usurper usurp him—he even financed the fellow. He's very good at that sort of thing. Actually, of course, what he was doing was retiring from public office, but it looked less suspicious that way.

"Sebastian, stop gawking at me like that. What can be so—wait! He had a son. No, a nephew. A nephew out in the province named...I don't believe it!"

"Neither will Desmontes. I can't wait to tell him. But how did you end up here in Rome?"

"When Desmontes and I parted I took a job as housekeeper for a friend of his, Demetrius Antipater. Demetrius's mission in life was to circulate the Scriptures, and I became one of his couriers. I had brought a parcel of scrolls down here to Rome when I learned he had been raided. Raided and executed. With nothing calling me back to Milan, I stayed here."

Sebastian's head swirled. Had the Holy Spirit not intervened, she would have been lost on that very first raid. He would have...this beautiful woman...and Desmontes. Desmontes and this lovely flower. A perfect match. Then why...?

"Irene, Desmontes is a man of impeccable taste, not to mention fair justice. Why aren't you two...or shouldn't I...?"

"By law a harlot is forbidden to marry, and I was a registered prostitute. More important, though, by God's law a woman must belong to one man. I have belonged to many. When I, too, embraced the faith, we both realized—"

"Who put this in your head? Desmontes?"

"He's right! It's very clear that—"

"He's wrong! When you become a new person in Christ the old is put away. You have a fresh start. You're free to—"

"The old nature is put down," she cut in, "but it remains as long as the flesh remains; just as a scar or physical deformity would. I'm content. I really am. Please don't try to stir up old fires."

"How can my dear old uncle mess me up like this?" He scratched his head and smoothed his hair down again. *Stupid helmets,* he thought irritably. "What does Caius say about this?"

"He's uncertain because he hasn't read all the writings yet. He says I must trust my own convictions, so I am."

"Then you consider yourself an authority on Scripture."

"No, not an authority...What I mean is..."

"If an authority gave you a learned opinion, would you accept it?" Sebastian asked her.

"Of course." After a pause she added, "Depending on the authority, I mean."

"Felician? Ever meet a gentleman in Milan named Felician?"

"Certainly. One of Desmontes' best friends."

"Will you trust Felician's judgment? If I write him by private post and he sends back an opinion, will you heed it?"

"Well, I suppose...," Irene said haltingly.

"Will you trust Felician's judgment?" Sebastian coaxed.

"Yes. I suppose..."

"Then I'll send the letter tomorrow."

"Now wait just a moment! If he says it really is all right for me to start over, like you say, I'll...uh...I'll reconsider. But if he says I'm correct, you must abide by that. You must abandon this...this insane courtship idea. Agreed?"

Sebastian nodded. "Agreed."

He would have to be very, very careful in his phrasing of the letter to Felician. If ever he needed a gift for words...

9

"You sent for me, Your Clemency?" Sebastian closed the chamber door behind him.

"Good day, Sebastian." Diocletian sprawled out in a chair and scratched his chest with both hands. His eyes were starting to look sunken again. "How do you like Rome?"

"She truly is the queen, sir. Nothing else like her."

"Indeed," the emperor concurred. "But noisy. Nerve-wracking, after a fashion, just like a woman. Ever meet a real queen?"

"No, sir."

"I did once. Zenobia of Palmyra. Ever hear of her?"

"Vaguely," Sebastian answered.

"Nothing vague about her. She was dark; a classy lady, a beautiful lady. But strange. Called herself Queen of the Orient. You can't imagine her dress, her jewelry, the make-up. She headquartered in Palmyra and claimed she had conquered

Egypt and the whole East, every shrouded barbarian in it.

"Aurelian captured her when he took Palmyra. Kept her handy, exhibited her a while in Rome when he returned. His triumphal entry was...oh, I don't know—ten years ago?"

"A little longer," Sebastian informed him. "I left Milan for Narbonne right after that. A little longer."

"Right. Anyway, he displayed her and then built her a villa out around Tibur, not too far from Hadrian's Villa. And he sent a Praetorian maniple out now and then for guard duty and maintenance. That's when I met her. Beautiful woman. Gorgeous. Bawdy. And strange."

"Sounds just like Rome, sir—right down to being served by the Guard," Sebastian quipped.

Diocletian chuckled. "By glory, you're right. Never thought of that. And strident. Don't forget strident. I have to get away from this noise and confusion a while. I hate noise; even the palace is full of it. Pick yourself ten good men—either cohort—and put them on horses to accompany me out to Hadrian's Villa tomorrow. Don't worry about tents or supplies. There's a fully equipped praetorium on the grounds. We'll leave the side gate here at dawn."

"You did say ten."

"Ten. I know, I know. The emperor is supposed to travel with a retinue a mile long. Do you know what an incredible burden a retinue is? I'm trying to get away from it, not take it with me. Just the twelve of us on horseback—be there in two hours. Thunder and fire, it's only fifteen miles!"

"Ten men and me, dawn tomorrow, on horses. By your leave, sir." Sebastian saluted and turned toward the doors.

"Incidentally, Sebastian, what's your opinion of Carinus?"

Sebastian turned back. "I've passed him now and then, discussed business on two or three occasions, but I don't know him, really."

"You don't have to know a man to form an opinion of him."

"I do, Your Clemency."

Diocletian snickered. "Dismissed."

That afternoon Sebastian personally picked out the biggest

horse in the west side stables for Prometheus, but he still looked ridiculous on horseback. Primus took a dim view of soldiering from four feet off the ground, but he accepted the offer because he wanted so much to see the fabled Hadrian's Villa. If Prometheus could make it fifteen miles without splitting, so could he—probably.

Castor accepted for the same reason. Quinn particularly liked cavalry and horses and being a Lancer. Sebastian hated to ask Thaleus, but knew he should. He privately rejoiced to hear Thaleus was out of town on leave. He filled the final six positions with Dacian Lancers, just so there would be someone along besides himself who could stay on a horse in an emergency.

He drilled his motley crew two hours that evening. At dawn the next day he still had serious misgivings about his "handpicked" escort. But Castor and Primus fell in at either side of Diocletian, thanks to well-drilled horses. The six Lancers formed expertly into two rows behind. And Quinn and Prometheus joined Sebastian at the rear as if they were born to horse. Quinn especially was good. Sebastian was so relieved, he didn't bother to mention to Prometheus that the gentle giant's reins were accidentally crossed.

Peace. Silence and peace are not synonymous, but very nearly so. No wonder Diocletian was so content out here. The villa, built by Hadrian and maintained by the emperors who succeeded him, spread out for nearly half a mile. It could be a distracting little city, but Diocletian purposely kept the numbers down while he was there.

Sebastian spent hours wandering among the gardens, the halls, the splendid Doric peristyle. Hadrian had loved the arts and it was all here—statuary, fresco, mosaic—all still here. The scale boggled him most, from the full-size Greek amphitheatre on the east to the reproduction of an Egyptian river town on the southwest. Two baths, a private stadium—all in polished marble.

Twelve days after their arrival they were still there. Sebastian could understand Diocletian's reluctance to return to the tension and intrigues of the palace in Rome. But, God permitting, Felician's letter would be arriving soon in Rome. Sebastian was confident he knew Felician's mind in the matter. But what if Desmontes' opinion prevailed? The waiting was making an old man of him.

So was boredom. He organized whomever he happened upon into work crews and directed minor repairs. He maintained a strong guard, of course, but there was really little to do.

Late in the evening of three before nones, Sebastian found himself wandering out into the small formal garden beyond the Philosopher's Gate. A lark rose off the hillside beyond the garden wall, singing good-bye to the sun. This was Sebastian's favorite place, this garden, and his favorite time of day. The place was stately, sedate, neatly trimmed, silent except for the crickets under the hedges. A marble bust of Elagabalus watched stoney-eyed over his shoulder as he sat down on a marble bench and stretched his legs out. Twittering swifts swirled in and out among each other across the clear gold sky.

Peace.

He felt the movement rather than saw it—someone nearby. He leaped to his feet, wheeled, and jerked to attention.

By the Philosopher's Gate Diocletian snapped his fingers. "Thought for sure I could catch you napping. Better luck to me next time." He pushed the gate open and stepped inside.

"Just leaving, Your Clemency. Enjoy the evening."

"Sit down."

Sebastian sat.

Diocletian stretched out on a bench as Sebastian had done moments ago. "It's a pleasure to just sit and pass the time with someone who isn't currying my favor for political reasons. You'll never know what a treat that is. Aye, Sebastian, I did some checking—talked to Primus this afternoon. He says you have no politics."

"That's about it."

"You're lucky. You're sharp—quick. You could aspire to high office and achieve it, probably in a very few years. Look how fast you rose in the military."

Sebastian smiled, "With a little help from my friends."

"Of course. How do you think I climbed to the top? By stacking furniture? You have the potential to be very big politically, and that's why you're lucky you aren't interested. If I had to start over...Know how old I am? Thirty-eight. And I feel like an eighty-year-old pensioner."

"High office isn't worth it?"

"That's right. In some respects. The empire's a mess. The only reason the barbarians haven't destroyed us is that they're in just as big a mess right now. And the only reason we haven't collapsed from the inside is Aurelian. *Was* Aurelian, I should say. His influence is dying.

"I have a plan, Sebastian. A good, solid, manageable government. Two emperors heading up an efficient double-regency system. I have it pretty well worked out in my head. Once it's set up and rolling, I retire."

"To Hadrian's Villa here," Sebastian presumed.

"No. I'd love that. But I'll leave this for my successors. I'm building my own, in Dalmatia. I grew up in Dalmatia, you know. My wife, she prefers Nicomedia, but I love Dalmatia. Going to go home and raise cabbages."

Sebastian studied him. "Cabbages?"

"Cabbages," Diocletian repeated. "Do you realize how versatile a cabbage is? How many people who eat cabbage develop scurvy? None. Ever taste sauerkraut? The only good thing the barbarians ever invented. Cabbage grows anywhere, prepares quickly with a minimum of fuss. What the world needs with its wheat gruel is the perfect cabbage—a variety that grows to a large size quickly; thick leaves; hard heads; sweet flavor. There is much possibility for improvement in cabbages, as there is in men."

"Then there's got to be something wrong with cabbages, as with men," Sebastian observed. "Nobody's perfect."

Diocletian chuckled. "You're mocking me."

"Not at all. I don't mind saying I have never had any enthusiasm for cabbage."

"Neither has Galerius—my son, you know. I suppose there are problems, like you say. Pretty much frostproof, for example, but they tend to wilt in heat. And there's cabbage worms, of course."

"Dust them," Sebastian suggested.

"What's that?" The emperor looked puzzled.

"Dust your cabbages. Gets the worms every time." Gentle Taurus's words came back like yesterday. "Take a jar of lime maybe so big. Add a double handful of ashes, like this or so. Mix it up, of course, and dust it on your cabbages after a rain. Or while they're dewy."

"Never heard of it. Sebastian, if the worms get fat I'll have your head in a basket. And if it works I install you as the next emperor, political interests or no."

"I promise I won't make you eat those words if I don't have to eat the cabbage."

Diocletian laughed and squirmed down onto his spine, a relaxed monarch. The swifts seemed to be giving up for the night. Sebastian was uncertain whether his presence was intruding or pleasing.

Suddenly Diocletian spoke. "Sebastian, you're sitting beside a murderer."

"What emperor is not one?" Sebastian replied blandly.

"Now that's a comforting philosophy. And practical. Carinus will not step down, though he has proved himself incompetent to run half an empire efficiently. His first mistake was thinking he was better than Carus. His second was failing to take the hints I've tossed about. His third will be when he feels he can operate the business by himself and tries to put me down."

"You won't let him make three mistakes."

"Precisely. Carinus is in Illyricum. I shall be, also..."

Peace.

The lark song was ended, the twittering gone. To the west, toward Rome, the sky swam in the sun's daily deathblood. It is an honor to die in the queen of cities even if you are the sun.

For the fiftieth time Thaleus paced across the atrium to stare unseeing at the marble bust of Servius Cannius Emptor. The bust stared back unseeing. Thaleus had been influential once and he would be influential again. Cannius was erring in making him wait about like this.

A toddler came waddling through the tablinum with a blank expression on his wet face. Why was this little wet-nose untended? Belatedly a sullen nanny appeared from the ala and scooped the child up. She stared at Thaleus briefly, turned and walked out with the child screaming under her arm. The cry faded and buried itself in some distant room.

Irritating place, Thaleus thought as he paced about the tablinum. He resented being kept waiting like a person of no consequence.

At last a young man stepped into the tablinum. His mien showed him to be master of the house. *It's about time,* the soldier thought. Thaleus crossed to him. "Servius Cannius, I presume."

"My father is out of town on business. I am Marcus."

"Ah. When will your father return?"

"Not for several weeks, kalends at least. Come in." The shaggy hulk of a man led the way into the peristyle. Thaleus found him vaguely unsettling. Was it the built-in swagger, or the menacing air, or the suggestion of power unmoderated by good sense...?

The benches around the fountain were ornate, obviously costly, obviously uncomfortable. Thaleus chose what looked to be the best of the lot. Cannius took his own chair. Slaves appeared instantly with inlaid tables, *mulsum,* a very nicely arranged relish dish. The Cannii knew how to buy house staff.

Thaleus cleared his throat. "I understand we have a common acquaintance in the imperial palace."

"Indeed?" Cannius poked a finger through his dish of figs.

"Sebastian, nephew of Desmontes here in Milan."

"He's in the imperial palace?" Cannius replied disdainfully. "I should think the emperor would have enough slaves to scrub the floors."

"Captain of the Fifth Cohort, Praetorian Guard."

Cannius froze, open-mouthed. His fig slipped from his fingers. "Impossible! He's a common foot soldier in Moesia."

"One would think it impossible, given his innate abilities," Thaleus said dryly. "He is there by a fluke. He won favor with Caesar, and..." Thaleus spread his hands helplessly.

"That I can believe," Cannius sneered. "He fancies himself a real charmer. With the ladies, in particular."

"Oh? I've been doing some checking, but I didn't come on that. Tell me more."

Cannius was not a speaker. He picked over his words as he picked over his figs. "Short weeks after my wife and I were estranged—and within hours of his arrival from Narbonne—he was in her company. I stop at her father's villa unannounced and in he walks. Before the final settlement, I might add. Does that say anything?"

"Adultery is not the crime for a man that it is for a woman, of course. But then," Thaleus adduced, "if the men who rule the praetorium are not of good moral character they should at least be circumspect. Don't you agree?"

"Speak frankly, friend Thaleus. You don't approve of his position in the palace."

"Speaking frankly, friend Cannius, he is a usurper. The position is mine by right and justice."

"And you are, ah, amassing information on this usurper."

"Exactly." Thaleus leaned forward. "I understand from reliable sources that you supported a candidate other than Diocletian to succeed Numerian."

"Is that so?" Cannius's guard was up as obvious as a bronze shield.

"I did also," Thaleus admitted. "In fact, certain candidates superior to Diocletian are even now waiting in the wings. You may have heard that several attempts on Caesar's life have been thwarted."

Cannius was even slower than Thaleus could have hoped. *This boor probably considers himself a political genius too,* the soldier thought. The beetling brows crowded closer together; after a few moments Cannius spoke, "If Sebastian rose under the favor of Diocletian he will fall when the emperor falls."

Thaleus permitted himself a sly smile. Playing this toad was like playing a stringed instrument. "I am, as you say, gathering facts. Please understand, friend Cannius, I am not simply looking to topple this Sebastian. I have a greater purpose. I am seeking alliances, men outside the military with influence and foresight. Men who can be trusted to act for the good of the empire. Your name was recommended."

Cannius swelled visibly. *The damnable toad,* Thaleus thought. "Of course," Cannius said when he grasped the soldier's meaning. "Sebastian is only a side issue—I understand that."

He wouldn't know what was good for the empire if you engraved it on his peristyle wall, Thaleus mused. *But to testify against the captain, our common enemy...*

"What," asked Cannius, "is the emperor's attitude toward the Christian cult?"

Thaleus shrugged. "He reigns under the hand and power of Jupiter. Stamps out the cult where it appears, of course, but not with any particular vitriol. His wife prefers the eastern gods; I hear she hates the cult with a poisonous hatred. But Diocletian himself? Moderate. Why?"

Cannius hesitated. He feared, obviously. *Whom did he fear?* Thaleus wondered. *Certainly not me, since he clearly considers himself my superior.* "I think...I think you would be wise to investigate the religious associations of our captain," Cannius said.

"The Christian cult? I talked several hours to his uncle and got no inkling of that. Perhaps I should go back to him and ask..."

"No!" Cannius blurted out nervously. "Ah, the captain's— that is, our acquaintance's religious activities here were minimal. I am sure you'll find the facts you need in Rome."

So it's Desmontes he fears, the soldier thought. Thaleus had overstated it; actually, he had spoken with Desmontes less than an hour. But in that brief time he had discerned that this Desmontes possessed all the attributes Cannius lacked—wit, insight, and a sharp political sense. He seemed an adversary worth avoiding, as Cannius here was convinced.

Thaleus stood. "Should the need arise, for the good of the empire, I might ask your support. Could you come to Rome if needed, perhaps even on short notice?"

Cannius swelled to the point of glowing. Beckoned to Rome for his political influence? He smiled broadly, a smile incongruous in such a dark and brooding face. "Possibly, friend Thaleus. For the good of the empire, of course."

Thaleus extended his arm. "To a lasting relationship profitable to us both. A blessing on this house, friend Cannius."

"Go in peace, friend Thaleus." Cannius gripped his arm. "And good fortune."

As Cannius's sour slave closed the gate behind him, Thaleus was startled to see his own slave sitting by the wall. The horse the boy held looked half dead from exhaustion. Sweat both fresh and caked marked rivulets the length of its legs.

The boy leaped up. "Master."

"You bring news from Rome?"

"Aye, master. I killed one horse and had to buy this second. And I have had terrible trouble finding you..."

"The news?" Thaleus asked anxiously.

"I didn't know if I should come, but I thought it might be ...that you might find the news worth rewarding—"

"Tell me your news!"

"The man you are enquiring about—that Sebastian..."

"Well?!"

"He's in the Mamertine prison, master. The Guard arrested a meeting of the Christians and he was among them. I came right away. I don't—"

"Shut up! Go to the house of Claudius where I am staying and take my baggage home. I am leaving immediately for Rome. I must be present at his torture and execution. I may be too late already. Go! Go!"

Marvelous! How simply marvelous, reflected Thaleus. *Sebastian ruined by his own folly and no shadow fallen on my head! But this Cannius is too pliant an oaf to let slip by. I'll invite the toad to Rome to share the demise of our common nemesis. Then I'll use Cannius as a painter uses a rag.*

Sebastian, destroying himself not by political intrigue but by a useless association with a vile and treasonable cult—in all his dreams Thaleus could not have conceived so beautiful a vengeance.

He was as good as captain already.
Sebastian was as good as dead.

10

Dampness. Dampness and gloom. Dampness, gloom, ticks, and fleas. And these were the nice cells. The real dungeon lay beneath. Far above his head, a small window glowed crisscross with afternoon light behind the bars. Midday, and it was dark as night in here.

Sebastian shifted his shoulders against the wet stone. He longed to get up, to pace his cage as Marcellian was doing, to work the corners off his square and freezing backside. But Castor needed his lap more than he did.

The Greek muttered something and rolled his head. Sebastian scooped a handful of water out of the jar and sloshed it across Castor's fevered face and neck. He was getting worse—much worse. Typhus? Probably, like a dozen others in the cohort, but it was too dark to look for the rash.

"Sebastian? Who's here?" Castor muttered.

"Same old bunch. Marcus and Marcellian. Quinn. Victorinus and Castorinus. Are you sure you and Castorinus aren't related?"

"Tell them I'm sorry."

"We're all sorry," Sebastian said. "Sorriest looking crew I've seen in days."

"I'm sorry," Castor repeated. "Rotten headache. If I had been feeling better I could have cut our way out. We might have escaped."

"You weren't armed, sword-slinger, remember? Just as well, too. I don't think the Guards realized we're soldiers, and that's good. We know you were sick. You were feverish even before we left camp that night. You still are."

"'Tell them I'm sorry," the Greek mumbled again.

"Let's feel sorry for Quinn, if anybody," Sebastian said somberly. "Here he is locked up for the faith, and he doesn't even have the faith. No prospects for escape and no guarantee of eternal life. He lost both ways." Sebastian glanced over at Quinn brooding in the far corner. He made no response.

Marcellian paused in his pacing. He was a boy yet by any standard, peachfuzz cheeks and a squeaky voice. "You're so sure! How can you be so sure? I don't feel Jesus here and He said where two or three are gathered. Here we are, gathered, and He's not here."

"He is," Sebastian said with conviction. "I assure you He is. But fear sometimes gives you tunnel vision. Quinn! You know how Diocletian is doing that repair work on Hadrian's Villa? Renovating?"

"Mmmm."

"Let's draw up a letter; see if we can convince him to do a little something for good old Mamertine here," Sebastian said cheerfully. "This hole is at least two hundred years older than Hadrian's palace. It could use a little sprucing up."

Quinn snorted. "What's Hadrian's Villa got that we haven't got? Besides a formal garden, stadium, two baths, and a theatre?"

"Cleaning ladies," Sebastian told him. "Do you realize this is the prison—maybe even the very cell—Paul was in? The apostle Paul. Saul. And it hasn't been swept since he left. Who's writing all this down? I'm dictating—who's writing?"

"I'll scratch it on the wall and we'll send the whole granite block to the palace," Quinn offered.

"Good. That'll carry more weight than a scroll." Sebastian rubbed his hands. "Where were we?"

Castorinus burst out laughing and Marcellian giggled.

"About these ticks, fleas, and lice," Sebastian went on. "We want a guarantee. Nothing smaller than a hedgehog permitted in the cells."

"Nothing smaller than a hare," Quinn corrected. "I found a tick on me this morning as big as a hedgehog."

Marcus, Marcellian's older brother, looked up from his corner. "Nothing smaller than a horse."

"Perfect!" Sebastian approved. "Men are smaller than horses. What else?"

"Baths?"

"Baths." Sebastian nodded. "We have baths, but they're installed sideways. How about: no water permitted on the walls. It all has to be in the bath."

Quinn scratched under his arm. "There isn't a bath that big. Caracalla wouldn't hold it."

"Caracalla has a library. A library would be nice." Marcus was getting into the spirit.

"Right," Sebastian agreed, "once we get all the water off the walls and into the bath so the pages don't stick together."

"And lamps." Marcellian was brightening a bit.

"Bigger windows would be better. Floor to ceiling windows."

"With no bars."

"This wide."

Castor jerked and flayed his arms. Sebastian grabbed one and glanced to Quinn. The mood, warming a moment ago, froze icy.

"Hold me!" Castor's voice was like dry, cracked stucco. "I can't hold on, hold me!"

Quinn dropped down beside him.

"They're coming." Castor raised his eyes toward the dripping, gloomy ceiling. His face opened into a smile. It expanded into a grin—a huge, radiating grin. "They're here, Bass. They really come for us. They're reaching out. Oh, my Lord...oh, my precious Lord!" The radiance faded gently, like a door slowly closing.

Quinn laid the slack arm across Castor's breast and wandered back to his corner.

Sebastian leaned back against the bleak stone. The tears felt hot on his clammy cheeks. Marcellian stood in front of him right by his feet. He was screaming. "If death is nothing to fear, why are you crying? Why is your Quinn over there sobbing if death is something a Christian is supposed to welcome?"

Sebastian closed his burning eyes. "Are you just screaming to listen to yourself or do you really want to know?"

"We're going to die. Every one of us! He's the lucky one. You want to cry? Cry for us! Why cry for him?"

Victorinus came over and hunkered down at Sebastian's feet. "I really want to know."

"We cry for the same reason Jesus did. It's a natural consequence of death. Ever read John's gospel?"

"Parts of it."

"Same here. Polycarp (that teacher over on the west side; brilliant old gentleman), Polycarp read that part about Lazarus when he was teaching about the resurrection. Jesus and this Lazarus were friends; Lazarus and his sisters Mary and Martha. Anyway, when Jesus got word Lazarus was sick, He deliberately waited until He knew Lazarus was dead. Then He went up to his house.

"Jesus knew ahead of time He was going to raise Lazarus from the dead. And still, when He saw Lazarus's sisters and friends all standing around crying—even though He knew He was going to be eating dinner with a healthy Lazarus that evening—He cried. Jesus cried. He knew Lazarus was going to walk out of his tomb alive and He cried anyway. Crying is that part of death that is played by the living."

Victorinus smiled. "Thank you."

At the far end of the block keys rattled. An iron door creaked. Sebastian followed with his ears the footfalls coming down the passage, watched the dull orange glow grow brighter. The turnkey stopped outside their barred door. He raised his torch. "Marcus and Marcellian, sons of Tranquilinus?"

Marcus stood up. Marcellian looked terrified. "Here."

"Step forward, you two."

Marcus hesitated, wild-eyed. Sebastian squirmed out from under Castor's head as the door closed behind the two boys. He pressed against the bars to see, to hear.

The keeper of the roll stood beside a gaunt, haggard woman and a balding man. "Tranquilinus, these are your sons?"

"They are. Aye."

"How 'bout letting us out, like those two? We're deserving, too, y'know," said a scraggly fellow in the cell across the passage as he leaned against the bars. All up and down the passageway people were pressing against the doors, listening, hungering for the freedom they saw in the passage.

"Quiet, scum," the turnkey said. "You're here for theft. Y'can't recant of theft."

The keeper of the roll stepped forward and faced Marcus and Marcellian. Sebastian knew him casually. He was one of the more efficient employees at Mamertine. "Your father says you two boys were led astray by evil practitioners of the Christian cult. That you aren't really believers; you simply got caught in the raid. I'm a just man. If this be true—if you deny that Jesus and worship Caesar properly, you may go."

Marcellian looked at Marcus. Marcus looked at Sebastian. *He's going to,* Sebastian thought. *He's going to throw it all away to—*

"No!" Sebastian shouted. He caught Marcus's eye and held it. "Did Jesus let Castor die here all alone, or did He take him away in glory? You saw yourself. He won't abandon you. You can only abandon Him."

"Shut up, atheist!" The turnkey thrust his torch at Sebastian's face. It threw sparks when it hit the bars and singed the stubble on his cheek. He held his ground.

"I—I saw Castor." Marcus was studying Sebastian. "He was...he...but he died."

"This man is perverting my sons! Silence him!" Tranquilinus pleaded desperately.

"Come lads! Speak up, that I may free you!" the keeper said.

"I don't know," Marcus said hesitantly. "I just don't know..."

"You do know, Marcus." Sebastian kept his voice low and silky. To shout now would bring the turnkey and keeper both down on him. "Visit any temple in the city—the Vestal Virgins—offer any sacrifice you ever heard of to any god in the city. None of that guarantees you a place in paradise forever, and the priests will be the first to admit it. And especially they don't claim to represent any supreme God. They offer no hope, no salvation. You've read the inscriptions on all those tombs outside town. Pick any road, any direction, any tomb. What does it offer? 'Stop, traveler, and remember Fabricius, confined to this tomb forever.' That's how much hope the gods of Rome give you. Even your parents here, who deserve honor for giving you life, can't give you eternal life. Only Jesus can. So you live another fifty years by denying Him. Then what?"

"I don't want to die," Marcus said.

"Neither do I. I want to taste roast beef again and wrap myself around a girl again and soak in a warm bath and maybe spend an afternoon at the races and watch my favorite team lose. My favorite teams always lose, but what does it matter? Those are momentary things. You know that. Fun, but they can't satisfy.

"No, I don't want to die. But I'd die for the emperor today if I had to just because he's emperor. I'd die for Rome, filthy and stinking as she is, just because she's Rome. She'll never do a thing for me. The emperor never promised me anything. But Jesus. Now He's worth dying for. He gave everything for you before you ever met Him. Rome takes, the emperor takes, but Jesus gives.

"Even if He didn't give, He's the only perfect life that ever lived, the only One who actually deserves dying for. And He loves you. You can't turn your back on Him."

"If he loves me, why are we suffering?"

"Oh, come on, Marcus! You know the answer to that. Let's say that if you convert and believe in Him, He'll give you a villa and twenty house slaves. No pain. No infections. No typhus. Everyone would want in on it. They wouldn't be loving Jesus; they'd be devoted to what He could do for them. So He lets Satan make it tough on us. When you love Him you really love *Him*—you stick to Him because he's worthy, not so He'll do you a favor. Remember what He said? 'Blessed are you when they persecute you and tell all kinds of lies about you for My sake.' He saw this coming. What did He promise you in the same breath? Tell me."

"Rejoice. Be happy. Great is your reward in heaven."

"Isn't that worth holding onto at any cost?"

Silence. A drop of water from the ceiling blipped at the boy's feet. Sebastian felt drained and tingling simultaneously. . . . a bit giddy, even. The torchlight wavered.

Everything floated in unreality. He had spoken out. He could not force the boys to respond, and he knew God would not. He wanted to reach out and touch, grab the boys and physically man-haul them down the right road. But he could only speak. He felt a helplessness, a futility. He leaned against the cold, unfeeling bars.

What use was power? Castulus put his feet up on the emperor's table and pondered the inefficacy of power. Carinus and Diocletian, co-rulers of the Roman world—the most powerful men on earth—were both in Illyricum. And for what? A power struggle out of which only one would return. As head over all the legions, Castulus was the most powerful man in the empire apart from the caesars, and what was it getting him?

Prestige? He had enough of that as a centurion. Wealth? He had enough of that from his father's estate. Honor? He would die in Rome rather than out in Bavaria. But even rabble and seditionists died in Rome if chance so dictated.

Power could not cure his persistent stomach pains. It could not return the son that had died in his arms. It could not save his Marcia. He still missed her. A year, and he missed her desperately.

"A woman to see you, sir."

Castulus jumped. He hadn't heard the soldier enter. "It's late. I'm not hearing anyone else today."

"She is persistent, sir. She claims friendship with an important person of military rank whom she will not name. Says her matter is of personal importance to you."

"Tomorrow maybe. No, dissuade her altogether. I'm going to my apartment now."

A curt nod. "As you wish, sir." The soldier left.

Castulus heard arguing outside the doors and decided to leave the back way to go to his "apartment." It sounded modest enough, if you did not know it comprised the whole ground floor of the back wing and included a private garden. As he approached the side doorway a guard pulled the curtain aside and opened the door for him. Another benefit of power—instant service. But he could get that for the price of a slave.

He paused awhile on the balcony to soak in some late-afternoon sun. *Miserably dank, that audience room,* Catulus thought. The apartment would be empty. He owned nine slaves including the concubine—all present, all bustling—and still, without Marcia, it would be empty. He descended the stairs slowly.

From nowhere she appeared—just popped out of the shrubbery in front of him. Startled twice within the hour—his stomach would complain bitterly about this. She dropped to a knee immediately and bowed her head. "Your Clemency."

"I am no one's clemency. The clemencies are in Illyricum. Stand up so I can see you."

She did so instantly. He was struck at once by the lovely figure and the luminous gray eyes. "I ask a boon, my lord."

"Your persistence has won you a hearing. Say. But quickly."

"Eight days ago certain men were arrested—Marcus and Marcellian, Victorinus, Castor, Castro—"

"Enough," Castulus interrupted. "I can't remember names strung out so freely. The courts will see to the matter."

"Not so, my lord. The charge is perpetuating the Christian cult."

"We arrest hundreds. What's different about these?"

"They are special to you," the woman said earnestly.

"And to you?"

"Yes sir."

"Then you're a Christian, too."

She hesitated. "I am, my lord. Arrest me. Torture me. But let them go. A word from you is all that is needed to—"

"Come with me."

She fell in behind obediently and he continued around to the side door of the apartment. He led the way out to the portico and garden. "Sit down."

She sat. Castulus wished that some of his officers obeyed with her dispatch. Festus placed a drink in his hand.

"Your name."

"Irene."

"Your trade or business."

"I sell willow baskets and broomstraw toys."

"Your whole life?" Castulus asked.

"I was registered as a harlot in Milan," Irene said evenly. "I turned away from that profession when I became a Christian."

"By reputation the Christians specialize in harlotry." Castulus watched her face closely as he spoke.

"By reputation the Christians do many things they do not, my lord."

This was insane. The whole conversation was insane. He sat down beside her and deliberately laid his hand on her knee. "You just offered yourself up for torture. What else do you offer yourself up for?"

The only thing steadier than her gaze was her voice. "Nothing, my lord. Unpleasant as torture is, it is honorable. An unholy bed would offend my Lord Jesus, the Christ. I came to beg a favor, not to bargain. I know you are just."

"I can't believe a lady as lovely as you can be such an utter fool," Castulus said incredulously. "I can take you now and your lengthy list of prisoners still be lost."

She smiled sweetly. "Oh, I realize that, but I have a hidden advantage. You see, you can take me only if my God permits. On the other hand, if I am under His protection you can't touch me. I know my appeal normally would have no merit. But one on that lengthy list as you call it is a personal friend of Caesar's. Therefore, it would be to your own advantage to free them."

"Which one?"

"Sebastian."

"Sebas— How did he get caught in a snare? His job is to set them. You said these prisoners were special to you also. I assume you aren't telling me to free Sebastian just as a favor to me. Who's special to you?"

"Sebastian, my lord. All of them, of course, but..."

"Ah, you two are lovers," Castulus said knowingly.

"No, my lord. He wants to court me. He has written to a

friend—an elder in the church—in fact, he just wrote a second time because the man didn't respond to his first letter. If the man says I may marry—"

"Why can't you?" Castulus broke in.

"My lord, a harlot..."

"No one pays any attention to that law anymore."

"We are a law-abiding people, my lord—a higher law than any constructed by the Roman Empire."

He gave her knee a squeeze, stood up and crossed to the portico pillars; he leaned against one, absorbing the late afternoon sun. Festus refilled his cup. She looked so serene sitting there.

"My first impression was wrong, my dear. You are the consummate fool. You feed me one impossible line after another and expect me to swallow them. Incredible."

"My lord, I don't care whether you choose to believe me or not. I have spoken the truth in every respect. He is not my lover. But if he were, it would make no difference. I ask you to intercede for him and his companions because of his value to you and to Caesar."

Castulus walked out into the garden. Marcia had been an honorable woman. For a time she was the only woman at court unspoiled by ugly rumors. She had been strong and true to him, a pure woman. He had despaired of ever finding another.

Leave it to that Sebastian, whose life seemed charmed anyway, to meet the only pure woman left in the world. *Pure and yet experienced; lovely...a real prize,* he reflected. Castulus knew the young captain only through the daily routine of work, but he liked him well enough—good soldier, enthusiastic, smart, a little headstrong—a whiz at making out schedules. She was right. He was of great value to the Guard, not to mention a favorite of Diocletian's. But then again...

He returned to her. "So Sebastian wants to court you. I assume he's in love. You seem absolutely irresistible."

"So he says." She smiled.

"And your feelings toward him?"

"I don't see...he's very charming, of course. And attractive.

My lord, what has that to do with my petition?"

"Go to your home, Irene. Back to your willow baskets, is it? I shall consider your request."

She stood up, hesitated, then looked at Castulus with eyes he found irresistibly lovely. "I appreciate very much your audience, my lord. May you prosper in our Lord's peace." She honored him and followed his slave girl out the door.

"Festus." Castulus took the *mulsum* jar from his slave's hand. "Festus, follow her discreetly. I want to know where she lives. Also, whether she really sells baskets and if so, where. And anything else you happen to dig up."

The man nodded and hurried out the side door.

Castulus leaned on a pillar, savoring the lingering thought of her. It would be nice to do Sebastian a favor. The boy was loyal enough—and handy, when the holiday schedules became completely snarled up. His religious bents, if he was one of the cult indeed, did not tarnish his usefulness at all. But what about the woman? Castulus would investigate her. He would test her purity, try her honor. And if she tested true...Castulus made two decisions simultaneously. Should she be as she now seemed, Irene was worthy of being courted, worthy of being an officer's wife. And Sebastian, the rival, could rot.

Thaleus could barely contain himself. Success was so close. For a week he had been waiting and entertaining the toad from Milan. It was nerve-wracking—not just the company of Cannius but the pretense Thaleus had to uphold that he enjoyed the churl's companionship. Now, Diocletian was back and Thaleus would be in the audience room in a matter of moments, on his way to a position of importance again. He glanced over at Cannius. The dark colossus looked back, smug and self-confident.

The ponderous doors drifted open. "Thaleus, you are to be heard." Thaleus motioned to Cannius and strode forward with the pride befitting an officer. His three slaves (actually, two of Cannius's, one of his; who counts?) carried the books and documents.

"All hail, Your Clemency!"

"Thaleus," Diocletian began, "your petition says your matter is of immediate importance to me as well as the empire, so I squeezed you in. But make it fast. Yours is one of about a hundred pleas I'm supposed to hear today."

"I present Marcus Cannius, son of Servius Cannius Emptor, a business scion of Milan."

Cannius stepped forward and bowed as he had rehearsed. Thaleus assumed a dramatic stance. "Until recently you had a traitor in your midst, Your Clemency. He is now imprisoned for the good of the empire. I refer to Sebastian."

Diocletian's face hardened, darkened. Even Cannius, the master of the stormy visage, stiffened. "Present your case."

"Cannius here will testify to the fact that, while still in Milan, this Sebastian engaged in adultery with his wife, among others." Thaleus waved toward his slave. "I have been to Milan. Here are letters from persons who know him attesting to his instability and lack of leadership qualifications. And this..."

Thaleus took from a slave a huge, musty ledger. "I stopped by and picked this up on the way over this morning. It is the current roll from Mamertine. You will find on three before nones a list of prisoners taken in a raid on a meeting of the Christian cult. Sebastian's name is here."

One of the scribes dumped his own records and set his writing table before Caesar. Thaleus plunked the clumsy ledger down with secret gratitude. He should have left that to the slave. Diocletian rose and stepped off his dais. The title page confirmed the ledger's authority—Mamertine roll over the signature of Nicostratus. Thaleus knew Diocletian recognized that name.

The emperor flipped to the final page and commenced working backward. He must be at the right point now. Thaleus took a deep breath and waited.

"Here's a list of names whose offense is perpetuating the Christian cult, but I don't see Sebastian."

"Three before nones." Thaleus hurried to the emperor's elbow. "Here. No, that must be a different listing. The names are unfamiliar. Back one page...here...no..." His heart was pounding against his breast. "Your Clemency, this roll has been tampered with! I visited the prison personally three days ago, immediately upon my return form Milan. I looked at his name right there. I went down into the middle prison and saw his face. This page right here! He is there!"

"Hassan, fetch Sebastian. If he's not in the palace, look for him in Mamertine," the emperor ordered.

"At once, Your Clemency." A dark, wiry centurion ran out. This vile little foreigner held the place Thaleus had once held. It wouldn't last.

"While we await the man himself, may I present Cannius and his testimony with—"

"Adultery? Instability? Bah!" the emperor said contemptuously. "It is on this charge of being in the Christian cult that your case will stand or fall." Diocletian thumped down on his throne. "You had best pray for your own sake, Thaleus, that your case stands. I see too much petty vindictiveness from this chair to countenance yours."

Thaleus knew when to press and when not to. He bowed and stepped back. He would wait. He had waited this long. Wait for Sebastian, filthy and unshaven and reeking of moldy stone walls...

Hassan reappeared and held the door. "Sebastian, Your Clemency. He was in the west room with the other captains discussing the holiday calendar."

Impossible! Thaleus's mind whirled. *What flummery was this that—?*

Sebastian appeared in the doorway, cleanshaven and freshly barbered. His breastplate shone. He crossed to Diocletian with easy confidence and dropped to one knee at the dais. "I rejoice in your safe return, Your Clemency. Welcome back!"

"Thank you. Thaleus here—incidentally, do you know this Cannius?"

"Aye, sir. He and I met frequently during our childhood in Milan. His wife, too, is an old childhood friend. Welcome to Rome, Marcus. Good to see you."

Cannius made no reply. He was fuming. Thaleus was more

than fuming. How could this warlock break prison?

Diocletian continued unruffled. "This is the Mamertine prison roll. Thaleus claims you're in it."

Look at him! Look at the blank expression on his face. Pretense! Thaleus's mind screamed.

Sebastian shrugged. "What can I say? I have not recently committed any thefts, murders, mayhems, adulteries, seditions..."

"Christian cult?"

"Except for a small raid three weeks ago, I haven't committed any Christians, either. Besides, we put that bunch in Esquilene, not Mamertine."

Thaleus's head pounded. This trickster! This word-weaver would talk his way out again!

"Where were you a week ago?"

"With a sick friend. In fact, Your Clemency knows him well. Castor, who acted in your behalf in that assassination attempt; who rode at your right hand out to Hadrian's Villa. He died of typhus a few days ago."

"I'm sorry. He was a good soldier."

"And a good friend. I miss him sorely."

"He died in prison, you high priest of Calliope!" Thaleus shouted. "You warlock of the glib tongue! Castor was one of the names! One of the names that aren't there now! He died in Mamertine prison and you were in there with him!" Thaleus had never been this enraged, had never felt an all-consuming emotion as perfect as this complete hatred.

Diocletian turned on him, skewering him with his glare. Cold fear dashed water on the fires of fury. The emperor did not speak immediately. First, he let the silence grow eloquent. Then, "Ah, yes. That assassination attempt. Now I remember. I was trying to place where I'd heard that before—the phrase you used a moment ago, 'for the good of the empire.' Same phrase my would-be assassin used, the man you yourself let through the doors. There wouldn't be any connection, would there?"

Thaleus found himself speechless. Now, of all times when he

must speak or lose his head, when he must be eloquent as never before...

"Your Clemency, may I speak?"

"Say, Sebastian."

"I don't know what's going on here, but I can understand that Thaleus might feel vindictive. Might even have some political intrigue in mind. But there's no evidence. Your Clemency, too many heads roll despite a lack of evidence. As you well know, I am not his supplanter by choice, nor have I ever asked a favor. I ask a favor now. Excuse him. Disregard this curious petition of his. The fact that it is preposterous suggests that he's too callow to be capable of any effective plotting. I beg your forgiveness on his behalf."

Diocletian flopped back in his chair, sighed deeply, sprawled out. If Thaleus burned before, he glowed like a crucible now. He wanted to speak and could think of nothing to say. His worst enemy, this bitter enemy...and now Diocletian was boring into him. No wonder he was Caesar, victor over Carinus, first among all. Those eyes.

"Granted," the emperor said. "Thaleus, take that blighted book back where you got it. Get out of here while I'm still in a forgiving mood. And Thaleus—watch your step."

His slave snatched up the ledger, and quickly stuffed it clumsily under his arm. Thaleus bowed deeply. He had to prod stupid Cannius. The churl. As he started toward the doors, Diocletian behind him was saying, "Dismissed, Sebastian. Oh, say. Tell the other two captains you three are invited to the banquet. Scribe, make sure the three captains are on the guest list."

Thaleus reached the doors as Sebastian was saying, "Are consorts provided or may we bring our own?"

"Bring your own. I look forward to meeting her."

"Thank you, sir, on behalf of all..."

The doors closed.

Thaleus led down the hall, through the doors at the far end into the reception room. He shoved his slave aside and waited. Footsteps—the doors opened—Sebastian paused as the doors closed behind him. Cannius scrambled to stand beside Thaleus.

142

"I saw you there!" Thaleus hissed. "How did you escape? How did you alter the roll?"

"Thaleus, Thaleus," Sebastian said kindly. "Learn the difference between petty vengeance and worthy goals. You have the ambition. You need the diplomacy. And love and forgiveness as taught by the Christ."

"Aha! You admit—!"

"To your ears privately. Quote me in public and see how many listen. Any word you say about me from now on will be attributed to jealousy. One other thing, Thaleus. You are no fighter. Cannius here is, but I can beat him. So don't send him or anyone else after me. Especially, don't try to have me murdered, or you'll answer to Caesar. I'm sure you're smart enough to know that. Go in peace, both of you."

Words! Thaleus suddenly despised words almost as much as he despised this posturing swaggerer. Particularly he despised accurate words. It was true. His vengeance must bide awhile. He would wait.

11

The sun paused, then slipped behind Janiculum. She would be closing up her stall now. Sebastian urged his horse faster, squeezed past an oxcart in the middle of Carmenta Gate. Behind him the ox driver spoke some unkind words. He left Flaminia Way by the temple of Isis and Serapis and cut across the back alleys. There she was, just leaving. He slid off and fell in step beside her.

"Good evening, prettiest flower in the empire."

"Good evening, Sebastian."

"No epithets? Where's 'Good evening, brassiest captain in the Guard'? Or my favorite: 'You armor-plated octopus with eight hands'? What's bothering you?"

"You read me very well. You came for a reason. State it."

"My sails are left without wind." He took her hand and laced his fingers through hers. "You're right. We are invited to a state banquet at which Diocletian will present the successor to Carinus; I because I am captain and you because I love you and want you at my side."

They walked in silence a few moments. He stopped and turned her to him. "Come on, Irene. What's wrong?"

She twisted away and kept walking. "I already am invited. Thank you anyway."

"To where?"

"The banquet."

"By whom?!"

"Castulus."

He yanked her arm. She forged ahead doggedly.

"Irene, you don't even know Castulus!"

"It happens, captain, I do. He sent his messenger this morning with an invitation by his own hand and I accepted. I'm sorry, Sebastian. I didn't even think you would be going."

"How can...You can't do that!"

She wheeled on him. "Sebastian, you owe him a considerable debt. Now don't—"

"I don't owe him a thong for his caliga."

"He got you out of prison!"

"He didn't even know I was *in* pri—" His heart turned black. He grabbed her shoulders, feeling for all the world like shaking her beautiful teeth out. "You went to him! You petitioned Castulus himself! Told him where I was and..."

"Yes!"

"...and why I was there!"

"Yes. I—"

"The army's job is to arrest Christians. So you go to the head of all the armies and announce that I'm a Christian!"

"It's not like that, exactly."

"Then what is it like, exactly? And exactly what did you offer him in return for my release? Or should I be a polite proper gentleman and not ask that?"

It was no lady-like slap. She knocked him back about two feet. She started walking away from him again, her shoulders bobbing. She was crying. He darted in front of her, blocking her way. As a safety precaution he grabbed both wrists.

"I can't believe you! I can't believe you'd sell out to a rank, even if he is chief of armies. But while you're snuggling up to him, keep in mind it's all for nothing. He didn't have a thing to do with my release. Don't believe him when he takes the credit. He didn't lift a finger."

He turned her loose and stepped back. "Enjoy the banquet, Irene." He swung aboard his fidgety horse and dug his heels in. He didn't care which way it went, just so long as he left. My God, no wonder Castulus looked so flabbergasted when Sebastian walked into the west room this morning!

What could he do now? Desert and sneak off to Arabia. Show up on the doorstep of the Fifth Legion in Moesia and apologize for being two years late. Grow a beard and become a hermit like that Anthony in Alexandria. Go home to Milan and hide in the warm bath at Desmontes' house and forget he ever heard of the Praetorian Guard.

And what if Thaleus gets wind? Thaleus's case was without merit until now, until the chief of armies could be called to witness. Castulus would surely hear about Thaleus's audience, too, and the ledger. Sebastian pulled his lathered horse to a halt. He must quit this raging and think. And quickly. The Sallustia Gardens spread out between him and Salaria Gate. Being so near the swine market, these gardens didn't smell exactly country fresh. They weren't silent, either, like the garden at Hadrian Villa, but they were quiet. He slid off and walked down the nearest path, down into the gentle folds of the gardens. The insides of his legs were wet with horse sweat. His head throbbed. How could she do this to him?

He must put himself aside. He must protect the others. Foremost he must protect Nicostratus, the keeper of the roll—Nicostratus, who walked into the cell block as a favor to Tranquilinus and walked out a brand new Christian. What a glorious thing that was!

In the silence after his appeal to the boys, the sobbing, and then their mother Zoë's crackling voice—how could he have known what a miracle that was? She suddenly regained her voice after suffering six years a mute. It was glorious!

And the conversions tumbled one after another in the midst of questions, tears, more questions. Nicostratus, Claudius the turnkey, the boys' parents—both of them—his cellmates Castorinus and Victorinus who reaffirmed a mislaid faith, plus fourteen of the thieves and rabble in the other cells all knew the Christ now. All were bound for glory.

What a marvelous moment for God, for His Holy Spirit! Castulus indeed. It was Nicostratus who put his life on the line and freed them, freed all the believers both old and new. It was Nicostratus who removed that page from the ledger and forged another with Sebastian's help—the page that would have damned them all had it not melted into ashes in the office fireplace.

The sun was gone. Behind it came the cool twilight moments he loved best. Tonight he must warn Nicostratus and Claudius and send them into hiding. Irene. Castor. Castulus. Things were piling up again.

Off to his right beyond an open hedge, a boy and girl paused. They pressed together, tangled together. The hem of her stola began to rise like a theatre curtain.

Sebastian knew the pleasure of being oblivious to everything in the cosmos except the one pressed against you. He ached. *Irene. How could she? he thought. In innocence, that's how.* Hers was a stupid stunt but done in innocence. Actually, she risked her life to plead his. She could not have made that appeal to Castulus without revealing her own connections with the faith. And he hadn't even noticed that.

So Castulus knew. But he didn't know for sure. He couldn't prove it, nor did he care to, it seemed. Perhaps they were safer than he first thought. What was there to warn Claudius and Nicostratus about? He would tell them what had happened, but what could they do? The best course was to continue with life as though nothing had happened—cautiously, of course.

Tonight Nicostratus, Claudius, and all the others were meeting outside town to be baptized. He must speak to them first thing tomorrow. And tomorrow he would apologize to Irene, asking her forgiveness. He turned his back on act one beyond the hedge, swung aboard his horse, and started home.

Sallustia Gardens was close to the camp, but he rode the long way around to cool his nervous horse. He reached the southwest gate near the end of first watch, gave the password, paused to pass a few pleasantries with the sentries, and led his horse down the principal way. Things didn't look quite so hopeless now. He kicked the night stableman, who was not supposed to be sleeping, and handed off the reins. It was nice to have private quarters. A bit cramped, perhaps, but solitary.

Two men stood at guard attention outside his door. Were they waiting for him with an arrest order signed by Castulus? Face it square on. He walked up to the guards. "Are you two protecting my quarters for any particular reason?"

"You have guests, sir. They claim to know you and we were uncertain what to do. They seem harmless, so we let them in."

"Wait here." Sebastian opened the door and stepped inside. It took but a moment to recognize the man sitting at his table in the lamplight. It wasn't Desmontes, but it was second best.

"Felician!"

The old man stood up. Sebastian's enthusiastic embrace lifted him off his feet.

"Ah, lad, the military has done wonders for you—turned you from a gentle thinker into a hulking brute!"

"Right! Study shrivels the brain, as you well know. Just a moment." He crossed to the doorway and dismissed the guards. He barely remembered in time to learn their names and compliment their handling of the situation.

He was closing the door behind him when he noticed the other. The guards had said "guests," plural. Felician motioned her closer to the lamp. She was young—fourteen or fifteen—and disfigured by a puckered white scar that extended from her cheek to above her left ear. One side of her head was scarred bald. Pity. She might have been a pretty girl. He stepped up to her and lectured himself sternly to look past the scar.

Felician smiled. "You know this young lady."

"Give me a moment. You do look familiar." Look beyond the scar. No wonder it came to him so slowly. The scar did not mask recognition so much as did the inner change. The twinkle was gone, the impishness fled. She looked haggard and old from the inside out. He drew her to himself and wrapped his arms around her in a smothering clasp. His mind filled up with memories, overflowed, and poured into tears. Taurus tossing those useless crutches away, Flumma bleating, howling fire, lances disappearing down the well.

Alyssa.

He held her for a long time; her small form was rigid as a board. When he at last released her, he walked over to his table where bread was laid out. Sebastian fumbled for a knife. He couldn't find the bread knife. *Oh, forget the bread knife!* he said to himself as he drew his sword and hacked the loaf into chunks. He put the honey pot out on the table and drew cups of *mulsum*. She was watching him as a mouse would watch a cat.

The armor! Everything about him must remind her of...He unbuckled his sword and cast aside the breastplate and pauldrons. The helmet he had shed when he first came in. They sat down, and Felician raised the bread and blessed it. He slopped honey across it with a broad, happy smile. The old man was hungry.

Now that he thought about it, so was Sebastian. "Uh, did you get my letter?"

"Both of them. I apologize for not answering. But since I was coming to Rome anyway, and of course visiting you, I decided to appear in person. I look forward to meeting your Irene. Desmontes told me much about her. I would like to talk to her, of course."

"Of course." Apparently that was all on that subject. "And how is Desmontes?"

"Fine! Healthy and happy. He finally found John's gospel. He took a week copying it for you. I brought it—also Alyssa here. We knew you would want to see her."

"I certainly do. I—"

"No, you don't." They were the first words she spoke.

"Why don't I?"

"Look again," she said coldly.

Sebastian snapped his arm out and grabbed her chin before she could pull away. He held her tightly. "Know what I see? Alyssa and Lavinia and Taurus and Bos and Galba and even Flumma. I see the finest family I've ever known. That one day with you changed my whole life. Your uncle and father are constant examples. I remember word for word your sister's lecture on the sanctity of marriage. I remember you and your egg basket and that giggle. Sure, your face is a mess. I'll not deny it. But it's the least part of you."

He kissed his fingers and laid them on her lips. "Thank you for coming to see me. Now tell me how you found me. It must have taken a piece of work."

"Where were you when they came?"

"Up on that little hill beyond the house, in the woods. That's where I got Lavinia's lecture. She went back down and I stayed. I liked the place. And besides, I was still feeling pretty shaky. I watched it happen from that big oak tree with the hollow knot. Know where I mean?"

She nodded. Her eyes locked onto his. "Did you send them?"

How could she possibly think such a thing? Then again, how could she think otherwise? He survived. He wasn't there when they came. And he was a stranger. "No. I swear I did not send them, nor did I know they were coming. Have you spent two years seeking vengeance?"

Her eyes fell. "That's one reason."

"Well, you found me. If you're convinced I'm guilty, you can run me through right now. I'll put the sword in your hand."

"Please don't make fun of me."

"I'm not." Sebastian assured her. "I mean it."

"Did you really love my whole family?"

"I still do."

She stared at the bread in front of her a long time. It lay there untouched, absorbing her gaze. Finally she half-whispered, "This isn't the way I pictured it. I don't know what I expected when I found you, but this isn't it."

"How did you find me? You still haven't said."

"I woke up near dawn and went to Ignatio's. They lived about a mile away. They took me in, but they're Christians too, and I was afraid it would happen again. As soon as I could I went to Milan, as soon as the burns healed over enough that the infections went away. I worked in a bakery. I'm very good at bread-making. Lavinia did the cooking but I made the bread. No one had to look at me in the back of the bakery." She sat quite still, her face listless.

"Which bakery?" Sebastian asked.

"The one on the street called North Star, up from the river."

"Specializes in those big loaves glazed with honey."

Her eyes flickered the least bit. "That's the one. You like the bread?"

"Love it," Sebastian said.

"I made it. I took over making all of it when his wife got sick. All I knew was your name. If you were connected with those soldiers the army ought to know you, so I tried to find you through the army. I asked around, you know? Do you realize how many soldiers are in Milan?"

"Two cohorts of a thousand men each, Lancers, Archers, auxiliaries and the army training camp," Sebastian recalled.

"I forgot—of course you'd know how many. And they wouldn't tell me anything. They said they don't give out that kind of information. Then I thought perhaps you weren't a soldier, you were only an informer. I spent weeks going up and down streets, stopping in shops and asking if they had any regular customers named Sebastian. I asked all the *ostiarii* at the baths. But I gave up. Finally I just gave up."

"When did you meet Felician?"

"A few months ago. That's the funny part. You see, I thought I was done with Jesus. He cost too much. Then the baker sent me to deliver a big order of bread to the cemetery. The cemetery! Felician met me at the gate and paid me extra for my trouble. He had very kind eyes—I asked him if he was a Christian. He was, and they wanted the bread for the Lord's table. All of a sudden I was in it again."

"And you happened to learn just by accident that Felician knew the man you were looking for."

"But by then I wasn't sure I wanted to find you. After all that time and work, I wasn't sure. Christians don't hold grudges and I belonged to Jesus again. And yet..." She shrugged.

"Do you regret coming back to Him?" Sebastian asked.

"I guess not. Especially since I know you're one too."

"You *guess* not! What kind of devotion to Jesus is that?"

"That's what Felician says too."

"I know you paid a very heavy price," Sebastian said gently. "But you weren't overcharged."

"That's easy for you to say. Look how nice you live here. And your face is handsome."

Sebastian was at a loss for words. Eventually he said, "I know what you mean. But my condition may have just changed." Then he asked Felician, "Do you two have a place to stay here in Rome?"

"Desmontes gave me the name of a man named Tycho north of the Campus Viminalis. We haven't tried to find it yet."

"It's very near here. A recent turn of events makes it dangerous to know me, much less be here. You must leave first thing in the morning. I'll take you to this Tycho's. Alyssa, you may have the pallet over there. You look ready to drop. Felician and I will make ourselves comfortable in the other room."

He left the lamp on the table for her. It would burn out shortly; it was nearly dry. Felician stood and Sebastian realized with alarm how doddering the old man was. A step at a time he shuffled into the back room. Sebastian gave him his cloak and toga. They lay in the blackness on the cold floor and talked of Desmontes and old times most of the night.

The next morning Sebastian's mind considered fleeing, but his body rode to the Palatine as always. It struck him that this was an act of faith, in a way, a putting of himself into God's hands. But then God's hands might be too full already. He was halfway to the west room when the nunciator hailed him in the reception hall.

"The governor wishes to see you straightway, Captain."

"Do you know why?"

"No sir. Privately in his chambers. He did seem anxious."

Sebastian reversed direction and crossed down the staircase to the governor's house nearby. Why Chromatius? The only thing he could possibly want would be the use of the Guard to decorate the forums during the upcoming holidays. He and Sebastian locked horns on that about a third of the time. The other two-thirds of the time, Chromatius locked horns with the other two captains.

There were two slaves in the governor's foyer. Magus, the governor's favorite, Sebastian knew. The other looked vaguely familiar. Magus conducted him directly to the governor's private rooms. No waiting.

"Your lordship, Chromatius. Good morning!" Sebastian greeted him.

"Good morning, Captain. Close the doors behind you, Magus. No interruptions." The rotund governor scratched the gray stubble above his ear and reached for a goblet. He held it out. "Refresh yourself."

"Thank you." Sebastian glanced at the governor's foot, propped on a stool and buried in a thick swath of wrapping. "Sorry your gout is kicking up again."

"I appreciate the sympathy. And the pun. Just wait until you get old."

"I'm counting the hours," Sebastian said lightly. "How many troops do you think you need and where?"

Chromatius chuckled. "This is not a business call, Sebastian. Sit down."

Sebastian took a bench nearby. "If not business, what?"

"Religion. Your religion."

"What do you fancy my religion to be?" Sebastian tried to make his voice sound as casual as his words.

"Jesus the Christ. And don't bother to put on a sham for me. A reliable informant attended a baptismal meeting north of town last night. He told me all about it. Fascinating."

"I wasn't there."

"Come now, Captain. I don't—"

"I wasn't there. Really. You'll have to tell me what happened. Through your informer, of course."

"He'll be along directly. He's breakfasting with our houseguests. He told me all about that incident in the prison too. A score of persons hear your exhortation and leave the security of the gods of Rome for an uncertain future with the God of the Jews. Fascinating. You must have a remarkable gift for... You look pained."

Sebastian grimaced. "It seems if you want to tell the world, just hide in middle prison and whisper it. The world will hear."

"Your secret is safe here. One of those converted was Tranquilinus, the father of Marcus and Marcellian. He was baptized last night."

The doors opened. "Ah, Tiburtius." Chromatius twisted in his chair, shifting his achy foot. "Sebastian, you know my son here. Tiburtius."

"Very casually. Tiburtius." Sebastian stood up and extended his arm. The boy's face was familiar, though he'd grown lately. He was probably now his full size.

The boy smiled a radiant smile and accepted his arm, hesitated, then dropped to one knee. *What's this?* Sebastian wondered.

Aloud he said, "Get up, boy! What's going on?"

"You are a man of God."

Sebastian scowled at Chromatius for an answer. "The boy is being a bit melodramatic," the governor said with a smile, "but he's right, for all that. He's the informer I mentioned. He was at the meeting last night outside Flaminia Gate."

Sebastian nodded and sat down again. "Investigating or convinced, Tiburtius?"

"Almost convinced." The boy pulled a stool alongside and plopped down. "I have certain questions. I'm half the reason Father invited you here."

"If I can't answer them, I know some people who can."

"Polycarp?" Tiburtius guessed. "I met him last night. Wonderful person."

"Polycarp and others." Sebastian looked at the governor. "And what is your attitude toward the Christ, Chromatius?"

"I'm not certain. Sebastian, does your God do favors only for His own? Or might He grant a boon first—before full faith—to a doubting inquirer?"

"You'll have to explain better than that."

"Ah, well, uh...you see...Tiburtius?"

"Last night Tranquilinus walked into the water to be baptized, suffering as my father suffers." The boy's voice was filled with awe. "He walked out whole."

"Aye." Chromatius cleared his throat. "I suppose what it comes down to is this: I would give my soul to be free of this miserable gout. Do you suppose your God would, uh..."

Sebastian felt the same excitement once again, and the same helplessness. He wanted to touch, to do. And he could only speak. "Well, I suppose God might allow you to work some kind of deal. Scriptures say He healed a leper named Naaman who was neither Jew nor believer. He cures your gout, then you commit yourself to Him. But I tell you a better way. Commit yourself to the Christ first. No guarantee of reward. Resign yourself to gout if need be.

"Take Paul for instance—an important first-century leader. His letters are considered as strongly directed by the Holy Spirit as anything in the Jewish Scripture. He had the gift of healing—healed lots of people—but suffered from some sort of affliction himself he never could get rid of. He considered it a blessing because it brought him closer to God and taught him something about himself he would not have learned otherwise."

"I don't want to learn any more about myself! I want to be rid of this blasted gout!"

"Chromatius, I love your flamboyance! If my men enjoyed standing in the sun while their heads baked, I'd give you all the glitter in the world. But they don't, so I fight with you. You can do great things for Jesus. Big, splashy things, because that's the way you operate. He needs you. You..."

"We weren't talking about what I'll do for Jesus. We're talking about Him doing for me!"

"Very well. Very well!" Sebastian started pacing. He had a strong impulse now. On impulse he had spoken out at the Donkey's Tail and Castor died gloriously. On impulse he spilled a Lancer's horse and met Irene. It was impulse that had hurtled him into the military in the first place. And now he found himself saying,

"Chromatius, God speaks to different people in different ways. To announce the birth of the Savior He hits the shepherds over the head with a bolt of light and a celestial army. All the wise men needed was a star. Everyone has a different conversion story. If you'll take the Christ as your savior only because you owe God the favor, then let it be so. If that's God's way of dealing with you, amen. Let your cure be a first step to full salvation."

Chromatius wore the face of a man perplexed. He stared at Sebastian. He broke off and stared at Tiburtius. His face melted. He might have been a child promised a treat and then denied it. Or had he been denied? His lips quivered. Suddenly he snatched at the bandages around his propped foot. He tore at them like a madman, with trembling, faltering fingers. The wraps loosened. He dragged them down off the heel, snatched them away from his toes—healthy-looking pink toes on a normal, healthy-looking foot.

The governor gazed at his foot a long time. When he looked up, the tears were flowing freely down his cheeks. "God is so kind to me, a sinner." His voice was soft, padded with wonder. "He trusts me, Sebastian. Don't you see? He delivered His half of the bargain first. He showed me He trusts me. And I trust Him. I am His."

A thousand petty and insignificant details stole his time. He settled half a dozen trifling squabbles between centuries, made a dozen inane and inconsequential decisions, worked out a major tangle in the schedule. Sebastian hated this triviality, and it consumed his whole day.

In that day he had passed Castulus once and spoken a word of greeting. There was no sign Castulus was going to behead him within the hour. Rather, the man was absolutely magnanimous. He saw Pavo once, but Pavo was absorbed by weightier matters than Sebastian had to offer.

It was nearly dinnertime before he could break free and go back over to the house of Chromatius. His business as far as the world was concerned was to deliver the completed holiday schedule to the governor. What he really wanted to do was to encourage, to talk, to build up this brand new believer—two believers, for Tiburtius, too, had come to the cross.

"Tiburtius has gone off to find one Polycarp," said Magus, "but the governor is about. He will see you shortly."

Chromatius appeared just then. He gamboled about like a chubby spring lamb, reveling in the joy of two good feet. "Ah, Sebastian! So good of you to drop by! Don't go away. I've matters to attend for a moment but I'll be right back—be right with you. The schedule? Splendid! Wait, I beg! I'll be right back." He flounced off into a side room.

The house's sumptuous peristyle was a relatively quiet retreat. Sebastian could use some quiet; his nerves felt unusually frayed. He told Magus where he would be, tucked his helmet under his arm, and wandered off to the peristyle.

Nearly all fountains contained lotuses. Most had fish. But Chromatius fancied frogs. Out near the middle, a small, sleek green one squatted on a brown seed pod, its toes spanning the holes. A large brownish one turned its clammy face to him and tried to stare him down. Sebastian saw several pairs of eye bumps protruding from the water around the edges. The longer he sat on the rim of the fountain and searched, the more frogs he saw. *There must be scores,* he thought idly. It was just like the church—invisible to the casual eye but populating every corner, everywhere.

The noise behind him was a much softer rustle than the frisky Chromatius would make. Sebastian leaped up and wheeled as she spoke.

"I thought the back of that head looked familiar. Sexiest helmet rack in Rome, definitely."

He had trouble finding his tongue. "Chromatius mentioned houseguests this morning. That would have to be you and your father. Greet Melitus for me and welcome to Rome, Melita."

"Thank you. Mother is here also. Since Father came on business she insisted we come too. She's trying to dig a husband worthy of me out of the Palatine. Why don't you toss your name into the grand lottery? The worst that could happen is that you'd win."

"You've grown bitter since I saw you last." Sebastian side-stepped her question.

"Not really. Perhaps it just shows more."

He extended his arm. She laid her hand across his knuckles, and he escorted her to a bench in the shade. She had toned down her make-up considerably and, if possible, developed even more fully those attributes that make a woman's figure so special. Her stola rose and fell in exactly the right places, bounteously.

Her breath cooed honey-sweet, like *mulsum*. "So you are a captain in the Guard. There aren't many captains, are there?"

"One per cohort."

"Two in Rome."

"Three, for the moment."

"Are the captains invited to that banquet or whatever tomorrow—where the new Caesar gets introduced?"

"Aye, we are. Have you been invited?"

"No." She giggled. "And my father is fuming because he isn't, either."

"Your father can sit at home here and throw stones at the frogs. I'd be delighted to escort you."

Her white teeth dripped calculated gratitude. "Why, Captain, I would be honored."

"I would have to call for you early. I must be there well ahead of time to get my cohort squared away. I think every soldier in the empire is going to be lining the walls."

She smiled with the glowing sparkle of a million sapphires. "I'll be ready. Sebastian, m'love, it is so good to see you again."

He would wait a few days before apologizing to Irene.

12

Melita, to Sebastian's amazement, was almost prompt. He didn't have to wait more than a quarter hour or so making small talk with her parents. They poured syrupy praise over his uniform, gushed, grumbled with smiles, and otherwise let it be clearly known that they were sorely offended by being inadvertently left off the guest list. An oversight, of course—still, it rankled.

He had awakened that morning with half a headache. Thanks to Melita's parents it was now a full-blown headache. It didn't help that he was worried about Prometheus; the giant looked bad and felt bad. Sebastian needed him, but he had sent the hairy aide to the infirmary and made do without him. He hadn't had a chance to check on him since lunch. Then Melita appeared and thoughts of Prometheus fled.

They would take a litter to the palace, of course? Absolutely not. It was only three hundred paces. Diocletian himself avoided litters at every opportunity. It was the coming thing, the fashion, to walk—as set by the imperator himself. Oh, well, in that case...

Sebastian, with Melita in tow, made the rounds from floor to floor, checking every century man by man. He was gratified to see that every man had taken the trouble to tie his thongs straight. He paused awhile with Primus, swapping jokes. Aye, Prometheus is doing poorly, but not frighteningly bad. And would you believe that the Third Cohort used up all the rouge in Rome to polish their armor and left none for the Fifth. Laughter. Serves you right.

Sebastian noticed that Primus might have his ear, but Melita held his eye.

The banquet hall filled simultaneously with guests and noise. The guests stood in knots and bunches and little circles. The noise, untrammeled, pervaded everywhere. Sebastian thought of the quiet frog pond, the quieter Sallustia Gardens, the quietest garden at Hadrian's Villa. Perhaps, instead of dreaming about what could not be, he should simply endure and thank God there weren't more of these affairs.

Every time someone laughed his head rang, and everyone was laughing. Sebastian might be out of his element, but Melita was right in hers. She shared her mother's gift for talking easily to perfect strangers. She didn't gawk at the ornate splendor of the hall. She didn't gush over the delicate music and the gorgeously arrayed tables. She fitted in as though she were born to it; no doubt she was sure she was.

There was Castulus talking to Pavo, Irene at his side. Melita's beauty was gaudy, eye-stunning. Irene's was serene, mind-stunning. Sebastian found himself equally awed by both.

A vortex in the moving, standing sea of people belied the presence of Diocletian. He was there, then here, meeting the ladies, jocular. Sebastian presented Melita almost mechanically. Too many thoughts were swirling around inside his head. She played it perfectly, turning on charm and humility both at once.

Aggion, Diocletian's personal slave, handled seating. The morose Greek memorized the place of every guest. Military brass took the end of the wing table. Melita, of course, reclined beside her escort. Irene ended up straight across. Sebastian wanted her to feel out of place, to be as unimpressed by the night as he was. But she blended right in, perhaps even more smoothly than Melita. She gave Castulus the same warm smiles and easy wit she gave Sebastian. No, she was enjoying herself far more than he wished, far more than he himself.

The Furies were shrieking between his ears, but he kept the smile pasted on. He would rather die than let these two women know he was anything short of enthralled with the whole affair.

After interminable rounds of *mulsum*, exotic foods, *mulsum*, rich sauces, toasts, jokes and *mulsum*, Diocletian finally got to the business at hand. "Our new caesar is a man who...a man who...a man who...the man I now present."

Maximian was shorter than Diocletian by far, darker, quicker, more smug, more intense. He spoke well, savored attention, appeared impeccable in dress. He struck Sebastian as a cross between Primus's build and Cannius's demeanor. And Sebastian could not have cared less. The only man who ought to be Caesar was content to crack the whip over a maniple in the Third Cohort. Aye, at the next shift of power Sebastian must recommend Primus. He would be the perfect emperor. Peaches—not too dignified a name for Caesar, but had "Caligula" been any better?

Primus would probably do better in choosing a consort too. Maximian's escort was plain in spite of make-up, flat despite the careful folding of her stola. Quiet. Lustreless. Formalities finally ended and the guests churned about. Maximian's consort disappeared completely. *Lucky lady*, Sebastian thought.

Melita whispered in Sebastian's ear. He smiled, happy to get away from this hot, howling madhouse if only for a few moments. He showed her the women's closets and availed himself of the men's, since he was there.

His headache was spreading into his arms and legs. Why couldn't this stupid gathering end soon? Why couldn't he, like Maximian, have an escort who wanted to go home early? He knew Melita's kind too well. She'd be there until the last lamp was put out.

Melita came out into the main hallway. He grabbed her elbow and turned her the other direction.

"Where are we going?"

"There's this nice little garden just off the east wing. I'd like to say I want to steal away with you, but mostly I just have to get away awhile. Read into it what you wish."

"Aren't gardens very dark this time of night?" Melita asked.

"They'll have torches out at one end of this one."

The finest of tonics was clear night air. It always made him feel better; not good, mind you, but better. His body would be days getting over this miserable party. The pathways were lined with sweet alyssum, perfuming the whole garden. Alyssa. Smelly little flower indeed! They ambled to the dark end, slowly.

"Know what's wrong with soldiers, Sebastian?"

"I know a thousand things wrong with soldiers. What's your opinion?"

"Hard, cold metal covering that soft, warm heart," Melita purred. "It's extremely difficult to snuggle up properly to a man in a brass breastplate."

There was an olive tree in the corner. Sebastian sagged against its cool, smooth trunk and pulled her in close. "Brass breastplates protect tender hearts from arrows, swords, and fickle women. Not necessarily in that order."

Her fingers began absently to toy with his ear. "I am not a sword or an arrow or a f—"

"That's two out of three," he teased. "Don't press your luck."

"You don't think very highly of me, do you?" she pouted.

"On the contrary. You very nearly got yourself married and dragged off to Moesia."

"Oh, yes. Moesia." Melita's warm breath was close to his ear. "It's just as well I never got around to writing the letter you asked for. It would have been a waste of time, since you never went to Moesia to get it."

"Mustn't waste time."

"I agree." She kissed him a sweet peck. "We've wasted too much time already."

As he drew her into the kiss he forgot the noisy party instantly. The headache faded, almost. Too bad this sort of medicine was not immediately available on any occasion. She melted against him, totally soft. Years. He'd been living like a hermit for years. How could he have gone this long without—no matter. The hermitage was past.

Time and place disappeared. In their stead were now and darkness.

Now.

She whispered, "Let's go home, m'love. Come home with me."

No, now.

"Right. And have a cup of *mulsum* with your father while I explain to him why we came home early."

Now.

"No. My rooms are separate. We'll have the whole night together alone. No interruptions. The only two people in the world. I want to be there with you."

Right now.

"Please take me there." She smiled and tickled his ear. "And the first thing we are going to do is get rid of that damnable breastplate."

They kissed once more, a promise, and started back toward the torches and the noise. His headache returned instantly, worse than before. Ah, but now he knew the cure. Shortly...

As they entered the banquet hall, Sebastian hopped up onto a foot-high bench and surveyed the room. "Diocletian is in that far corner, but Aggion's right here by the tables. We'll take our leave of him." He stepped back down and very nearly spun out. Melita's hands, surprisingly strong, held him steady until he regained his balance.

"Sebastian?" she said with concern.

"I *hate* these noisy crowds!"

Again Melita was smooth as silk as she expressed her enjoyment of the whole affair. Sebastian thanked Aggion, who memorized everything, and asked that his gratitude be passed on, confident that this was one message that would not be forgotten. He turned to leave and almost bumped into the new caesar.

His tongue fumbled a moment as he presented Melita to the stormy little man; then they were exchanging pleasantries. It gave him time to get his head back together.

Shortly now. Very shortly...

He realized suddenly that Maximian had spoken to him twice and he had answered. And he had no idea what he had just said.

"I say," Maximian repeated, "If this were just some ordinary occasion, of course I wouldn't ask. But my own escort is ill. She left early, perhaps you noticed. And it really isn't proper that I stand alone tonight. It's just for this one evening. Surely you don't mind."

"What?" Sabastian said incredulously.

"If you will, that I, uh, borrow your escort here."

No! Sebastian's mind snapped back to reality. Melita was already standing closer to Maximian than she was to him. *No!*

His thoughts weighed, paused, fell into line. "You will find,

Your Clemency, that I don't deal in subterfuge or phony words. You'd better believe I mind! This lady is mine and we were just leaving. I realize you have the privilege, if you choose to use it. But you're going to have to pull rank to take her."

Maximian nodded slowly. "Very well, Captain. I just did." He smiled. "I admire honesty. We'll get on well together." Effortlessly he swept Melita away on his arm. They melted into the crowd, were gone that quickly.

In that foul, hot, smoky, crowded, noisy, churning room swarming with laughing, screaming, talking, mingling, bumping, jostling, lewd people—he was alone.

He walked out into the main hallway and stumbled past the flickering torches. He shivered—compared with the banquet room, the hall was dank and chill.

It took him a while to find Primus. The centurion was shifting his men around a little, just to keep their circulation going. Sebastian leaned his back against the cold stone wall and closed his eyes. Primus stopped beside him.

"Ah, lad. I see you love crowded rooms every bit as much as I do. I'll take on a whole troop of northern barbarians before I'll take on that toga bunch."

"Let me know when you leave," Sebastian told him. "I'll walk with you."

"You and your lady don't want a fuzzy old m—"

"I didn't say lady, did I?"

Yes indeed. Primus would make a perfect emperor. He could size up a situation instantly and accurately. "Look forward to it, lad."

Sebastian wandered into the reception room and stretched out on the long scribes' table—anywhere to rest his pounding head. He accidentally kicked an inkpot off, heard it bonk and splat, but didn't care. He dozed. He dreamed. They weren't satisfying dreams of soft skin and beautiful ladies to mollify his aching body. There were horrible things in them—horrid, uncontrollable things. When Primus shook him awake he couldn't remember what they were.

They strolled together through the damp night air made

moist with the smell from the sewers. Primus kept up a running patter for a while. Quinn looked terrible—sent him back early. Can't tell if it's illness or hangover. So-and-so was escorting the widow of so-and-so. Probably not so much a romance as a military alliance. Her father was so-and-so. All those togas trying to learn the inside doings of the palace. If you want to know what's really going on, be a centurion. The guards in the chambers hear it all. You can learn anything you want to know if you ask the right people in the praetorium.

Their caligae gritched in unison on the flat pavingstones of Tiburtina Vetus. They matched strides unconsciously from long practice.

"Know what, Peaches? Think I'll get married."

"That'd put an end to this snatcher business. But there's a disadvantage to it—one or two."

"Everything has its drawbacks. Three girls. For a year there I was nowhere. More than a year. All of a sudden, three of them. Irene's first choice, of course. Castulus is no threat. He's not in the faith..."

"He's sympathetic, lad. You know all the orders against Christians come from Pavo, not Castulus. Not even Diocletian. Castulus doesn't go out hunting."

"...so she won't marry him. But if the worst happens and she refuses me there's Melita. She never once said she loved me, you know that? Irene, I mean. And the Lord knows I gave her chance enough. There's Melita."

Sebastian stumbled on the rough stones, then picked up the stride again. "But then, why should Melita work her way to the top if she's already there? No. Maximian's married. I think. I can get her. But if the worst happens and I can't, there's always Alyssa."

"That little girl with the scar?"

"Nice girl in spite of the scar. Not luscious like Melita or svelte like Irene, but nice. Unspoiled, I think. And she's getting big enough now. Twelve-year-old's too young. I never agreed with that. They don't have their growth yet. If they get pregnant, they have all sorts of problems. But she's fifteen. That's old enough. Out of three of them I ought to get one."

"I met that Alyssa yesterday evening. Met Felician, too. They're at Tycho's. Elegant gentleman. Say, did you know Marcus is getting married?"

"Marcus Tranquilinus?"

"Aye," Primus affirmed. "To that Rhoda over in the west side congregation."

"Good match," Sebastian said. "She's a little heavy, but it's a good match."

"And now Marcellian all of a sudden is looking for a wife. Bet the cub never even thought of it until his brother jumped into the quicksand."

Primus kept talking but Sebastian wasn't listening. He'd heard the term "blinding headache." This one was both blinding and deafening. Besides, he didn't care what Primus was saying. He already knew Felician was an elegant gentleman. He'd known Felician for years, for crying out loud.

Primus's armored shoulder bumped into him, muscling him down a sidestreet.

"What are you doing? We just passed Viminalis Gate. We're not home yet."

"I know that, lad."

Sebastian stopped. "I don't want to admire the scenery. I want to go home."

"We're not going back to the camp. We're going to Tycho's."

"Tycho's! It's third watch. They're asleep. And I don't feel social; I'm going home." Sebastian tried to turn around and nearly spun out again. Suddenly he wasn't certain which way he should be walking.

Primus tugged his arm. "All right. Home. This way, lad, remember?"

They walked on in silence. Primus seemed grim. Even wrapped in the shroud of his own aches, Sebastian could see that. Primus muttered, "I don't understand it. Winter's the season for typhus, and it isn't winter yet. Prometheus, Castor, and now Quinn. He says it's a hangover, but I know better. Well, I'm taking no chances with you, lad."

Why weren't they coming back out on Tiburtinus Vetus? Sebastian stopped. "We're going the wrong way. Peaches, I want to go home."

"Not far now. Here. You sit down right here. Rest a moment. I'll go check where we are and be right back."

Sebastian protested just to argue, but it sounded good. He didn't want to walk any more. Riding in a litter has its advantages. You just lie down and next thing you know you're there. He was shivering in earnest now, swamped by cold night air.

He closed his eyes. They still burned from the torch smoke in that crowded banquet room. He thought of Melita's perfumed bed, soft and comfortable. And thinking of soft comfort brought to mind Melita herself.

A torch flared near his face. The sudden light made his eyes water. Primus's square hands were gripping him, pulling him to his feet. Who were the others? Tycho. One of them was Tycho. Now why was...?

"Peaches, I thought we were going home."

"It's all right, lad. Come along now. A few feet more. Not far."

His knees buckled. He straightened and walked against his will, braced between two strong men. The room was nearly as bright as day. Why were they burning so many torches? Small, cool hands pressed his cheeks.

"Stick out your tongue." A girl's light voice—a pretty, melodious voice. He stuck out his tongue.

The splash of a white scar waved in front of his face. The light voice sighed audibly.

"Peaches, where are you? I want to go home," Sebastian mumbled.

The breastplate and pauldrons fell away. The corselet was gone now. Good. His chest itched. His sword—where was his sword? The greaves scraped his calves and disappeared. His legs felt lighter. He was prostrate in a cool, soft bed. It was not so inviting as Melita's, of course, and not perfumed, but comfortable. Could it be hers? Perhaps his wildest longings were coming true after all. Cold water splashed all over him, and he waved his arms around to make it quit.

Then floated a long, fast succession of faces, some in bright light and some in torchlight: Tycho, Primus, Alyssa, Primus (only occasionally, never when you asked for him), a couple faces he'd never seen, Irene, Alyssa quite a bit, Rhoda once, Desmontes a few times. Once he perceived Dexter trying to help him drink. Why dream of Dexter, of all people?

Faces and voices kept trying to force food down him. Couldn't they understand he had just come from a banquet? He wanted dawn to come so he could wake up from this nightmare. Several men were clustered over him wagging their heads. Two of them resembled Desmontes and Felician, but not quite. *The spots are spreading too much.* What spots? More faces, some known and some unknown.

At last day broke. Sunlight coursed through an open window beside him. A slight, cheery breeze stirred the air. His face felt wet. In fact, his whole body seemed wet. And there sat Dexter on a low stool beside him. The black face split into a toothsome grin. "Master? Master!" The boy hopped up and ran out.

Desmontes appeared in the doorway smiling and crossed to him. The long, lanky body looked so real. And the ultimate touch of realism: no toga. He plumped down beside Sebastian and the pallet bobbed a bit. He picked up a rag from nowhere and wiped off Sebastian's face. He laid a cool hand against his neck, his head. He fingered the damp, tangled hair aside. He certainly felt real enough.

Sebastian reached out and touched Desmontes' face. He was indeed real. No dream, this. Here was a happy reality better than any dream.

"Am I in Milan or are you in Rome?"

"Rome. Tycho's house, remember?"

Sebastian closed his eyes. They didn't burn anymore, and the headache had subsided to a dull heaviness. "I told Primus I wanted to go home—back to the camp. He must have known you were here." He opened his eyes. "That's it! It was a surprise! Sorry I didn't appreciate it better, Uncle. Too much party. Miserable night."

"Eleven of them."

"Eleven what?"

"Miserable nights," Desmontes told him. "This is the twelfth day. We about lost you two or three times."

"That can't be!"

"The same night he brought you here, Primus sent word by fast military post to me in Milan. I got here four days ago."

"Twelve days! Diocletian's going to think I sank into the earth."

"Diocletian should be in Nicomedia by now," Desmontes informed him. "Primus told him before he left that you were ill and promised to send him word. Maximian is holding down this end of the empire—not to mention some other things."

Desmontes drew the cover aside and poked at Sebastian's chest and ribs. He tucked the cover in again. "Listen, son. Your fever broke, but it's not gone. The rash is still there. You're going to have a couple more miserable days until this thing runs its course, and then at least another week in bed before you're safely out of it."

Safe. He felt safe now. He raised his hand to scratch his itchy chest but it wasn't coordinated enough to handle the assignment. Long bony fingers wrapped around his, and he fell asleep.

13

"Master, you have guests. Castulus and Irene."

"Thank you, Dexter," Sebastian said. "See them in." He really should rise. This was his superior officer and bride-to-be. But he couldn't find the energy to throw his heavy legs over the side. He was sitting up. That would do. He squitched himself back to slightly-more-erect.

Irene. He hadn't seen her in a fortnight. It was just as well. The Subura lay between her apartment and Tycho's. It was no route for a woman to be taking after dark. And while he was thinking of her, he asked another blessing upon Felician. The gentle scholar had spent hours talking to her, teaching and hearing, until both he and she were certain it was permissible in God's sight that she marry. There was nothing haphazard in Felician's approach to the faith.

And what problem was bringing Castulus? He had visited only once before, for advice in handling some sticky dispute in the Fifth. Had he come with Irene today (a thoughtful gesture if he was accompanying her for her protection), or had random chance propelled them both through the door at the same moment?

Castulus was not in uniform; his white toga sported a narrow and sedate band. Sebastian admired him for never flouting his position. Irene was more beautiful than ever. She flowed from there to here like liquid silver. He extended his hand to her. When she took it he drew her down for a discreet peck on the cheek.

Dexter and one of Tycho's slaves appeared with chairs and a fruit basket.

"I trust the empire is surviving without me."

"Barely. Tottering on the brink." Castulus smiled a forced sort of smile. "We look forward to your return so we can get back on an even keel."

"So it's that bad, is it? Irene, you look wonderful."

"I wish I could say the same for you. You look absolutely terrible. But then that's a thousand times better then you looked last week. Praise the Lord's name you're finally picking up."

Castulus smiled again, still forced. "I wish I could do that, Sebastian. You just told her with your eyes to be more careful and your expression hardly changed at all. It's a gift. But you needn't worry. I'm one of you now—or rather, one of His. I was baptized last night."

Sebastian extended his arm, mentally checking to make sure his smile was genuine. "I rejoice in your salvation, Castulus!" At the same time he was wondering, *how you ask a new brother tactfully whether he is a rival for the hand of your intended?*

Castulus took his arm. The smile was unforced this time. "You can't rejoice more than I. And now that I'm meeting with other believers, I find Christians all over the Guard. The whole military is riddled with them. Oh, before I forget..." Castulus passed him a small parchment. Sebastian recognized the seal even before he continued, "A personal note from Diocletian, included in the correspondence from Nicomedia. Primus has been keeping him informed of your progress."

"Thank you." Sebastian laid the roll aside for later. "Primus tells me everything is going smoothly with the Fifth, but he never said who's running it. So? Who's filling my caligae?"

"Primus, and doing just fine. He doesn't have your talent for making a complicated schedule sing like a cithara, and he hates desk work, but he's an excellent leader—privy to every thought and deed in the palace. I don't know how he finds all the dirt like that, but he's on top of a situation even before it happens."

Sebastian chuckled. "He has his ways. Keep him on as captain and I'll take over his maniple."

"Primus predicted you'd say that." Irene smiled. "Perhaps you'd better tell him about Thaleus."

"Ah, Thaleus." Castulus sat back. "He appealed directly to Maximian the hour he heard you were ill. Apparently he feels the captaincy is really his and everyone's ignoring him. Primus came to me immediately and gave me a run-down on you and Thaleus. Pavo actually had his pen in his hand when I stopped him. The last man I want heading up the Fifth is an ambitious conniver out to further himself at the expense of the Guard. So you might remember that you and Primus now have a common enemy."

Sebastian sighed. "If we count our enemies within, how can we fight our enemies without?"

Castulus shook his head. "Sit down and analyze the military objectively and how does it run at all? Errors, unwieldiness, pettiness, flawed officers—and yet, it's invincible once it gets rolling. Amazing."

"And the same with the church," Irene suggested. "Petty ego problems and flawed men. Still, God's work moves forward and souls are saved. It's just as amazing. Is Felician here?"

"No," Sebastian answered. "He and Desmontes left early this week, back to Milan."

"I'm sorry," Irene said. "I wanted Castulus to meet him. Desmontes went too? I thought that little black slave was his."

"Dexter is my get-well gift. Desmontes was certain I couldn't make it without him, and he was right. I'm so weak I can't even go...Dexter's very helpful. Uh, Castulus. What's Maximian's attitude toward Christians?"

"Despises us. But his hands are full of too many other problems to be planning pogroms. And I keep Pavo busy with other things."

"Years ago, Alyssa's sister was wishing out loud that the persecutions would end," Sebastian recalled. "Think her wish will come true?"

"Not while Maximian and Diocletian are in the chair," Castulus said. "It's not going to end until and unless you have the sympathy of the top. The very top. I'm almost the top, but I can't remand an order from the caesars. For the moment, though, there's respite."

He was starting to feel tired; a strange sort of tired, a heaviness. "I think about her now and then—Alyssa's sister. I think how nice it would be to just get married, buy some little farm, and forget the world. But duty calls. So I'll stay here and get married. And wait."

Castulus cleared his throat. "Now that you mention it, there is a reason we stopped by today. The two of us."

Sebastian glanced over at Irene. She was studying her hands in her lap, picking at her fingernails. Her face was tight and grim. He leaned back and closed his eyes. He should have guessed by now. He should have been able to tell from her visits (increasingly infrequent and reserved), from her attentions (at first open, then distant). He had attributed all that to a ripening, easy relationship. Why should it ripen? He should have been pressing his suit instead of glibly expecting her to wait for weeks on end while he vegetated. If she cared at all she would have waited. He certainly would have waited for her.

"I see. I hope you two will be very happy together." He opened his eyes. "I mean that."

"I feel guilty." Castulus was staring at the floor. "I'm no match for you when it comes to winning a woman. I don't have the charm, the quick wit. I'd never think of those clever attention-getters Irene has told me about. I'm not young anymore. When you got sick I grabbed the chance—jumped right in. Frankly, I played dirty, took unfair advantage of your illness. I made my own sales pitch, as it were, while your influence with her was minimal."

"Guilty? Unfair? A military man is expected to seize every advantage. Makes a good commander great, you know."

"Stop it!" Irene fairly screamed. "Stop taking this so philosophically! Yell at me or something, like you did when you heard about the invitation! Remember? Hit me! Pay me back that one I owe. I cried all night after I slapped you. And then to hear three days later that you were dying, and I hadn't even bothered to apologize."

She was dissolving. He'd better break this quickly. "Irene, I may be feeble, but I'm not blind. You never really loved me. *Eros?* It would have been fun. We both know what we're doing. *Phileo?* Maybe. But *agape?* Never. Castulus is right. I was trying to make it on charm, trying to sell you something you didn't really feel. That was stupid. Someday you'd fall in love for real and then the misery would start. Tell me that you two really love each other—that it isn't just attractive rank marrying attractive chastity—and go with my blessing."

Castulus leaned forward earnestly. "Love and more. When I first claimed the faith I thought I was doing it to please and win Irene. But I understand now how the sacrifice of the Christ pays for my sin. How much Jesus has done for me. If I were to lose her right now, I would remain committed to my Savior."

Irene snuffled. Castulus pressed on. "Even though you didn't mean to be, you are the instrument of my salvation and my happiness. I'll do my best for her, Sebastian."

If Irene had anything to say it was lost in the quiver of her lip. The gray eyes overflowed. She leaned over, kissed him wetly on the cheek, and ran out.

Castulus, nonplussed, begged his leave and followed.

Sebastian lay back drained. In a way, a weight was lifted and replaced by a heavier one. He should have seen this coming. And they handled it exactly right, coming to him together like this. They kept everything out in the open. She never really did love him.

And he would never cease loving her.

A surprise visit by Prometheus late in the afternoon raised his spirits considerably. The gentle giant must have lost fifty pounds at least—a hirsute skin draped over a towering skeleton. If Sebastian looked half as bad as he...and theoretically, Prometheus's illness had not been so acute. Quinn was very weak, but recovering. No one knew why the infirmary should be full of typhus this time of year. The Guard was stepping up recruitment. Primus would be by tomorrow...

Marcellian stopped by briefly as Prometheus was leaving. Without his older brother the boy seemed lost, a ship without a rudder. As on every other visit he sat around a few minutes, could think of nothing to say and took his leave. Sebastian wondered why he bothered to call at all.

A few days later when Chromatius came calling, Sebastian was able to rise and greet him properly in the peristyle. The spherical gentleman still bounced.

"Ah, Sebastian! I stopped by a few weeks ago but you were sleeping. You're making fine progress, I trust."

"Absolutely. I can walk to the closet without tipping over now. How are Tiburtius and your wife?"

"Splendid! Just splendid. Growing in the faith. We all are."

"You couldn't bring better news."

"I bring some almost as good. Sebastian, my young friend, I am retiring."

"What kind of good news is that? Rome needs you. And besides, the position of influence you have now..."

"Influence? Bah! So I am governor of the grandest city the world has ever known. The slave who unloads grain barges by Probi Bridge will stand before the Christ no less glorious than I."

"No more glorious, either," Sebastian reminded him.

"True," Chromatius concurred. "All are equal before him. You remember all those splendid people who came to Christ at Mamertine? Not just Tranquilinus and Zoë, but the others— the rabble, if you will."

"Over a dozen of them."

"Splendid people. Not when they went in, of course, but when they came out. Every one of them has held true to the faith and growing. Well. I have this villa out in the Campania, a few miles out. It's run down. My father took it in payment of some debt years ago. Belonged to the Sublius family. Anyway, we're all going out there—me, my family, the new converts. Except for Nicostratus and Claudius, of course. They have their positions at the jail there. Eleven of them have families and two more are getting married. We're going to fix the place up and make it a center for study and instruction in the faith."

"Sounds wonderful. Library?"

"Better. We will all devote a part of our time to copying the writings. Tiburtius will remain here in Rome. He will be our supplier, you see."

"Told Maximian yet?"

"Only that I am retiring my prefecture. Not the rest of it, of course. I gave failing health as the reason. Didn't add that I'm getting sick of the job (heh heh). We're thinking of taking Polycarp out there as a teacher. Tiburtius says you should be the one, since you are our mentor so to speak. But you have your position in the Guard—can't just quit—I realize that. A teacher. Writings. Time to study and to contemplate. Serenity. It will be glorious!"

"Glorious! And how are your houseguests doing—Melitus and his family?"

Chromatius frittered with the band of his toga. "Melitus and his wife have long since returned to Milan."

"From that I take it Melita is still here?"

"Here in Rome. Not in my house."

"You're being devious, Chromatius. Where in Rome?"

"The imperial palace. She is now, ah, Maximian's houseguest. It came about as you were taken ill. Sebastian, what irks me most in the matter is her mother. That witch is actually pleased that her daughter is the adulterous consort of Caesar. And the poor young girl doesn't even realize that..."

"Chromatius, believe me. She realizes."

"Well. I suppose you know her better than I do. But it irks. I realize Rome is godless, but it irks nonetheless."

"Think how godless immorality irks our Lord. The fact that it bothers you simply shows that you are in tune with Him."

"I never thought of that!" Chromatius brightened. "Amen! I must leave now—on my way to another appointment. But I did want to drop by and tell you my good news. May God prosper your recovery."

"Thank you, Governor." Sebastian stood.

Chromatius bounced out and Sebastian sank back into his chair like warm wax. *Consort to Maximian.* Dashed were any hopes he might have had of making Melita his own. He had heard of Maximian's rages. It was not impossible that the imperator might simply put her aside eventually by murdering her. Even were Maximian to cast her out, he would not countenance an underling's taking possession of his reject.

Was Chromatius right? Perhaps Melita was essentially a child, too naive to realize how dangerous, how precarious, her position was. Then he remembered her polished performance at the banquet. She would outlive him and Maximian and the next three caesars and still be a successful courtesan at eighty. Melita knew exactly what she was doing.

He moped about for hours, Melita on his mind, before the perfect plan finally forced itself past thoughts of soft curves.

At lunch he obtained permission to use Tycho's litter. By the time he arrived at Chromatius's he was exhausted. How can riding around prostrate be so tiring? He was grateful the governor couldn't receive him immediately. It gave him time to sit on the rim of the frog pond and marshal his strength. Very peaceful, this bit of amphibian paradise.

"Good to see you up and out again!" Chromatius' voice boomed.

Sebastian jumped like one of the frogs. He took a bench as the governor sat down.

"Chromatius, you were talking this morning about a teacher

out in the campania. I'd like that position."

"But your captaincy here..."

"I have it on best authority that the Guard is riddled with Christians. It was great, but things have quieted down. They don't need me anymore. Besides, if I return to my captaincy Primus will have to step down. And he is worthier of that position than I am."

"Aye, perhaps, but—"

"There are other reasons. Personal reasons. The quiet and the physical activity will help build me back up—I didn't realize how weak I am until I rode over here."

"I'd love to have you, as would Tiburtius, but Polycarp..."

"Polycarp is not a personal threat to Caesar. I am. As far as Maximian is concerned, Melita was once my lady. Frankly, it was only the Lord's intervention that kept it from being so in truth. Whether he trusts her fidelity now or not, the day will come when he will not. And I don't want to be anywhere around when that happens."

"I can see a possible problem there..."

"But the most important reason is that I want to help build up the believers, work with the writings. I can't think of a better service to our Lord, and that includes the position I hold now."

"I don't know what to do," Chromatius replied, perplexed. "I can't take you both. You both are equally...I just don't know what to say."

Sebastian stood up. "I apologize for dropping a thing like this so unexpectedly, for putting you on the spot. I didn't expect any answer now. But I do want to be a part of your exciting work out there, and I hope you'll consider me. Thank you for hearing my petition."

"No apologies, my boy!" Chromatius bounced up. "You do my heart good to warm up so enthusiastically to my little project. I will put your request to careful consideration, I promise! Greet Tycho for me."

In a giddy swirl of similar greetings, Chromatius disappeared into his back chambers and Sebastian found himself at the gate. He paused to lean against the wall and to reflect on how such a quiet place as the frog pond could exist in such a boisterous house as Chromatius's.

The next morning Sebastian considered seeing Chromatius again, seeing Polycarp, seeing Primus (just to see him), and vetoed them all. He considered going over to Etruscan Street to browse the book stalls and shops, perchance to find a really nice thank-you gift for Tycho. Too much effort was involved for that; it meant more reading. He was sick of reading. There is a boring weariness to convalescence.

It was Irene who saved his day from ennui. She appeared, lithe and lovely as a lily, around the third hour. "I'm going exploring, and Castulus suggested you might wish to come also."

"Castulus suggested?"

She laughed. "I think he still feels guilty. And he made a special point this morning of expressing his trust in us. And mostly, I suspect, he wants you strong quickly. You should see the muddle his Lupercalia schedule is in."

"Where are you exploring?"

"South side. I know this north end pretty well, but I've never been south of the Circus."

"Ah! My end of town! I shall be your guide—if I can make it that far."

"My litter awaits you," Irene announced.

He brought Dexter along. He knew the boy would like to see the Caracalla Baths.

Marriage suited Irene well. She bubbled, acted ten years younger, and tempered that marvelous serenity with a brand-new enthusiasm. Marcus and his bride Rhoda were now living in Irene's old apartment—she had spoken to the landlord when she moved out. Castulus was receiving increasingly frequent communications from Nicomedia. Obviously Diocletian would be returning to Rome shortly. And that would mean another special guard schedule (you don't know how sorely you are missed). Two of Castulus's slaves converted. And Caius received a letter from Felician last week...

They watched wagons being loaded at Livia Market a few minutes, then followed the wall down to Dripping Arch. Sebastian enjoyed this end of town. It possessed an antiquity, a sedateness, the other districts lacked.

Sebastian called a halt at Scipio's tomb. "There's Appia Gate. We have just run out of city. Go or turn?"

She didn't hesitate. "Go! The gate looks brand new."

"Aye. In fact, the wall isn't quite finished in spots. Chromatius says that ever since they started it, this wall has been one big pain in th—let's say he uses his favorite expression every time he talks about it. And I don't mean 'splendid,' either. One foul-up after another."

As with all the major trunks of Rome, Appia Way was lined base-to-base on both sides with ornate marble tombs, a solid and imposing forest of spires and blocks. Sebastian flopped down on his back and watched the sunsheet bob. He was getting tired already. "What do you think of when you pass the tombs along these ways?"

Irene thought a moment. "Not about death. For me there will be no death. Sometimes if I'm terribly pensive I'll feel sorry for all the souls represented here who never heard of the Christ—or worse, laughed at Him. But mostly I just look them all over and try to find a tasteful one among all the garish displays."

"Have you ever visited the burial tunnels?" Sebastian asked.

"The ones up north of town beyond Nomentana Gate. We've laid several friends there. I understand the biggest are down here."

"That little dirt path there leads to the first one. There are others further down the road. I've visited a couple times at the ones half a mile beyond here."

"You visit burial tunnels?" Irene asked, puzzled. "You mean, as in 'stopping by'? Why?"

"I don't know, exactly. Same feeling I had when I was in middle prison at Mamertine, where Paul had been. You know, Catacumbas up ahead there is where they put Peter and Paul for safekeeping—what's left of their remains, I mean. Caius and some of the other believers were afraid the pagans would

178

desecrate them. Caius brought me out here once; he showed me the grotto where they're laid."

"You like Paul, don't you."

"Peter no less," Sebastian told her. "I read more of what Paul wrote, of course. But I feel like Peter a lot. Walking on the water, for instance. 'Here I come, Lord....Uh, hold on there a moment.' That business with Chromatius's gout one day and almost falling with M—...uh, some young lady the next.

"Here, Dexter. Lead off that way. See the path?"

They left the marble tombs behind. Here was the torchseller's stall. She was one of Sebastian's favorite people. She never forgot a name. She was asleep now, her withered old body scrunched up under her awning.

"Stop here."

"Sebastian, what are we doing?" whispered Irene.

He swung off the litter, paused to firm his balance, and tapped the woman's shoe.

"Eh? Ah, you're young Sebastian. You'll take one."

"Two this time. I brought some friends."

"Not your wife?"

"Bride of a friend and brother, Festa. Two torches, please."

"Two. Fresh pitch too. Here you are. Suppose you want to borrow a flint." The old woman squinted through watery eyes. "Friend. You sure she isn't a meretrix?"

"You have a good eye, Festa. She used to be but she quit." Sebastian fished through his purse. "Here," he lied, "the smallest I have is a sestertius. Keep the change."

"Bless you. You mind yourself in there, hear? Bad ideas come natural to boys your age. She quit, eh?" Festa curled up again. She was dozing by the time Sebastian was back in the litter.

They stopped at a tunnel mouth overgrown with brush. The flint was worn nearly to the nubbin. Dexter couldn't make a spark so Sebastian took over. He had to strike it a dozen times, and he began sweating from even that simple exertion. He gave one torch to Dexter and led with the other.

The only sounds were of torches hissing and grit crunching under their feet. The walls were as gritty as the floor. You could rub sand off them. As he turned into a side drift he glanced back and laughed. "Dexter, if your eyes get any bigger you're going to need another head to hold it all."

"I revere the dead, master—what remains of them."

"So do I, but not unduly. The pagans are too superstitious. They won't enter these burial chambers at all. That's why the remains of the apostles are safe here."

"I feel fresh air," Irene whispered.

"We'll do better than fresh air. Here's a cubicula clara—a grotto with a skylight punched out."

Irene stepped into the cubicle and looked up at the intricately painted dome ceiling, at the shaft of light far up. "This is almost spookier than darkness. You can't help but see how far down you are."

She gasped and nearly broke his arm squeezing it as they passed the Portiri family grotto—the skeletons were right out there for all to see.

Sebastian found himself shaking again in the dry cold. His trembling hands made the torchlight smoke and dance. Finally they were there and he could sit down, fold his arms across his knees, and rest his head on them.

Irene took the torch and knelt awhile in prayer.

Sebastian had nearly forgotten Dexter until he heard his voice. It started as a whisper: "*Paulos desmios Christuo Iesou kai Timotheos ho adelphos, Philemoni...*" and grew to a gently, fluid, faultless Greek. The boy had it memorized—Paul's whole letter to Philemon. "*...egraphe apo Romes dia Onesimou oiketou.*"

Enclosing, peaceful silence.

At length Sebastian said, "That must be your favorite scripture. Why?"

"It doesn't just preach love, master, it demonstrates love."

"For a slave."

"Aye, master."

"Do you suppose Philemon took Paul's hint there and freed Onesimus?"

"I wish so, master."

"Do you want to be free?"

Hesitation. Then, "Aye, master. But only if Sinister be freed as well."

"What would you do with your freedom?"

"Preach the word, master."

Sebastian looked over at Irene. She was smiling at him. *You're as transparent as a fishpond, soldier.* He read her thoughts. He smiled back. "A preacher must first of all be a student. Keep studying, Dexter. You're coming along very well."

"Thank you, master."

"And incidentally. I heard somewhere that not only was Onesimus freed, he later became a bishop in Macedonia." Sebastian was getting stiff from the cold. "Let me show you some of the most artful cubicles. I suggest then we start back. There's a little stall by the Appia Gate that sells tasty roast-mutton pastries. Let's eat lunch there, spend an hour or two at the baths, and go home."

Irene smiled. "And you're going to head straight for the Laconicum."

"The hotter the better, to drive the chill out of these bones." Sebastian lurched to his feet, Irene floated gracefully to hers, and they started on. Dexter was slow coming. Sebastian glanced back. The boy was taking one last, long look at the sarcophagi of the two apostles. Sebastian distinctly heard him whisper, "Thank you, Brother Paul."

It was the common baker's sign displayed outside the door of every bakery in Rome—the spool-shaped wheat mill and the donkey (head and tail only) that turned it. But beneath it hung a new sign freshly painted. It portrayed a huge honey-glazed loaf. Sebastian walked inside. He deliberately picked this time of day to buy, when the bakery was filled with the wonderful aroma of warm, fresh bread.

The proprietress grinned behind brown-stained teeth. "Well, look at you! Finally starting to pick up a little weight again. What will it be today? One loaf? Two?"

"Four."

"You're celebrating something."

"Aye, going home—back to camp. And a few friends will be dropping by my quarters. I've been Tycho's guest long enough. How's business?"

"Just wonderful! You know, so many people come asking 'Is this the bakery that makes those glazed loaves?' that I put that sign out. I sell everything the girl bakes."

"I never did hear how she ended up here."

"Walked in one day. She said she'd been a baker in Milan and may she show me her specialty. She set one of those big loaves on the counter and the customer standing here scooped it up—at the price she asked. I asked, 'Who can vouch for your character?' and she said, 'Tycho who lives a hundred paces up the street,' and that was good enough for me."

"May I speak with her?"

"Surely! Go right on back."

Sebastian slipped through the curtain into the back room. Alyssa was up to her elbows in flour, kneading for the next baking. And she had an audience.

Sebastian smiled, "How are you, Marcellian?"

Marcellian stood up from his stool in the chimney corner. "Well, sir. And you look much better." He sat down again.

"Thank you." This was just like Marcellian's truncated visits at Tycho's. Nothing to say. And obviously he wasn't leaving, either. "Alyssa, I have a letter here from Desmontes. In it Felician sends you greetings."

"My greetings in return," she said amiably.

"I'm answering it in the next week or so. Shall I include anything else from you?"

She paused, her lips pursed. "No, I can't think of any news he hasn't already heard."

Marcellian whispered coarsely, "The date?"

"He knows that." She smiled brightly. "Thank you, Sebastian! You're very thoughtful."

He smiled back, happy to see a spontaneous grin from her. "Go in peace, Marcellian, and greet Tranquilinus for me. Have fun with your mud pies, Alyssa."

"Mud pies! You eat enough of them, you—"

But he was out the curtain.

Dexter was trotting out the door with the four loaves. This time Sebastian really didn't have the right change. "I don't know when you first met her," the proprietress said to him, "but she was sour as a pomegranate when she first came here. Despondent. It's wonderful to see her so cheerful."

He found a sestertius. "How long have you been displaying that statue in your chimney corner back there?"

The lady giggled as she poked through her money box. "Doesn't he look silly? When he first started coming around I thought, 'Oh, dear!' But they never try to sneak around or, ah...He just sits there and watches, all very proper. So I can't object. She says they are waiting until the wedding. Not many young people are that moral, not these days."

"The wedding?"

"Isn't it grand? No travail comes but what it doesn't bring a blessing. Why, do you realize if you hadn't gotten sick like that, Alyssa probably would have just gone on back to Milan. She wouldn't have stayed to help; she wouldn't have come here to work; I wouldn't be making so much money. And that young Marcellian, I understand, got to know her on his visits to you. I'm sure he never would have gotten to know her otherwise, with that scar and all. Turns a boy off. Now don't take this wrong, but I think it's wonderful you got sick. It brought those two young people together. Fine young people. Fine girl."

"Aye. A fine girl."

"You look weary. Like a flower that needs watering. Wilted. You should go back and take a nap, right now. You mustn't exert yourself too much yet, you know. Have a nice time with your friends tonight."

"Thank you," he answered glumly. He walked outside, squinting in the bright sunlight. A chubby woman, obviously someone's slave, paused beside him to study the sign. She waddled inside. *Fine girl, Alyssa.* He reviewed briefly the memory of her skipping out the farmhouse door, her egg basket, her solemn eyes as she sat at his table that night. No wonder she had brightened up to being the old Alyssa. She was in love, and not with Sebastian, either. Marcellian's abortive visits suddenly made sense.

How many doctors know that one of the most devastating side effects of typhus is an acute loss of marriage prospects?

Just before he left for camp, Chromatius stopped by. Unable to make the decision, he had put the problem before Caius for arbitration. Caius suggested Polycarp should go. Sebastian thanked him for his concern and consideration and tried not to let it sound hollow.

At his quarters that night he urged his friends to finish off the fourth loaf. "And don't let the last of the wine rot the bottom out of the keg," he urged them. He left them to their laughter and joking and went to bed.

Alone.

14

Behind him in a niche posed a three-foot-high statue of Venus, clad only in a coating of gold leaf. Beside him in another niche stood Juno. Sebastian wondered idly if the women's portion of the baths was similarly adorned with male statues. Stretched prostrate on the tiled table, he gazed up at the vaulted arches overhead, the intricate red and gold geometric designs on the ceiling.

The masseur grunted "Over." Obediently Sebastian flopped over. Primus, on the table beside, yelped and took a wild swing at his masseur.

Sebastian chuckled. "He pounds a hundred bodies a day, Peaches. He's not going to remember that little knob on your ribs." A moment later his own masseur hit the knobs on his. He yelped and swiped at the stupid jerk.

"Know what this is?" mused Primus. "The lull before the storm. I feel it deep down inside."

"Good. I'm ready for a little action. You push just so much parchment around and you begin to wonder why you're in the Guard."

"I said it before and I'll say it again. The happiest day of my life was when you came back to the west room. I don't see how you can stand it."

"Easy," Sebastian drawled. "Write with your eyes closed so you can't see what you're doing. Heard when Diocletian is getting here?"

"Aye. Private runner came in early this morning; says he's already halfway up from Brundisium. Minturnae tomorrow, or maybe even Fundi, Forum Appii the next."

"Bet he makes it to Three Taverns. He'll be traveling light. And here the next day. What else do you hear?"

"Nothing," Primus said. "Except he has Galerius with him."

"Think he's going to try to get king-making out of the barracks and back into dynasties?"

Primus grunted. "Doubt it. He wants a good, solid government, remember? If you think Maximian has his ups and downs, wait'll you meet Galerius. Just like his mother."

The rhythmic splacking stopped. Sebastian sat up slowly. Yes, he was certain he would prefer the heat of battle to the cold of making out schedules. The bath was his only escape. He came with eagerness and left with reluctance. Primus wrapped a towel around his waist and led the way out. They dressed, spoke a few moments with the *ostiarius* on the way out, and started the familiar walk back toward camp.

"Did Castulus say when he's going to approach Diocletian about legalizing the faith?" asked Sebastian.

"No, but he probably doesn't know himself. He'll test how the wind lies and pick the perfect time and place. He's good at that."

"Isn't he, though?" Sebastian thought briefly of that visit by Castulus and Irene many months ago. Tactful. Nothing, if not tactful. "What's Caius talking about tonight? Do you know?"

"Origen."

"Again?!"

"My feelings too," Primus agreed. "Enough is enough. I never was strong on philosophy."

"Caius is, though." Sebastian stopped. "Here's where we part company."

"Quinn and I are going over to Domitian Stadium before the meeting to watch the Lancers rehearse for Caesar's homecoming. I think I mentioned Quinn wants to join the Lancers. Sure you don't want to join us, lad?"

"Thanks but Tiburtius has this houseguest he's sure I want to meet—a lady named Lucina."

"He's still trying to match you up?"

Sebastian snickered. "With his rejects. Why not? I'm in the market. I'll meet anybody once."

"Ah, say." Primus cleared his throat. "You don't happen to have a bit extra?"

"Bronze or silver?"

"Bronze's fine."

Sebastian spread his change out on his palm and Primus borrowed three asses. As Sebastian turned his back to the Flavian Amphitheatre and walked off, he heard Primus's voice hailing a *cisium*-for-hire. The paunchy little centurion was getting lazy in his old age.

Lucina was charming, Tiburtius grave. Lucina was probably always charming. Tiburtius was certainly always grave. Sebastian waved a finger toward the liquamen cruet and Dexter quickly sprinkled more sauce on Sebastian's fish. Tiburtius was expounding on the evils of Plotinian philosophies and the failure of Plotinopolis. Sebastian didn't really care. Obviously, neither did Lucina, but she handled it well. Although, Sebastian noticed, Tiburtius did not.

Tiburtius jarred Sebastian out of his thoughts. "What do you think of the matter?"

Sebastian shrugged. "Anthony went down to Alexandria about the time Plotinus was coming out. I wonder if they ever met and what they would have thought of each other."

"Anthony. The old hermit is wasting his life. Plotinus may have been misguided, but at least he got out there and acted. He did something."

Lucina gaped at her host—a calculated gape. "You really believe Anthony's life is wasted?"

"What did he do to further the cause of God?" Tiburtius challenged.

"Devoted himself to God," Lucina asserted.

"Yes, but what did he *do?*" her host persisted.

"That is sufficient," she maintained. "You give yourself over to God and He uses you as He sees fit. If he chooses to perform a very obvious work in you, as He did in Paul, for instance, fine. If He chooses that you die young in His name, that is no less to His purpose. I submit that he marked Anthony for a special life in hermitage because that is the capacity in which He needs him."

"I understand your point," Tiburtius conceded, "but I can't see that hiding in a cave can bear fruit for God."

"There is much we can't see this side of the veil."

Tiburtius's face sat blank as he sought a response—or at least a point with which to renew the conversation. The table lapsed into silence. Sebastian kept his own face straight, but inside he was chuckling. Lucina was not a woman he would look at twice; she was too raw-boned, and too heavy. But this was the third time she had stopped Tiburtius's rambling philosophies cold. There was much more to her than met the eye.

Sebastian let the silence get heavy just to give Tiburtius the hint, then bailed him out. "Lady, what is your favorite part of Rome?"

"My favorite part of Rome, Captain, is outside it. Catacumbas, down south of the Appia Gate."

Sebastian glanced over at Dexter. The rapt boy was in love. "Why, lady?"

"What it represents, I suppose. Our heritage, with the apostles and church leaders interred there. Our hope, our respite, our industry and devotion. All symbolic, of course, but all there. Primarily, though, I enjoy quiet. It is quiet."

Sebastian smiled. "I don't know what Tiburtius's intentions toward you are, but if he doesn't marry you, I will. You have superb taste."

The slaves set out bowls of fruit and nuts. Tiburtius waved

them out. "All of you are dismissed." He studied Dexter. "You may wait outside."

"By your leave, Tiburtius," Sebastian interceded, "he's studying for the ministry. Might he stay?"

Tiburtius scowled at the boy. "As you wish."

Even when Dexter kept his face sober, the joy leaked out visibly.

The young philosopher became grimmer, more serious. "I learned from friends in Nicomedia that Galerius is bringing with him his mother's wishes—to stamp out the Christian cult, to wipe it from the face of the earth. She worships the Persian gods and is convinced that Christians are her arch enemies. We face wicked times, Captain."

"She isn't Caesar. And neither is Galerius."

"She might as well be," Tiburtius retorted. "Diocletian has her ear and she his, and he believes her completely."

"Maximian is unpredictable—half mad, at times. But Diocletian is a reasonable man. He doesn't go for Persian gods, being an emissary of Jupiter, and he has several persuasive speakers at his elbow. Speakers to support the Christ."

"Including you," Tiburtius said meaningfully.

"As the Spirit leads. Let's not worry about frying before the pan gets hot."

"Hmph." After a pause Tiburtius asked, "What do you know about a centurion in the Third Cohort named Thaleus?"

"Now why do you ask that?"

"He is a new convert. Sincere. In fact, he is so zealous he strikes a discord."

"I would imagine they said that about Paul," suggested Lucina, "right after his conversion in Damascus."

Thaleus. Thaleus! Sebastian thought. *Anything is possible. Look indeed at the apostle Paul, that ardent persecutor of Christians. Primus the Mithraist, for that matter. Thaleus.* Aloud he cautioned, " 'Ye shall know a tree by its fruits,' Tiburtius. Check the apples very carefully on this one."

Thaleus. The conversation drifted to lighter topics, all touching the faith. As the lamps came out Sebastian begged his leave.

Thaleus, he mused. *Conniver. And yet, if the conversion was genuine* ...Dexter fell in beside him as they walked the Tiburtina Vetus back to camp. *Thaleus.*

"Master?"

"Hmm?"

"Are you truly going to marry her?"

"Who?" Sebastian said, coming out of his reverie.

"That lady. That Lucina. Master, she's perfect."

"Why should I marry her? You're the one who's in love with her," Sebastian teased.

"Master!"

"I saw you. She said the word 'Catacumbas' and you melted like warm tallow."

Dexter's big eyes glanced up and away quickly. *He's lucky*, thought Sebastian. *People of his race don't blush.*

Diocletian arrived amidst formal fanfare, worshiped at each of the temples of Jupiter, and conferred in closed chambers with Maximian for two days.

Sebastian spent the time trying to figure out how his cohort could go on annual maneuvers and still keep the forums from being carried away by whomever the Guard was guarding the forums from. Late in the afternoon of ten before October kalends, Sebastian felt like personally burning every scrap of parchment in the imperial palace. He sat back, ordered a cup of cold water from his orderly, and rubbed his weary eyes.

Prometheus tapped his arm and handed him still another parchment. "Letter from the prefect of the Dacian auxiliary. Wants to know if you recommend Quinn for appointment to the Lancers."

Sebastian reached for the inkpot. "Wish they were all this easy." He penned a few well-chosen words extolling Quintillian and gave it back to Prometheus. The giant dispatched it immediately with an idle aide. Quinn was as good as in.

Castulus appeared in the doorway. Sebastian's blood ran cold. The man was white, pure marble white. "You two come to my apartment. Bring Primus."

Sebastian poked the captain of the Third. "Where's Primus?"

"Front annex drilling the new palace guards. We'll send him right down there."

Sebastian and Prometheus took the back stairs down.

"What's up, Bass? Any guesses?"

"From the look on his face, the empire just collapsed."

Irene met them at the door personally. She started to speak; instead she melted against him sobbing. It was several moments before she could shudder, "It's started. It's worse than ever."

Sebastian studied his huge companion and Prometheus returned the scowl, equally confused. Sebastian turned her around and piloted her gently into the peristyle.

Primus came jogging up behind, winded.

Castulus was pacing like a caged lion from pillar to pillar. He was still as white. He wheeled on them. "The whole legion! And he didn't stop him. The whole blessed legion!" Prometheus grabbed the man's shoulders and dragged him to a standstill. Like a small boy, Castulus sank down on a bench and buried his face in his hands.

Sebastian dropped to one knee in front of him. "Start at the beginning. What's happening?"

Castulus's whole being shook, from body to voice. "The Theban Legion. They were Christians, Sebastian, every man. Maximian sent Pavo out to check out the rumor. Not one of them would burn incense to Caesar or claim the mysteries of Mithras. Pavo ordered them decimated. Six hundred good men gone, just like that.

"They went over his head. He ordered a second decimation. They made formal appeal to Maximian. I read it, Sebastian. It was eloquent. They swore fidelity to Caesar and the empire, swore to serve to the death—but as Christians. Maximian flew into one of his rages. Told Pavo to cut them all down."

"Oh, come on, Castulus! Even Maximian couldn't destroy a whole legion. You're talking about six thousand men. Diocletian would never—"

"He *did!* He concurred with Maximian. I couldn't reach him, couldn't even talk to him. Six thousand loyal men and he concurred. If this is the beginning of the madness, by all that's holy, what is the end going to be like?"

Irene was doing an admirable job of putting the pieces back together. She snuffled and wiped her eyes. "Apparently Diocletian feels...I don't understand what he feels, except that he got the ideas from his wife. He know that Caius is bishop of Rome and he knows where Caius is. Caius and others. He has a list."

"Now how could he get something like that?"

"How should I know? He has it. And as soon as Pavo gets back he's going to start raiding. Caius will be first."

Things were whirling again in Sebastian's head. "Why doesn't he send one of us out right away, before Caius could flee? Are we on the list, do you think?"

Castulus wagged his head. "I saw the list. He has them all. And where to find them. But it's a big secret. Only Diocletian and his closest advisers have it. He figures he's got all the time in the world, I suppose." He whispered. "Six thousand."

Sebastian grasped his arms just to draw his attention. "The list, Castulus! Any military on it?"

Castulus looked at him for the first time. "No. No military. Not one. That means the informer is a civilian."

"No! It means the informer is military, and protecting himself lest the pogrom reach into the palace and the Guard."

"It could be any one of hundreds of men. You or me. Anyone. Maybe someone who's not in the faith but knows someone else who is."

Sebastian stood up. "Peaches, what do you suggest?"

Primus was standing there numb. "A whole legion," he whispered.

"I know that! Now start thinking!"

"Aye, lad. You're right." Primus's eyes misted. "Pavo won't get here for a day or two. We have a day or two. We have to get Caius out of town. Caius and the others. All of them."

Irene shook her head. "Caius won't leave. His flock is here. He'd never leave the city."

Prometheus nodded. "She's right. But he might go into hiding here."

"Where?"

"The Subura," Primus suggested.

Sebastian scowled. "No. You can buy an informer there for an as and get change. It'll have to be on the other end of the economic scale."

"Tycho's."

Castulus shook his head. "He's one of the names on the list."

Sebastian leaned against a pillar and looked out across the peristyle, awash in late-afternoon gold. This was it! He wheeled around. "Here!"

"What?"

"Here in the imperial palace somewhere. If you're Pavo, where's the last place in Rome you'd look for refugees?"

Primus brightened. "Aye! Safest place in the city. Caius can come and go when he has to through the kitchen, like all the greengrocers and bakers and butchers."

"Fine!" Sebastian was pacing now, but from excitement, not despair. "Now. Where's the best place in the palace?"

"Right here." Castulus stood up. He was composed again, his old rock-steady self. "We'll bring them here and house them in this apartment. There're enough cubicles. And even if Pavo suspects something, he won't dare to enter without my permission. I'll double-check the list and make sure we don't miss someone. I think there were eleven names."

Sebastian considered a moment. "Tranquilinus?"

"Marcus and Marcellian, but not Tranquilinus or his wife. What's her name?"

"Zoë. The boys have been coming to meetings regularly, but Tranquilinus has not. He's been stuck at home with arthritis."

Primus snorted. "Then our informer is probably a recent convert who wouldn't know about Tranquilinus."

A recent convert.

In the Guard.

Thaleus.

"Are you sure he'll come?" Sebastian was getting nervous. Prometheus mumbled, "According to Manlius he comes this way every evening, out to buy a drink at that tavern on Nomentana Way. You're fidgeting, Bass."

"Well, it's late and he hasn't—"

"Psst! There he is!" Even Prometheus's whisper rumbled.

"How can you see in total darkness?"

"I see."

Footfalls came closer. Sebastian held the cone over the lamp, blotting out its light. Prometheus stepped away from him out into the street. There were scuffles, a muffled yelp. The giant was at Sebastian's elbow again. Sebastian lifted the cone away. Prometheus had the boy pushed flat against the quaestorium wall. Sebastian shoved the light into his face.

"You're Thaleus's personal slave."

"I—I—I have no money, sir. I did nothing. I—"

"Do you read?"

"Aye, my lord. A bit of Latin."

Sebastian stuck a parchment under the boy's nose. "Whose signet is this?"

"Caesar's, my lord. Diocletian's."

"Read the parchment."

The boy scanned the lines, hesitated. He took the parchment into his own hands and read it carefully, incredulously. He looked into Sebastian's eyes, confused. "My lord, my name is there. That's my description."

"And what does it say?"

"It gives me my freedom, my lord. It would set me free. I don't understand."

"Understand this. I give you my word that if you answer certain questions satisfactorily you will have this. By edict of Caesar you will be free and Thaleus can't take you back. If you refuse to answer, or if you lie, I touch the tip of this sheet to the lamp here and we'll watch it burn up together."

"My lord, I know nothing."

"Is Thaleus of the Christian cult?"

Silence. The boy stared rapt at the parchment. He licked his lips. Finally, "Aye, my lord."

"How do you know?"

"He attends the meetings. He reads certain forbidden writings studied by the cultists. And he has urged me to be one too. He says it's the only way."

193

Sebastian looked at Prometheus. The man shook his head. Sebastian tried a more direct tack. "I say he is a false brother—an informer for Caesar against Christians. What say you?"

The boy glanced at Sebastian, his eyes glistening. "I don't...I don't want to...what shall I say?"

"Say truthfully, boy."

"I don't see how he could be. He believes."

Prometheus poked his arm. "Has he talked lately of being promoted?"

"He always talks of that, my lord. He says a usurper named Sebastian stole his place and he shall have it back. Though, he hasn't been saying that lately, not since his conversion. He hasn't said anything about a new position since his conversion."

"Has he extra money to spend?"

"No, my lord. His former slave died of typhus. Buying me took all he had."

Sebastian stepped back a little. He handed the parchment to the boy. "Here you are. Also, here are three asses. Rent yourself a room for the night. Don't return to Thaleus. Do you know where the tablinarium is?"

"No, my lord."

"Find your way to the old forum on the Sacred Way. Stand in the Augustus arch with your back to the temple of the Vestal Virgins. Walk straight ahead, past the rostra on your right and Vespasian Temple on your left. The building ahead of you is the tablinarium, the hall of records. Present your parchment there to be enrolled as a citizen."

The boy rolled his parchment with trembling hands. He dropped to both knees and smeared Sebastian's hand with tears. "Thank you, my lord!"

"Go quickly!"

They listened to the footfalls hurry out the southwest gate.

Sebastian blew out the lamp. "That's not exactly what we expected to hear."

"Mmm. Masterful forgery too," Prometheus grumbled. "Work of art. For naught."

"Think confronting Thaleus himself might be fruitful?"

"No." Prometheus scratched his shaggy head.

"Neither do I." Sebastian pushed away from the wall. "See you in the morning." He thought briefly of stopping at Thaleus's barracks, but Prometheus was right. Either the conversion was genuine or Thaleus was canny enough to put on a total act, even for his slave.

He walked off into the blackness.

Diocletian's aide appeared in the west doorway. "You, Captain. Come."

Sebastian motioned to Prometheus and headed for the door. His bulky aide fell in behind. They followed the orderly down to the main audience room, through the high doors. Inside, Diocletian paced back and forth. Sebastian noticed Galerius off in one corner—a petulant young man.

Diocletian turned, a parchment in his hand. "You know any of the names on this list?"

Sebastian studied it. Here was the list Castulus had seen three days ago. The first name was Caius. Which names ought he to know and which not? Sebastian carefully arranged his face. "This first name. Caius. I met him at Tycho's house, I think. Aye, here's Tycho sixth one down. Strange man, weird ideas. Marcellian. I don't know if it's the same one, but a boy named Marcellian hung out at Tycho's some too."

"How do you know Tycho?"

"Primus and another guardsman took me there when I got sick last year. It happened to be the closest house along the way. Tycho lives just off the Tiburtina Vetus."

"Primus knows him?"

"He does now. He didn't then. But the other fellow did—Claudius something. There're a million Claudiuses in Rome and I must know two thousand of them."

"The turnkey at Mamertine," the emperor said sharply.

"Then I know him," Sebastian replied matter-of-factly. "And Nicostratus, of course."

"When did you see them last?"

"I haven't seen Tycho since I left his place, about five weeks after I got sick. Sent him a thank-you gift, of course. Caius and Marcellian the same. Claudius and Nicostratus last week when we jailed that purse-cutter. I take that back. Four days ago. Three unregistered harlots operating in Trajan Forum."

"Where do Claudius and Nicostratus live?"

"I have no idea, Your Clemency. If their faces weren't framed in prison stone I probably wouldn't recognize them."

Diocletian was studying him intently. Sebastian returned the gaze amicably, kept himself relaxed.

Caesar nodded. "I believe you. These people are Christians, ringleaders in the cult."

"So what?" Sebastian shrugged.

"What!" the emperor thundered.

"I thought we were giving up on that. We haven't chased after Christians in months."

Diocletian took his list back. "My negligence. I didn't realize the hideous threat they are until just recently. They must be stamped out. Destroyed. They are a cancer that will erode the heart of the empire if they be left to proliferate. Atheists, anarchists, seditionists. Removing the menace is now our primary objective."

Sebastian nodded, "All right, then, let's start with your list here. I'll pick a score of good men and we'll bump them off right down the line."

"They're gone."

"Who? The list? All of them?"

"I sent Pavc. Someone warned them. They've disappeared."

"The whole list? Then you have an informer in close here."

"That's right," Diocletian said in a foreboding voice.

Sebastian rubbed his cheek. He strolled over to the window and looked out toward the cattle market. He turned. "Your Clemency, you must have obtained that list by the hand of an informer in the first place. Could he have had two copies and sold one to each side?"

Diocletian's face brightened like dawn. "A prospect worth investigating, well worth investigating. And I know the man I'll put to it. As for you, I want you to seek out these men. Find

196

their haunts, the places they frequent, their friends. Track them down. Make arrests freely, coerce freely. But get them."

"I'll do my best, Your Clemency. Oh, and sir? If I come across someone who visited Tycho's frequently but isn't on the list, shall I arrest him? That is, by association?"

"Absolutely. The list is surely incomplete."

Sebastian saluted. "By your leave, Your Clemency. Good day." Prometheus followed him out.

They walked the length of the hall. The far end doors opened and closed behind them. Prometheus jogged a little two-step and fell in beside. "That last little request was brilliant. A touch of genius. That's the kind of quick thinking I wish I could do. It would take me days to come up with that."

"Not as long as it would take me to break a door down. Every part of the Body has its gifts, brother."

"Amen."

Sebastian said loudly, "I want the whole cohort in formation before taps tonight. Spread the word."

"Aye, sir!" Prometheus saluted and ambled off.

Sebastian took a long, deep breath—smiled smugly to himself—and broke into a cold sweat.

15

It was a roomy, comfortable chair. Sebastian slouched down on his spine and stretched his legs out. He took another sip of *mulsum* as he watched Irene gracefully slicing bread. She did everything gracefully.

"...and so we loaned all the slaves except Festus out to Sylvester, since he needed help anyway. Castulus felt we shouldn't have the slaves here as well as our new guests—the quantity of food consumed would look suspicious."

"You seem to be getting along just fine without them."

She smiled. "You should see Marcus trying to clean house."

The door slammed behind him and Castulus stood by his shoulder. Sebastian and Prometheus started to rise, but Castulus stayed them. "Don't. You two look so comfortable I'd hate myself for expecting you to move. What's the news?"

"I have my maniples scattering out in fifty different directions—all the wrong ones. But I don't know how long I can keep them traipsing around the berry bush. Who's investigating our double spy?"

"Pavo himself."

"Has he realized yet that he's on the wrong track?" Sebastian asked.

"I don't know. Pavo hasn't confided who that informer is. Apparently he deals only through Pavo."

"Informers are known for their poor taste."

Castulus snitched a chunk of bread. "Have you any idea who it might be?"

"Sure. Thaleus. But Prometheus and I have tried half a dozen different ways to find some hint he's false. Nothing. He smells good any way we sniff him."

Prometheus followed his superior's example and grabbed himself a piece of bread too. "You're above Pavo. Tell him to tell you, so we can all investigate."

"I considered it, Prometheus, and I don't think I dare. Pavo is eyeing me very suspiciously. Maximian too. I can't appear to be too interested. After all, Diocletian himself assigned him the job. I wouldn't care so much if we didn't have the responsibility of all these people."

Irene set out the boiled beef and onions. "I invited Prometheus and Sebastian to dinner. Did Caius get back?"

"Not yet. I wish he'd stay here more." Castulus snitched another chunk. "Always out tending sheep, he calls it. He's going to get caught just by accident."

A fist thumped on the door. Castulus looked at Irene. They said *I love you* with their eyes. Sebastian's heart ached.

Primus bolted in unbidden. "They got Tranquilinus!"

"Who got him?"

"Sulla's century. They drew a crowd together, talked up how dangerous the Christians are, and stood back while the mob stoned him."

Prometheus nearly knocked Sebastian over in their scramble for the door.

"We have to get to Zoë before they do." Sebastian stopped and turned to Irene. "Can you tell the boys?"

She nodded, a little numb.

He paused, returned to the table, and laid his hand on her arm. "It's not the end. It's just the beginning. Don't forget that."

Prometheus returned to the table also, grabbed a chunk of boiled beef, and followed Sebastian out the door.

They stuffed their helmets on their heads on the run. Prometheus headed straight for the Lancer on horse who sat guarding the entrance. He saluted, reached up, and lifted the boy off his horse. Sebastian swung onto the horse's back as the boy left it.

He gouged his heels into the horse's ribs, drove it out across the Sacred Way and behind the temple of Venus. His horse skidded and slipped and balked at awnings.

Lubicana Way was clogging with merchants returning home. He took the back alleys—it was faster. There was Tranquilinus's house just ahead. Black smoke curled up through the atrium and boiled out the peristyle. Sebastian hauled in at the front gate and slid off. "Who's in charge here?"

One of half a dozen Guards snapped to attention. "I, sir."

"How many prisoners did you take?"

"We took four slaves alive, killed one, sir."

"Only slaves? There should be a wife and two sons here."

"We're certain no one escaped, sir."

"Name and rank," Sebastian barked.

"Pollitonus, sir, squad leader, first century, Third Cohort."

The boy's face, his expression—was Sebastian reading it right? The horse shook its head, spraying sweat. The bridle slipped a bit askew. "Here, soldier, help me."

The boy held the horse's nose as Sebastian rebuckled its

bridle. Sebastian casually struck an arc across the horse's lathered neck. The boy hesitated, then struck an opposing arc. Sebastian nodded, "That should do it," and patted his horse's neck on the sign. The fish disappeared.

He swung aboard. "Carry on, Pollitonus. If you do capture the wife and boys, send me word immediately. Sebastian, captain, Fifth Cohort. I have questions for them."

"Aye, sir."

They exchanged salutes, and Sebastian wrenched his horse around. Now where? Zoë's best friend lived two streets over. He tried that house. No one was home. He wished Prometheus were there to conveniently remove the gate. He called Zoë's name, called his own. No answer.

Where else? He paused on the corner to let his horse catch its second wind. Not only was it street shy, it was out of condition. *Stupid horse,* he thought irritably.

An old woman came trundling down the sidestreet, heading toward the villa of Tranquilinus. Sebastian left the horse where it stood and hailed her. She stopped, terror-struck.

"You're one of Tranquilinus's slaves."

"As you wish, my lord."

There were others in the street. He must take care. "Come with me, woman." He grabbed her arm and hauled her roughly to his horse. He led both out into the bustling, faceless Labicana Way. He drew the woman closer.

"Tranquilinus is dead, stoned by a mob, and his house is in flames. Marcus and Marcellian are safe so far. Where is Zoë?"

She stared at him wide-eyed.

"I am Sebastian."

"Sebastian!" Her eyes welled up. "Oh, my lord! They seized her. She was by the tomb of Saint Peter, in prayer for her sons. They arrested her, pulled her right up off her knees. I was a bit apart, so I stepped behind a pillar and fled. My lord Sebastian, can you help her? Surely you can."

"I'll do my best. Do you know which soldiers?"

"No, my lord. They all look alike to me."

"Which prison?"

"No, my lord, I'm sorry."

"That's fine," Sebastian assured her. "Do you have friends, a place to go?"

"Outside the city on Collatina Way..."

"It's getting late. I'll escort you to the Tiburtina Gate and let you out. Go to your friends. I'll send word when I can. Do the boys know this friend?"

"Yes, my lord."

"Come, then." Sebastian talked to her all the way to the gate, calming her shattered nerves. He could take all the time he wanted now. Zoë was lost.

As the lady lumbered off down the road, Sebastian spoke a word or two with the guards and turned toward the Esquilina Gate. He would send Prometheus out to find Caius; the shepherd must be sequestered in the fold. But Sebastian could not stay at the apartment, could not face the grief of Marcus and Marcellian—and Alyssa. She loved her in-laws as much as she loved Marcellian. How could God let her be hurt so much? How could He let this happen at all?

He arrived finally at his quarters well after dark; he paused outside his door. Light leaked out under the crack. Dexter must still be up. He pushed the door open. The mumbled speech inside ceased.

Dexter and Alyssa were sitting at the table. And Felician was with them.

The old man stood up. They embraced, but there was no joy. Sebastian hugged him one last time and let him sit. He himself plopped down in the only chair left, bone weary. "I'm delighted to see you, Felician. Now turn around and leave. I'll see you out the gate." He pulled his hot, sticky helmet off.

"You needn't bother, lad. There is no safety in Milan."

"Desmontes?"

"Alive when I left. But the church in Milan is next to gone. Sepio..." His voice stopped. He continued, "I came down seeking Caius. Now I find Caius gone. Not only he, but Tycho."

"Tycho and Caius are safe. We have them—"

"No they aren't." Alyssa's eyes, all puffy and red, were even sadder than they were that other night. "They're arrested, all of them. Someone betrayed Castulus and raided the apartment."

"Oh my God!"

"I think Maximian himself made the arrests, but I'm not sure. I was out in the garden, so I hid in the shrubbery and climbed the wall."

He felt his mind draining away. He must not lose it now. Think!

"All right, Alyssa. Who exactly? Who was there?"

"Castulus. Nicostratus and Claudius. Tycho. M... M...M..."

"Both boys?"

She nodded and sobbed again, a shuddering sob.

"Irene?"

"No. Marcus said he was going to go kill Sulla for ...for...and she went out to try to find you. She thought you could convince him not to."

"Primus was there when I left," Sebastian said.

"He went out right afterwards to help Prometheus find Caius. They were going to bring Caius back to the ap—" She stopped cold.

And they would walk right into a trap.

"I'll be back shortly." Sebastian swung the door open viciously, let the cool night air hit his face. He could empathize with Prometheus, unable to think quickly. He stood in the darkness and pictured a quiet fishpond in Milan. He pictured an insect falling in, the concentric ripples pushing out, the reflection of blue sky and clouds.

It didn't work. He couldn't think, let alone pray, could not speak to God. The Greater Mind must act on his behalf. He ambled casually over to the gate. The guards snapped to attention.

"At ease. Are you two the boys who let my guests in?"

"You, uh, seemed to approve the other time, sir."

"This time too. You did rightly. I just wanted to thank you.

What's moving out here tonight?"

"Nothing, sir, same as always."

"Your century was out looking for those people today. Any luck?"

"No sir. Might as well be in Britain for all we learned."

Sebastian leaned against the post. "I hear they made some arrests in the Guard itself. But I've been out most of the day. You hear anything like that?"

"No, sir. Are you sure? I can't imagine anyone in the Guard deserving arrest."

Sebastian forced a laugh. "If all the guards you know are pure and moral, we're not in the same army."

The boys laughed, winked knowingly, and elbowed each other in the ribs because you dare not touch an officer.

Sebastian left them. He could go down to the palace and hang about outside the apartment, hoping to intercept anyone who would be returning. Too late for that now. He could go over and warn Tiburtius. Why? The boy wasn't on the list and had no connection with Castulus other than common friendships. He should get Alyssa and Felician to safety, but where? Was he on the list now? Probably.

Perhaps in the morning he would choose some soldiers and try to spring as many prisoners as possible. He would not be able to reach Castulus, but he might be able get the boys out, perhaps Zoë and even Tycho. Were Primus and Prometheus in prison now? He could at least find that much out tomorrow. He disliked uncertainty and intrigue.

Just to make sure, he jogged over to Primus's barracks, to Prometheus's quarters. Of course they weren't there. He returned to his own.

Six eyes watched him enter. Six ears waited for his instructions. He didn't mind ordering a whole cohort about, but his decisions now would mean life or death to these, his closest friends. He stopped in the middle of the room. He couldn't even think where next to put his body.

"Felician, you and Alyssa can't stay here. If I'm marked they can come for me at any time. Quinn is in the Lancers now. You can spend the night over at the stables. No one will think to look for you there."

Alyssa stood up. "Do you think there's hope for Marcellian?"

"If not in this life, then in the next."

"I keep hearing that!" Alyssa cried. "Every person I've ever loved dies. I want to be able to touch someone today and know I can still touch him tomorrow if I want to."

Sebastian walked over and took her hands in his. "I'll probably be dead tomorrow. Touch me anyway. Remember the story of Hercules and the Hydra? Cut off one head and nine more sprout. It's the same with the church. They cut us down one by one, and we sprout new ones nine by nine. The severed head hurts but the body benefits. Serve Jesus, Alyssa. Be a willing member of His body, whatever God requires of you, and let Him take care of you in eternity. That's all that counts, you know. Jesus and eternity."

She pressed against him, so he held her close. "It's so hard to remember Jesus, Sebastian. Marcellian...he..." She allowed herself another of those soul-shuddering sobs.

"If Marcellian dies, he'll be waiting for you in paradise," Sebastian said. "None of our persecutors has that promise."

She sniffled a few moments. Suddenly she stood erect and giggled inanely through her tears. "Do you know, it's terribly hard to snuggle up to a man in a brass breastplate?"

"So I've heard." He hugged her close, pressed her head against his cheek. And remembered. "So I've heard."

Someone was thumping on his door. It couldn't be Alyssa or Felician. They weren't that strong. Guards, no doubt. His time was come. He rolled over, still too much asleep to fear. The door swung open and a hairy giant stood silhouetted against the blue-black false dawn.

"Prometheus...you're here." Maybe if he sat up he would awaken quicker. He struggled to untangle from his blanket in the dark. "Find a lamp. Bring fire, will you?"

"Thaleus is bringing fire," Prometheus told him.

"Thaleus!" Sebastian was awake.

As he swung his legs over the side, Thaleus paused in the doorway, his hands cupped protectively around a faggot. He crossed to the table and touched off the lamp.

Sebastian lurched to his feet, slumped into a chair, and scratched his heavy head. "What's going on, Prometheus?"

The colossus plumped down across from him. "Sit here, Thaleus. Bass, the world's coming apart. They raided Castulus, caught the whole bunch."

"I know. Alyssa got away. She's here. Did you find Caius?"

"Aye," Prometheus nodded. "What about Zoë?"

"They got to her first. Where's Caius?"

"Primus is taking him down to Catacumbas," Prometheus said. "We found Caius at Tiburtius's, along with Lucina. She's going to Catacumbas too. Tiburtius wasn't there. I was returning to the apartment when Thaleus here stopped me. He told me what had just happened. Bass, I would have walked right into it if it hadn't been for him. Then we found Primus and grabbed him before he went in."

"What about Irene?" Sebastian asked.

"We waited and waited for her and you. When the guards sealed the apartment we figured you were either safe or caught. Primus is going to smell around and see if we're marked. He expects to be here by first light."

"I don't know what to do," Sebastian said wearily. "You two have any suggestions?"

Prometheus snorted. "You do the thinking, remember? I bust doors." He picked up the lamp and walked into the back room. Sebastian heard him scratching around the shelves.

"There's half a loaf in that wooden box," he called.

The box lid thunked. The room lightened as Prometheus returned with the lamp and bread. Someone knocked. Prometheus left the lamp and bread to answer it.

"Excuse me, sir. A lady here to see the captain."

Sebastian called, "See her through."

"Aye, sir."

Thaleus wiggled his eyebrows. "A lady?"

"What kind of smart remark is that?" *Why can't I trust this fellow?* Sebastian wondered. Thaleus had just proved himself twice over. He had saved both Prometheus and Primus. And Sebastian couldn't even like him. "Thank you, soldier."

"My pleasure, sir."

Irene stood in the middle of the room with the whole world on her shoulders. She let her palla fall away. The gray eyes glistened luminous in the lamplight. "I didn't know where to go. Sebastian...?"

"I know." He crossed to her and she immediately pressed to him, her head on his chest. This was happening with astonishing frequency lately. Why couldn't it have happened in pleasanter times?

"I was out looking for you," she said. "When I came back they were just leading them out of the apartment. To prison. Sebastian, they have Castulus."

"I know. They missed Alyssa, though. She's here. So is Felician."

"Felician! What's he doing here?"

"Bringing news from Milan and looking for Caius," Sebastian told her.

She went almost limp against him. She surely had had no rest this night. "Sebastian, do you think Desmontes...I mean..."

"He was safe when Felician left."

Sebastian heard a clunk on the table. That would be Prometheus hacking bread with his sword. He closed his eyes, the warm and quivering body so close...

"Aha, lad! Just as I'd expect! A beautiful woman draped in your arms. I thought you were giving up on all that." Primus's voice lilted from the doorway.

Prometheus rumbled with his mouth full. "About time you got here. Want some bread?"

"Not now."

"Good." Prometheus chopped himself another chunk. He barely snatched the loaf aside in time as Primus slammed a musty ledger on the table.

"Thaleus, lad. Recognize this?"

"I'm ashamed to say I do. The ledger from Mamertine."

"Aye. Now we see who's here and who's not."

Sebastian's stomach was churning. How could Prometheus sit there and eat? But then, when you're stoking a furnace that big...

Irene pointed to her husband's name. "What's that little squiggle there?"

Primus shrugged. "Someone's initials. Bureaucracy, you know."

"But why?"

"I don't know, lady."

She latched onto his arm and turned him to her. "You do, you wily buzzard. You know everything of that sort."

Primus tried to meet her eyes and couldn't. He pulled his helmet off and threw it over on the pallet. "It means he's still officially in custody of the turnkey, but someone else has him temporarily."

"Who?" Irene demanded.

"The examiner, lady."

She took a deep breath and closed her eyes. Sebastian had always loved her. Now he admired her even more.

"Can you tell me more, Primus?" she said faintly.

"The squiggle you call it is Ferrus's mark. Ferrus is what you might say the chief in charge of torture. His speciality is the rack. But that's not to say for certain...I mean..." He walked over to the pallet and sat down with a plop. "This fuzzy old man talks too much."

Sebastian studied the ledger. Ferrus's mark stood beside the names of Zoë, Marcus, Marcellian, Claudius, and Nicostratus also. Usually prisoners languished awhile. Why was Ferrus getting them so quickly? Could they still walk if Sebastian were successful in reaching them? "Primus, do you know if we're marked?"

"I asked around. The best I have is no. Not yet. Especially not Thaleus. We ought to send him in ahead of us tomorrow morning to test the water."

Since he could not think, he would once again rely on impulse. "Prometheus, take Irene, Alyssa, Felician—Dexter too—he shouldn't be here with me—down to Catacumbas. It's the safest place available. Primus and Thaleus and I will try to spring as many as we can. We'll do some fancy forgery, phony transfers—whatever looks like it might work. You take care of these people. I don't think they can fend for themselves too well."

Prometheus nodded. "For how long?"

"How good are you at foraging? Enough to keep these people fed for weeks if need be?"

"Forage if I must, buy if I can," Prometheus replied. "Give me your purse."

Primus started rummaging. "I have a few sestertii too."

Prometheus stood up and sheathed his bread knife. "I know a few other purses I can tap for loans. I'll gather some things together. Where are the others?"

"With Quinn."

Prometheus took Irene's elbow on his way to the door. Beside her he looked very big and very protective. Sebastian felt better already.

Prometheus paused in the doorway. "May God preserve us." He disappeared in the blackness.

May God preserve us, Sebastian thought. *God grant us peace in this castastrophe. But what if God has other plans?*

16

Did Daniel walk into the lions' den under his own power, and if so, did it feel like this? Sebastian felt a certain security in having Primus at his side. Together they could vanquish the world. Still...

Nothing about the palace looked hostile or out of place as they strode up the long staircase. Thaleus had gone ahead a quarter hour before and had sent no warnings out. The two guards on horseback at the base of the stairs, the guards at the doors all saluted smartly and candidly. They were entering the massive, open doors as Thaleus came jogging out to them.

"They're onto us," Primus whispered.

Sebastian realized his hand was on his hilt.

Thaleus stopped close. "Ferrus hung three of them up as examples—hung them by the heels."

"Who?"

"That Marcus and Marcellian and their mother. Campus Martius by the sundial, apparently right after they were taken prisoner. They built a fire under the woman last evening and suffocated her. The boys are still there."

Sebastian's voice surprised himself. It was well modulated. "Peaches, get half a dozen archers out there as fast as possible."

Primus turned and ran down the stairs. Thaleus was calling to their backs, "They're under guard! You can't reach them!" But Sebastian was running down the staircase too, taking the steps three and four at a time. He saw Primus heading for one of the Lancers. Given sufficient motivation, even that old infantryman would take to horse.

It must have been the same boy as before on this nearest horse. The Lancer glanced back, moaned "Not again!" and slid off. Sebastian vaulted aboard and dug his heels in.

Part way up Flaminia Way, Sebastian's horse bowled over some gentleman in a bordered toga. Sebastian did not pause to enquire regarding the senator's disposition. Campus Martius by the sundial. Within sight of the peace altar. Right.

People in knots and groups were coming and going, shaking heads, muttering. Their casual disinterest sickened him. Out on the concourse three tall stakes were set. Zoë, suspended by her feet on the nearest, was turning black, her abdomen bloated. The fire beneath her head had burned to white-powder coals. Her hair once long was now a charred frizz on her scorched scalp.

The boys were nailed by the ankles, not roped. The dry blood traced black lines down their legs. Their faces were purple, their lips swollen. Marcellian's tongue bulged too big to fit his mouth. Their chests heaved periodically. Both alive yet.

A squad stood at parade attention, facing out, keeping spectators (and rescuers?) at a respectable distance.

Sebastian slid off his sweaty horse. "Who's in charge?"

"I am, Captain."

"Cut them down."

"I'm sorry, sir. I am under direct order from Pavo to respond only to his personal instructions. No one is to approach them, sir. Not even us."

Sebastian leaned against his horse and pulled his helmet off. "I figured as much."

Only a few moments more, boys. It is almost over. Your agony is nearly done. Caligae came stomping out onto the concourse double-time. Sebastian knew without looking it was Primus and his archers. He waved them over to him. Mauretanian Archers. The best.

"The guards are under orders not to move, and we're not permitted inside the line. Three on one between the guards. Line out."

The squad leader burst out, "Sir! This is not what Pavo intends, I'm sure."

"You just shut up and stand there and follow your orders like a good boy! Nock and draw!"

Six bows raised, six arrows shimmered.

"At will."

The agony ceased.

"Centurion, retire your archers." Sebastian swung up on his horse, dragged its head around, headed away from the concourse, away from the smell of blood and scorched flesh and singed hair that hung about the sundial.

He kept his horse at a walk. Shortly Primus came clattering up, hanging onto the mane of his mount with one hand. The horse fell in beside Sebastian's.

"If we weren't on the list before, lad, we are now."

"I am. You're not." Sebastian countered. "You were just following orders."

"I doubt Pavo will make that fine distinction."

"Did you recognize the squad?"

"No," Primus said.

"Then they probably didn't recognize you. How did you get there so fast?"

"I remembered target practice today in Domitian Stadium," Primus answered. "I just grabbed the first six I saw."

"You should be our next emperor."

"I wouldn't take that job if they doubled my pay." Primus looked so intensely uncomfortable Sebastian slid off his horse. The centurion slid off his gratefully. Impatient, Sebastian's horse waltzed its backside about and shook its head.

"Lad? You'll tell Alyssa?"

"Aye."

"Then you best tell Irene, too. They buried Castulus this morning. It's the talk of the cohort—archers told me."

Sebastian closed his eyes. "When did he die?"

"He didn't."

Sebastian stopped. His horse shouldered into him. "Even Ferrus wouldn't do that!"

"Twice stretched on the rack and still alive when they buried him. Pavo has a free hand and both Caesars behind him. Like you said, lad, it's just beginning."

"We'll split up. You get Tiburtius out of the city. If you have to bind him and load him on a wagon, do it. I'll go to Mamertine and see what I can do for the others, especially Nicostratus and Claudius. And Tycho."

"For once I disagree. Let's get Tiburtius on the road—he'll listen better to you than he would to me, anyway—and then hit Mamertine together. Two of us can cut our way out if need be. One can't."

Yes, Sebastian thought, *this man definitely must be the next emperor.*

The house of Tiburtius seemed so tranquil, so at odds with the holocaust around them. Sebastian always enjoyed its pleasant serenity, especially so this morning. This hideous morning.

By the peristyle fountain Tiburtius hopped to his feet in cheerful greeting. Didn't he know what was happening?

Sebastian's heart leaped and sank. "Felician! What are you doing here?"

"Delivering messages, which was my purpose in coming."

"Castorinus. Victorinus. You two picked the wrong time to come back to town."

"We're low on supplies out there, parchment especially." Castorinus beamed. "And papyrus, too. We're doing the short letters on scrolls, six to each. It's a glorious work, Sebastian! Just glorious."

"To be sure. But it's not glorious here. Tiburtius, Felician told you Tranquilinus was killed, I'm sure. And that the apartment was raided. We just turned our backs on the dead bodies of Marcus, Marcellian, and Zoë. Castulus is dead if God has any mercy at all. You four are leaving right now. Get out of town before someone connects you to the campania. Right now, Tiburtius. We'll—"

"Hold there!"

Sebastian wheeled and froze. He recognized the impenetrable cordon he had so often helped to forge: a trap, and he had walked right into it. He realized vaguely that his hilt was in his hand, his sword half drawn. He did not sheath it.

Pavo stepped forward. "My informer promised another big fish. I have suspected you for some time, Captain. But we miss your enormous aide. Where is he?"

"Ask your informer."

Sebastian sensed movement behind. Tiburtius had stepped in close to his right shoulder. Why?

"I can walk quietly to my slaughter like a nice, meek little lamb," said Primus, "or I can take you with me.... You devil!" He pivoted, sword in hand, not toward Pavo but toward the man behind Pavo. For the first time Sebastian saw Thaleus, saw the young man's sneering smile turn to cold terror. Thaleus was not a fighter.

Without thinking Sebastian lunged for the nearest—Pavo. A weight slammed into his back and knocked him aside. As he went down he saw Primus lurch forward, heard the centurion's iron breastplate clang against the tile.

A caliga mashed his neck down. The sword wrenched away out of his hand. What was the weight across his legs? The caliga lifted off his neck and he could raise his head. The body and toga of Tiburtius were sprawled across his legs, but the head lay several feet away.

Pavo was expounding on the nobility of giving one's life for a friend. Sebastian was on his feet again. The rest of the room dissolved into grey and formless background, made itself oblivious. There were only he and Primus in the world. The guard with the bloody sword had stepped aside. Sebastian pulled his helmet off and cast it away. Very gently he removed Primus's too.

He was not dead yet. In fact he was not even bleeding a great deal. Sebastian laid a hand on the bull-sized neck.

Primus smiled. "Foolish me. Forgot. 'Vengeance is mine, says the Lord.'" He coughed scarlet froth. "It's an honor to die in the queen of cities, lad, only if you're dying for...the King of Kings."

Sebastian waited for the pulse to disappear, the eyes to fade, before he stood up. "I hear you read some, Thaleus. Paul's writings?"

"Ludicrous philosophy. On the eve of his execution he's still talking about having the victory. Wearing crowns. Absurd."

"Ah, then you're familiar with his letters to Timothy." Sebastian caught Thaleus's eye and held it. "Greet Hymenaeus and Alexander when you see them."

Mamertine greeted them with its same clammy walls, same dank chill, same ticks and fleas. Castorinus was trying to explain how Tiburtius sensed the attack on Pavo coming and knocked Sebastian aside, taking the sword thrust meant for him, but the lengthy speech failed to register clearly. Sebastian was still seeing Primus turning white, the fuzzy cheek flattened against smooth tile made slick with frothy blood. He thought about that fancy Hydra speech he'd made to Alyssa. Was she right after all? Was this worth it?

Felician and he were conducted to the lower prison this time, where the only umbilicus between the windowless cell and reality was an air vent in the ceiling. The door grated shut on their six-by-six cell as two prisoners were dragged past into the next cell. Their legs hung useless, the shins smashed by a vice designed specifically for that purpose. As one remote, Sebastian recognized Nicostratus's face. He could not see the face of the other, but the build was Claudius's. Primus knew how to go.

He sat down in the dark on the floor and draped his arms over his knees. Felician's soft cloak settled close beside. The warm, soft arms wrapped around him and he around the warm soft cloak. And he cried a long time.

"Any idea what time it might be?" Even though his voice was nearly a whisper, Sebastian sounded loud in the darkness.

"No. Do you know when they feed you here?"

"It was late afternoon up in middle prison. Have they been yet?"

"You slept briefly, but I did not," Felician said. "They haven't come around."

"Felician, Castulus said there will be no rest until the very top is sympathetic. Maximian is co-ruler only as it pleases Diocletian. The man to reach is Diocletian."

"As a theory, adequate. In practice, however..."

"There was an affinity between him and me, a congenial—I don't know. I can't believe it's gone completely. You know, Felician, he might come around to the prison here. Not necessarily to talk me out of the faith; perhaps just to watch the torture. Or get inside information on why Christians should cling to Jesus in the face of this sort of thing. Maybe I'll get a chance to talk to him."

"This prison is very close to the imperial palace, is it not?"

"Very, if you cut through Trajan Forum."

"Mmm." The old man paused awhile. "I have heard—understand this is not scriptural—but I have heard that the apostle John was immersed in boiling oil somewhere around the south end of town here, and emerged unscathed. I also heard the incident occurred in Ephesus. I think if that happened to me, I would boil like any other chunk of meat."

"What does that have to do with us?"

"While I do not have the apostle John's faith, I aspire to it. But I do have his extreme age. I have no desire to be tortured to death, or even to have the opportunity to be miraculously spared."

"What are you saying?" Sebastian asked, perplexed.

"Between the two of us we just might be able to break you out."

"You mean give your life for mine? Tiburtius already did that. I'm having enough trouble with his sacrifice. No."

"Tiburtius died nobly," Felician reminded him. "And painlessly. If I were denied suffering I would not complain in the least. More important, do you not think that you might have been spared for a reason? Let us not second-guess God—or worse, play God."

"No. You might be freed."

"Nonsense and you know it. I have seen daylight for the last time. I believe you are correct. Reaching Diocletian is the only hope for a temporal peace in this world—the only respite from constant persecution. But I do not believe Diocletian will appear here. You must go to him."

"They will expect a fight from you, perhaps, but not from this doddering old man. You'll be surprised how weak I can look when I try. If I give you the opportunity, you must turn your back on me, break for freedom, and reach Diocletian."

"Do you realize what you're saying?"

"More than you do, I believe. I am not asking your opinion. I am an elder of the church issuing direct orders. You are to abandon me and run, and I will do my best to slow your pursuers."

Sebastian could not see his face in the blackness. He wanted to see the old man's face. "I don't think I can make myself turn my back on you and run."

"You can! I am going to be sacrificed in any event. Let us put that sacrifice to good, practical use."

Fatalistic, or immensely practical? Sebastian had no more time to consider the matter. A door creaked, and orange torchlight flickered at the far end of the passageway. Two burly, smelly men appeared at the cell door. "You boys are our next guests of honor. Come."

Felician stood shaking. His knees nearly buckled. Sebastian caught him, steadied him. The old man leaned heavily, scuffed one foot before the other. The two louts were unarmed save for the torch. The torch carrier was a baboonish man with grey chin-stubble. The real push-and-shover was nearly as big as Prometheus and hid behind a bushy red beard.

They made their way slowly down the passage and past the floor guard. Sebastian waited for Felician to make the move.

They climbed the stairs with extreme difficulty. Once in a while the brute with the red beard would shove impatiently, or the other would wave the torch at them. Breathing heavily, Felician paused at the top of the stairs. The middle floor guard stood by the stairwell, glanced at them, and turned away disinterested.

Redbeard pushed at Felician again and snarled some word of haste. The old man sagged against the wall. He looped his leg suddenly behind Redbeard's knees and pushed, toppling him backwards downstairs. His surprised yelp was cut short by the clunk of his head on stone. Felician grabbed the torch with both hands, twisted it—the baboon's hair was smouldering but Sebastian only smelled it, for he was diving for the guard.

He knocked the startled man flat, rammed his bare foot into his throat, and clanged his helmet into the stone. He yanked the helmet off, grabbed the fellow's hair and clunked him against the stone floor again. He gripped the corselet and rolled him over. At last he was armed, the guard's sword in his hand. It felt good.

He was sorely tempted to turn back to Felician, but he had his orders. He ducked down a side passageway and ran for the doors at the far end. He would be free soon if no one...He was halfway there when the big doors swung open. A massive, slouch-shouldered form paused briefly in the brilliant glare. Prometheus? And someone with him? The doors swung shut again and Sebastian could see the hulk's face. It couldn't be!

"Cannius!"

The beetling bulk stood cold, equally stunned. The prison guard beside him drew his sword and wheeled for the door.

"No!" Cannius snatched the guard's sword and backhanded him against the wall. He stomped his foot on the man's chest. "Go for help or interfere in any way and I'll decapitate you myself. *I* will deal with that man, do you understand? *I alone!*"

The guard shriveled, cowering.

Sebastian swung his sword up *en garde.* "I have no fight with you, Cannius."

The glowering face twisted into a half-smile. "That's what you think, provincial." He tugged his toga loose and swirled it around his arm, a makeshift shield. He feinted. Sebastian backed off. Cannius had always boasted of being the better swordsman and there was a time when he was. But Sebastian had since been the eager pupil of Castor. He realized he could use Cannius's overconfidence to his advantage.

"I don't give a hang about religion, provincial, yours or anyone else's. But when the killing started there was only one Christian in the empire I wanted to see dead, and you weren't in Milan. So I came to Rome directly. Thaleus told me you were here, and I was afraid I was too late. Obviously, I'm just in time. Just in time. This is delicious!" He feinted again. Sebastian backed away, hopping the still-prostrate guard.

"Fight me, you puny coward!"

"Believe it or not, I don't want to kill you, Marcus."

"Then let me tell you this. As I was leaving Milan I stopped by the praetorium. I talked to Victor Maurus himself. Told him where to find a fine library of forbidden Christian writing. Your uncle will no longer flout the law with impunity."

"Desmontes!" The anger exploded inside and Sebastian lunged at him. They locked hilts momentarily. Cannius twisted and thrust—Sebastian ducked barely in time. The sword tip clipped his sleeve. Cannius was laughing—a raucous, delighted, chortling laugh.

As Desmontes often said, *You rise to the bait too readily.* Sebastian must not let that happen again. Cannius would have killed him in that moment were he not playing cat and mouse. He must keep his head. Even more, he must pretend desperation—watch calmly inside, pretend frustration outside; frustration and near incompetence.

"Why, Cannius? Desmontes went out of his way to befriend you. Never once did he act against your best interests. Never."

The black face darkened further in the gloom. "Isn't that just grand of him! Because he's your uncle, that's why." He bore forward. Sebastian gave way. "You know what my father's like. How he treats the world. That includes his son, let me tell you. And my stepmother—both stepmothers. Even Melita has parents who care. She's a slut and they still care."

"So?"

"Why should you have two good families and I never have one? Why should you win every fight when I'm bigger and stronger? And better? Melita never let me near her until you went away and her parents insisted. Then it was my family connections—not me. Know what I heard for five years? 'Sebastian talked nicely to me.' 'Sebastian has a softer touch, you clod.' Even in our marriage bed, you black ass! You are less than I! And you have bested me my whole life! By deceit. By guile. With that snaky tongue. No more, you swine! No more!"

Cannius thrust forward suddenly in white fury. Had he been ready, Sebastian could have seized the opportunity. Another chance lost. *Wake up! Be ready!*

Desmontes kept intruding. *Desmontes. No, God!* Flames disturbing the gentle serenity of that house, smoke of burning books obscuring the sky reflections in the quiet fishpond...

"Why didn't you stay in Milan and take Desmontes's house as informer's spoil?"

"I don't need anything of that Gaul's."

"Couldn't be fear, could it? Like he told you, he's a formidable adversary."

"Afraid of him? Blood of Zeus!" Cannius lunged forward.

And Sebastian had his chance. A feint, a leap, a quick thrust. His hilt clacked into Cannius's. He pushed in closer and gave his wrist the double twist that was Castor's specialty. Cannius's sword rang as it struck the stone floor.

Wild-eyed, Cannius grabbed at Sebastian's sword arm. Sebastian chopped with his knee, caught the hulking swordsman square. Cannius fell backward, but Sebastian's fist in his throat cut his startled shriek short. Cannius was a fighter, but he was not a loser. His pride and fury faded behind a gray pall of cold terror. He was obviously not prepared to die, least of all by this man's hand.

Sebastian snatched up the second sword. "A few hours ago my best friend died trying to exact a vengeance that wasn't his. I've learned from his mistake, Cannius. You are spared in the name of my Lord Jesus, the Christ. I trust God to execute His own judgment for anything you've done against His servants."

Cannius raised his head, then dropped back with a strange, almost sobbing noise.

Sebastian wheeled on the guard. Did this churl have all his wits to start with? Probably not. The men chosen for guard duty in the prison depths were usually too dim for any other job. The guard stood with his hand on the door, totally perplexed. Sebastian waved a sword toward him. He understood that well enough. He backed aside, hugging the wall, staring rapt at the sword tip.

Sebastian hauled a door open and slipped through. The warm sun and fresh air stung his eyes. Felician. *I shall not see daylight again.* Felician's sacrifice must not be for nothing.

Desmontes. Might Desmontes, too, have escaped? Perhaps that elegant villa in Milan was still intact. Perhaps there were new owners—usurpers—but Desmontes was as wily and slippery as—no, wilier and *more* slippery than his enemies could anticipate. And his glib, clever tongue was quick enough to circumvent any calamity. Perhaps he was still at home, still being served by Sinister as always, still eating Bella's unimaginative cooking. Sebastian ran a hundred paces up a side street and disappeared into an alley.

He knew the palace grounds. He knew every door and wall, every window casement. He knew where the guards would be—and where they would not. What other useful advice might he have gained from Taurus, had he known him longer?

He looked at the sun; it was almost dinnertime. What would

Diocletian be doing now? He hopped the wall at the back gate, darted hunched-over to the kitchen annex. Now work along the south wall to the balustrade. Climb that large vine—careful, lest a trellis bar snap. Cross the balcony. This window opens into an unused storeroom. This one does not. He flattened against the wall by the window and listened.

The shutters were open. He heard muttering that sounded like Aggion. The door to the closet closed. The door at the far end closed. Was that someone entering or Aggion leaving? Silence. The closet door squeaked again.

Now!

He set a foot on the open windowsill, paused, and vaulted. The timing was excellent. Alone in the room, Diocletian wheeled to face him—stood transfixed ten feet from the tips of the two swords. Like Primus he could size up a situation instantly. The cold terror fled from his face as quickly as it had appeared. The face became noncommittal. His towel was still in his hands. He resumed drying, wiped his face.

Sebastian extended one sword slightly. "Go ahead and throw it. I'm ready."

Diocletian hesitated, then tossed the towel into a corner. "So. My favorite ingrate. Very well. Commit the ultimate act of ingratitude and run me through. In payment for Castulus? Or Primus? Or both?"

"They were faithful to you, Your Clemency. Loyal to a fault. You lost two of your best soldiers, not to mention the Theban Legion with six thousand men sworn to serve."

"Why all the talk? Do what you came to do."

"I came to talk." Sebastian took a step closer to the window and threw both swords out onto the balcony. He put himself quickly between the emperor and the doors. "I'm loyal to Caesar even if he did condone the murders of our mutual friends and mentors."

"I do what's best for the empire and with no apologies."

"You once told me in a tone of regret that you're a murderer. I supposed the blood of political enemies went with the throne. But not the blood of devoted followers who have never raised a hand against you. That's true murder—the death of innocents."

"Innocents!" His hand slapped the table. "Since you recall our conversations so well, recall my purpose in coming to the throne. I am not glory-hunting, take that or not as you will. This empire is on the brink of collapse, and the Christians are kicking out the last two props—one religion and one law. I intend to sit in this chair only long enough to set up a workable, manageable government."

"And then you'll retire and raise cabbage. I know."

Diocletian nodded. His voice dropped a notch. "The Christian cult denies any unifying religion and perverts the law. The new government is having enough trouble getting a firm start without that added difficulty."

"You're wrong, misled by some of those closest to you. Hear the other side. You can't run an empire without taxes. Jesus examined a coin, pointed to Caesar's face on it, and told us to render unto Caesar that which is Caesar's.

"Paul's letter to the believers right here in Rome says, 'Obey the law. The powers that be are ordained by God.' That includes you. And you want a unifying religion? The soldiers don't burn incense to the legati and tribunes and centurions—only to Caesar as head over all. Why worship Juno and Vesta and the lars and dozens of others when you can worship the one God that is God of gods and Lord of lords?

"Christians fill your coffers, serve the state, and are loyal to you—not to mention moral and law-abiding. Christians are the best citizens you could possibly have for your new, improved government. And because He promises to bless anyone who blesses His own, the supreme God is the only way your government will prosper. In fact, He says that unless He is in on the building of it, whatever you build is in vain."

Diocletian folded his arms and perched on the edge of his table. "You have always been a clever speaker, Sebastian. I admire that. I see in you many valuable traits I wish my Galerius possessed. That's why your ingratitude stabs so deeply—I had great plans for you." He raised his hand. "If you truly came to talk, let me speak as well.

"I knew, deep down inside, that you were a Christian ever since Thaleus pressed that suit. Incidentally, you've probably heard he has your captaincy now. Or perhaps you haven't, since Primus was your ears. Anyway, he's not stupid enough to haul that ledger in front of me and expect me not to examine it. He saw your name there and he saw your face in a cell.

"And yet, within a day or two you had not only broken prison, you had somehow altered the official roll. Now tell me. Is tampering with government records legal? For that matter, is jail-breaking legal? Does your Jesus teach you to obey the law or only to obey when it suits and erase the record to cover your illegalities?

"If you are loyal to me, why did you use my own archers this morning to thwart my wishes as expressed through my legatus Pavo? If Jesus teaches—"

"Your Clemency! You can't sit there and claim your wishes were to inflict such hideous agony on two boys!"

"Aye! As an example to others who might be considering this cult. If Jesus teaches you to obey the law, why do you belong to an illegal cult, itself an affront to the law? If Castulus is so loyal, why did he betray me in the matter of that list of state criminals—in his own apartment, no less. When your Christian friends are endangered, is your first loyalty to them as Christians or to me as the legal head of state?"

"You are misconstruing the ev—"

"I am not! I am stating the evidence. I have no use for religious double-talk. Christians are a practical threat to a government based on one law and one religion. They will be removed."

"They are *not* a threat! They're an asset, and given the chance, they can show you that to your satisfaction. Give us that chance! And are they being removed? Since the beginning we've been burned out, tortured, murdered—and why aren't we gone? Why are there more today than ever? Because our God is more powerful than anything in your Roman pantheon, that's why. Consider what God promises to them who turn to Him."

"I told you I have no interest in religious philosophies."

222

"Well I have interest in you. Jesus the Christ saves men's souls for eternity—even men who started their careers murdering the church—like the apostle Paul and you. Our God is truth, morality, mercy, and justice. Obedience in this life and glory in the next. These are all the goals of your improved government, and you can build your empire best by basing it on Jesus. And that's not to mention securing your eternal happiness as—"

The doors swung open. Aggion dropped his serving tray and ran out.

Diocletian waved a hand. "Our conversation is nearly ended. You have surprised me in many ways today. You consider me misled. I consider you misled, corrupted by the false leader of a false religion."

"Am I different now than what I was a year ago? You claim you discerned my religion even then. And yet you also claimed to believe me when you were talking about that list."

"I let my heart rule my head. It won't happen again."

"Then let your head rule! Your affection is not unrequited. I care for you. I'm going to an eternity of peace with God and you're going to a godless grave worse than Hades..."

The soldiers were there.

"...simply because you let people turn your heart against the Christ. Use your head! Investigate the writings and see how much solid evidence there is to support the Christ! Read His own words, not what others claim for Him. See for yourself..."

They were dragging him out the doors.

"...that He loves you. Don't let Nicomedia rob you of eternity and the just government you want so m—"

The doors slammed shut.

They were nearly through the reception room when the squad leader overtook them. "Hold. He's not going back to Mamertine. Caesar says he's too slippery to stay in it. We're to hold him right here under triple guard. I'm supposed to go find a certain six archers—somebody in the Mauretanian auxiliary. It'll take a while. Then we haul him up to the Campus Martius to be shot at sunset."

"It's a big campus, sir."

"They're supposed to use one of those stakes on the concourse, where they cut down the three bodies today. Hold him here."

"Aye, sir."

An iron breastplate clanked on the tiles across the room. A centurion crossed and helped the wobbly-legged guard to his feet.

"What's wrong, lad?" the centurion asked.

"I don't know, sir. I've been feeling dizzy all day—thought I was getting over it. I'll be all right."

"Go back to the camp."

"I think I'm all right, sir."

"I don't give orders twice, soldier."

"Aye, sir."

"Need an escort?"

"No sir. I don't think so." The boy wagged his head a little and walked out. Sebastian recognized him as he passed. It was the young squad leader he had met at the house of Tranquilinus: the Christian, Pollitonus.

17

Dexter felt miserable. He was still wet and shaky from running the length of the city. And Irene, beside him, was equally drained. The exertion did not seem to faze Prometheus a bit. It didn't help that Dexter had cried the whole way. Ever since Pollitonus and Quintillian had arrived at Catacumbas to fetch them, he had cried. He was cried out now—at least, he hoped so.

He stood between Irene and Prometheus in the shadows, watching the campus concourse. Irene adjusted her palla, shading her face in deeper gloom. She was recognizable. She must not be seen.

There was his master now, crossing the concourse in the midst of a squad of soldiers. Behind marched six archers. The news was accurate—Irene had feared a trap of some sort.

Now they were stripping his master, and Dexter knew Sebastian to be a modest man. His master was speaking, shouting even as they were roping him to the stake. Dexter strained to hear the words—he caught most of them. They were almost exactly what Stephen had said in the book called "Acts of the Apostles." Sebastian was forgiving them all. He was telling them the news of salvation, and forgiving them.

Dexter recognized with a shock the man in charge—he was wearing the captain's helmet that had once been Sebastian's. Thaleus. And his master was forgiving Thaleus too—forgiving that traitor with the hideous smile. Dexter's eyes burned hot again. He tried to pray and could not.

Thaleus yelped unintelligible commands. The soldiers fell away. The archers were lining up. *Please God, a miracle!* Dexter prayed as he discerned the arrow tips wavering a bit. The bows twanged as one. After dreading this moment for hours, Dexter found it somehow remote from reality. What he had imagined was not so quick and clean as this. His master relaxed and slipped quietly to the base of the rough-hewn stake. Behind Dexter's shoulder, Prometheus sobbed aloud.

Apparently Thaleus was now dismissing the archers. One of them hesitated, stepped up, and broke his bow across his knee. He dropped it at the new captain's feet and walked away. Another did the same. Four more bows snapped and fell. As one, the soldiers and auxiliary turned their backs on the captain and walked off.

Dexter started forward, but Irene grabbed his arm. Thaleus was walking over to the stake. He stood there long moments, staring down. Then he walked away, off the concourse, past the sundial, out of sight. The sun disappeared behind Janiculum.

Prometheus's bulk was much too obvious. He would remain in the shadows. Dexter and Irene would wrap the body and drag it off the concourse for Prometheus to carry to its grave. Since Alyssa's help was not crucial, they had left her at Irene's old apartment, just in case this was some sort of trap. They would stop by and get her on the way out to Catacumbas.

Irene stepped forward now and the plan was in action. She spread the shroud as Dexter cut the ropes. A snap startled him—another. She was breaking the arrows off.

She took the head, he the feet, and they dragged the rolled bundle across the concourse. Dexter had not expected it to be so heavy. And he had expected more blood than this. A dream. This was all so distant, like a dream. They were back in the shadows now. Irene whispered something in Prometheus's ear, urgently, then she ran off like a deer. No! Jesus was not sufficient for this moment. Dexter wanted her stability; he needed her. But she was gone before he could follow. The strain must have been too heavy for her—Castulus, and now his master, all in one day.

Tenderly Prometheus loosened the wrap around the head of the bundle. He scooped it up gently and lumbered off up the hill at a jog. Dexter could not see the need of hurry. As he followed the giant up the stairs to the apartment he realized what must be happening. Irene had discerned some imminent danger Dexter had missed. They would hide here a while before returning to Catacumbas. But why all the lamps if they were hiding?

Irene was already here in the apartment. Where was Alyssa?

"On the table there." Irene was ripping her palla into long thin strips. Alyssa pushed past Dexter, a water jar sloshing on her shoulder. Why was Prometheus unwrapping the body here in the apartment? Dexter did not want to see it.

"Prometheus, you're a master forager. We'll need more bandaging. This isn't enough. And I could use at least one more lamp."

"Be back shortly, lady." He hurried out the door.

"This one's bleeding worst. We'll start with it. Just put the bowl right there."

Dexter finally realized the twist this dream was taking. "Lady, you can't possibly save him! Even if he's still alive, wouldn't he be better off to die and be with Jesus? His wounds..."

226

"If God wanted him dead, he'd be dead. This isn't exactly what I prayed for, but it's a close second."

The shroud had fallen away over the edges of the table. These women knew his master was a modest man, and they were leaving him uncovered. They were working inches away from his most personal parts and they weren't even noticing. Didn't they realize...?

"Good, Alyssa. That's very good. Now let's go for that one in his chest. If it penetrated his lungs, we're done before we start."

Dexter pulled his cloak off, folded it precisely, and tucked it under his master's head. Even he could see the life now. His master's hand twitched. "Lady? Is there nothing I can do to help?"

"The best thing you can do is be his friend, Dexter. He'll need a friend this next hour."

Why do adults do that—say something like that to make you feel useful when everyone knows you're not? Dexter thought. He sighed and took hold of the clammy hand. The cold fingers tightened and clung to his. Now the women were working elsewhere. He stayed close to his master's head to avoid the embarrassment of seeing them so close to...His master convulsed, gasped. His head rocked back and forth. Dexter laid his free hand against his master's cheek. The cheek pressed against him. His master breathed heavily, swallowed.

"Dexter," Irene said, "he's going to lose his stomach. Keep his head turned well aside. It's important! He mustn't inhale any or he'll strangle on it."

Her prediction was accurate. Now how did she know that? The cold fingers squeezed tighter, hanging on as if to keep from falling. Perhaps this being a friend was not so useless after all.

The dreamtime solidified into practical reality. Dexter felt much better dealing in reality, however unpleasant it might be. By daybreak his master was feverish, by nightfall in delirium. The fever of typhus had left him simply comatose. Dexter was not prepared for this constant movement, muttering, flaying. Prometheus bound Sebastian's arms with a folded sheet to keep him from hitting Irene, who spent hours putting honey-water, a few drops at a time, between Sebastian's clenched teeth.

She lanced and drained the worst of the suppurating wounds. The apartment smelled strongly like dead rats. Reality began to weigh very heavy. Perhaps dreamtime had been easier.

Prometheus slept by day and prowled by night. Alyssa came and went. Irene stayed. Dexter ran occasional errands, but he hated to leave for even a moment. On the fourth day his master seemed a bit brighter, less restless. On the fifth the fever seemed obviously to be subsiding. Sebastian sent Dexter out to purchase writing materials, and Prometheus gave him three asses from a nearly empty purse. He returned with the supplies requested and two quadrantes change.

On the sixth day his master was able to sit propped up. He spread a sheet of parchment out in front of him. "Something I should have done long ago." Late in the afternoon, with a nap in the middle, he finished his writing.

He rolled the last of the sheets and beckoned Dexter over. "Pay attention here. Send this letter to Desmontes by private post. If he's still alive they'll find him. In it I'm asking him to give Sinister his freedom. Since Sinister belongs to him, it's the best I can do for you. Now this one gives you your freedom to—"

"Master!"

"...do with as you wish. Don't take it to the tablinarium here in Rome. Present it in Ostia where my name is not so poorly received. Now, while you're in Ostia..."

Dexter's heart thumped. "You're sending me there?"

"Just for these errands. You can be there and back in a day or two. Look, Dexter, you can't get lost."

"Master..."

"This one has three copies. I want you to deliver one copy each to the Matellus Warehouse, the grainbrokers' hall, and the Sheaf of Wheat brokers."

"Master, please. I don't want my freedom anymore. I want to stay with you."

His master settled back a bit, smiling. "Good! Please stay

with me. There's nothing I'd like better. Don't you think I will enjoy your company better as a freedman and my equal? Friends? I'm not sending you away—except tomorrow to Ostia, of course."

"Master..." For the second time that week he cried himself dry. But this time he could weep on the breast of his master, his friend.

Fog. Sebastian hated fog. Even under the best of conditions it invited claustrophobia. And now the cold and clammy air made his injuries ache. The five of them walked down the vertical canyons of brick apartment buildings and warehouses. The fog robbed him of perspective, even of his sense of direction.

"Prometheus, are you sure we're going right?"

"We're still on the Decumanus, Bass. Aye, here're the baths. We're right."

"Baths. Sounds wonderful. Laconicum. Warm."

Irene giggled. "Let's suggest to your friend that he needs a bath."

"Right. Sailors love getting wet—comes with the job. I just hope he's here. If he's been making grain runs he will have received at least one of my notes, but half the time he's ramming around some other place."

The water smell grew stronger, that unique smell that permeates the taste buds, that lurks in every serving of seafood, that tells you the sea is very near.

Dexter bounced beside Sebastian all excited. He had been here before. "I know where we are now, master! The wharves are right down this way. That's the grainbroker's hall there."

"Lead on, guide."

Alyssa romped ahead, matching stride for stride with Dexter. It was the first enthusiasm she'd shown since the raid on Castulus's apartment.

Irene clung to his arm. "I like Ostia, Sebastian. It's plain and solid. Good, honest, square brick houses. No ostentation."

"Some of the wealthiest people in the world live here."

"I know, and they don't flout it. It's compact. It doesn't ramble, like Rome. The streets are squared off nice and straight; you don't have to spend years learning your way around. Even Milan is all a-jumbly compared to this."

High buildings gave way to water lapping. A boat prow appeared in the gray. A second. They walked past one prow after another, peering into the mists.

"Well, praise His name. Here it is."

"Are you sure? They all look alike to me."

"I'd recognize that rail anywhere. I hung over it for three solid days. Of course, that Orion constellation painted on the bow helps. Orlestes?" Sebastian called. "Orlestes! Are you aboard?"

"Aye, lad!" A distant, muffled voice became stomping footsteps. The companionway slid open and yellow light dumped out into the gray fog. Orlestes emerged and hopped dockside. He pumped Sebastian's arm. "Saw your father just last month. Welcome aboard, all of you. Clio's fixing dinner and there's plenty."

Sebastian was getting very tired again. He could feel it coming on rapidly. He leaned on the rail, that Alyssa might precede him. If he stepped on a deck with trepidation, she was worse. He suddenly realized she had never even seen a large boat before.

Belowdecks he plopped into the first seat he found (which he suspected was Orlestes'; he didn't ask), arranged his protesting body as comfortably as possible, introduced everyone all around, and wished he were soaking in a hot bath. "Orlestes, if a Christian wanted to hide away, where would you recommend?"

"I recommend the Christian just turn himself over to the army and save everyone a lot of trouble." He snapped around to stare at Sebastian. "All the water in the sea, lad! Not you!"

"Not the province or Northern Gaul," Sebastian said, ignoring his remark. "Not Spain. Certainly not Asia Minor or Palestine. How about North Africa, maybe the west end of Mauretania?"

"There's no safe harbor for those atheists, but the empire's power is weakest in Britain and Germany."

"How would you get to Britain?"

"Sail out to Gades," Orlestes told him, "pick up a coaster going north."

Sebastian loosed his purse and flung it onto the table. He closed his eyes until the sudden stab of pain subsided. "Passage for four to Gades?"

Orlestes dumped the purse out and poked through its coins. "Is this all you have?"

"Aye. Prometheus here has a purse, but that would be to go north on."

Orlestes dropped an aureus back into the poke and tossed it to him. "I'll not take your last coin. What's here is sufficient for passage for four, but there's five of you. Who's not going?"

"I'm not."

"You gave me a start, lad. I thought for a moment there that you were one of—ah, of them."

"I am. I'm just not going. Orlestes, friend of my father, you suffer from the same misconceptions of the faith I used to have. I wish you could talk to Desmontes. Aye, Desmontes. He's been a Christian for years. And while we eat dinner I'll show you what I've learned about the cult."

It was dark when he left the *Star in Orion*, a soft and swirly dark. He was off the gangway when Irene came running down. Why was she doing that? He wanted the break to be clean and painless.

"Sebastian, please!"

"We're done talking about it, remember?"

"But there isn't any hope. Remember what Jesus said? Even if a man came back from the dead they won't listen. And that's exactly what you're trying to do. When He was telling them about the rich man and Lazarus in—"

"I know. Luke's gospel. Look, I'll wait at least another week, until I can run, but I—"

"Be reasonable! You weren't successful the first time. He got his message. You have a whole new life ahead."

"Irene, stop it!" The words were hard coming. The weariness had returned already. Why was he saying all this again? It had all been said to Prometheus, to Dexter, to her. "Two Jewish prophets preach to Nineveh. Nineveh repents for Jonah and ignores Nahum. Does that mean Nahum wasn't successful? No. He was. He preached the word as it was revealed to him, in good faith. It was up to Nineveh to listen. Diocletian may not convert, but he might reconsider and stop the murder."

"Because Felician sacrificed himself."

"Because of everybody. Desmontes, you, a thousand believers we've never met. I couldn't just hide away my whole life wondering if one more confrontation might have persuaded him. Right now I'm the only one who can bring the word to him. I promise I'll keep an escape route open, all right?"

She laid her head on his shoulder. "Would it do any good to tell you I love you? I really do, Sebastian. I'm not just saying this to dissuade you. I really do."

He tipped her face up. "I have always loved you, Flower, and I always shall." He kissed her—a warm, firm, honest kiss. "Wait for me. But don't wait too long."

He left her quickly, lest his own resolve break down. Why had he said that last? he wondered. He knew he would never see Britain.

Sebastian was dead and Sebastian reveled in the fact. So long as he did not frequent any place where he might be recognized, he could enjoy a semblance of normal life. He remained in Ostia four days, spending his time napping, walking the straight and orderly streets, soaking in the baths, prowling the sea- and river-fronts.

He had barely made it down here with Prometheus and Irene's help. He must have more strength than this to get back. It was the eve of the fourth day before it dawned upon him that for less than a sestertius he could ride to Rome on a river barge. The next morning he stepped onto still another deck.

River barges being towed upstream do not need milestones. The distance from Rome can be measured by the amount and smell of sewage in the water.

Irene was right. Ostia stood solid—trim and orderly. Milan bustled about in a conservative way—aloof. Raucous, ribald, wretched Rome stood alone in her charm and filth, a godless city full of temples, a wealthy city full of slums, a sprawling and desultory city that ruled the most orderly empire the world had ever known.

She waxed gluttonous on the flesh of those slaughtered in her amphitheaters and was never satisfied. She flung herself across her hills drunk with the blood of martyrs and getting drunker by the hour. This was foolish. Stupid. The squalid and glamorous city beckoned him as she had called Peter and Paul before him—a siren ever thirsty for more blood. She would take his and give in return nothing other than the honor of dying in her. He was resigned to that now. If only he could reach Diocletian, to touch the heart and mind of Caesar!

The barge bumped into a piling in a casual sort of way. Sebastian leaped ashore before she tied up. He knew these docks and warehouses. He was just upriver of the Aemilia Gate. He crossed between the walls on the south side and left town through the Appia Gate. He wanted to meet and worship again with whatever believers remained, to hear the news. Catacumbas was the place to find them.

Three days later, swathed in a gray cloak, he slipped through a wall by the fallen oak on the west side of the palace. He waited by the back staircase, near the garden gate. He thought of Primus and Tiburtius, who had died easily. Would Castor have survived typhus had he not been imprisoned? Marcus and Marcellian, purple heads and black tongues; Zoë, frizzy black and smouldering; Castulus; Nicostratus, Claudius, Castorinus and Victorinus, all thrice tortured and then drowned, their feet chained to rocks. No one knew for certain what had been done to Felician. Who said Romans were unimaginative?

The doors opened at the top of the staircase. Diocletian paused in the doorway talking to a senatorial toga. The toga followed him out onto the portico. Sebastian would prefer to meet him without guests, please, God. They talked, nodded; the toga disappeared back inside. With his easy, ambling stride, Diocletian started down the staircase, giving some lengthy piece of instruction to a faceless aide. He was growing lax in his old age. What was he now, forty? Forty-one? Sebastian wondered. Were Sebastian an assassin he would be dead in moments.

Sebastian stepped out. Diocletian may have been caught off guard, but the aide had sufficient presence of mind to spring between them. Sebastian backhanded him into the bushes before he could raise his own arms in defense.

"I want to talk to this man who rules by reason." Sebastian dropped the hood of his cloak. Diocletian stood stone still, staring.

"Zoë, the wife of a man who paid nearly twenty thousand sestertii in taxes last year, was hung by the heels and smothered by fire," Sebastian began. "Tell me how that served the empire. How did denying her burial serve? Not as example, surely, since only a few Christians knew it happened. The torture inflicted on your own chief of armies wasn't publicized, so how could that serve as an example to anyone?

"Don't tell me you're doing what is best for the empire. You're doing whatever appeals to Diocletian. What's worse, you're letting your underlings—aye, and your wife and son—do your thinking for you. You're inflicting pain and death on the very people who can make your dream-government work, just because your wife happens to like Persian gods."

He pushed in closer. The aide, groggy, was trying to disentangle himself from the hedge. Diocletian was still dumbstruck. He had moments, yet.

"God has called you to salvation through His Son, Jesus," Sebastian implored. "Neglect that salvation at your peril if you will. But for the love of all that's holy, give up this 'best-for-the-empire' fiction and start acting in the true best interests of the empire. If you must murder innocents, at least refrain from these hideous tortures that avail nothing. If you must eliminate Christians, why not just banish them to some country you don't like? They'll go. Confiscate their property for the state if you must, since they won't be around to pay taxes any more. But

234

stop proclaiming your inane cruelties to be in the best interests of your empire! Your pogroms are senseless, and they will eventually incite rebellion in those people with the common sense to see through your insane bloodlust."

"I was there...watching...I saw you." The emperor's mouth trembled.

"The faith is growing faster than any effort you can put out to destroy it. Accept reality! If you hope to build a lasting structure on a foundation of stupidity like you've been displaying so far, you're an asinine fool!"

"How can you speak...say those things!" Diocletian was stuttering.

"How can you engage in these outrageous cruelties and label it anything other than what it is—thoughtless barbarity and the empire be damned? The most powerful man in the greatest state the world has ever seen must act from wisdom, not the groundless religious prejudices of his wife and son! Stop and *think*, Your Clemency!"

The guards were coming down the stairs now. He had told Irene he would run when it got hot...and yet...he was striking somewhere close, he could tell.

"You like the title 'Your Clemency'. Start living up to it," Sebastian pleaded. "For the best interests of your empire, relax your cruelties and persecutions against the supreme God's people..."

The guards were dragging him down. They were much quicker than he had anticipated.

Diocletian's lips struck a thin blue line across his white face. "Arrows weren't b-b-big enough," he stammered. "Club him down. Club him down! Make sure this time. Then throw his body in the sewer. There will be no further r-r-resurrections. Not for this m-m-man."

Sebastian tried to wrench around to his feet, but he was being dragged by one leg. He tried to call out a parting word, but another guard was hauling him along by the neck. They were dragging him downhill past the flower beds. For some reason

Diocletian fancied flowers there. In all the years he had been in Rome, nothing beautiful had come of it. But the stakes were up again to keep unappreciative feet from trampling the new growth. They were big stakes this time—a good three feet long—to provide a greater deterrent, perhaps; or a stronger example for the flowers.

A guard yanked out four of the stakes as they passed. His head would roll for that. Belatedly, Sebastian realized why he had done so. They dropped him beside the duct that opens eventually into the Triumphalis line. He had been prepared for death when the archers faced him. No one had been more surprised at the outcome of that than he.

But this time? He would not survive this one. Peter and Paul had died speaking out for God. That was their honor. It would be his.

The guard's grip on his throat had left him voiceless. He forgave them in his heart, but he could not speak it. And Diocletian. Tormented, admirable in so many ways, careful in certain respects, boundlessly cruel and blind in others—Diocletian must be forgiven also. One of the flower stakes came whistling at him with another close behind.

Literature dating back to AD 350 testifies to the double martyrdom of Sebastian, as well as to the fates of the Theban Legion, Zoë, Tranquilinus, Primus *et. al.* According to that literature, Lucina recovered Sebastian's body from the sewer (guided by a vision, some say) and buried him *ad Catacumbas* near the temporary repository of the remains of Peter and Paul.

Once the name of that burial system only, *ad Catacumbas* has come to mean any and all such systems. There are seven catacombs in the immediate area of Sebastian's internment. His is now in the Catacombs of Saint Sebastian. The nearby gate in the Aurelian Wall, once Porta Appia, is today Porta Saint Sebastian.

What is truth and what is legend? An accretion of myth often blankets the facts about strong personalities in the early church. The facts of Sebastian's life may be obscure, but the reality of pain and death are not. The church was born in blood, and she will be translated in blood.

"Persecution" and "torture" are not words relegated to history. As the end approaches they will become as personal to us as they were to Sebastian. The tide will turn. We must be prepared.

GLOSSARY

As, short for *asserion*, a copper coin. See Money Equivalents.

Aureus, a gold coin of great value. See Money Equivalents.

Breastplate, called cuirass in later years, was the armor covering a soldier's front from collarbone to waistline. Depending on his rank, a soldier might wear one of leather, iron, or brass.

Caliga, plural caligae; soldiers' footwear. Heavy as boots, they laced much like high-top shoes but were open in front (no tongue or closed toe). The emperor Caligula was given his nickname when he was very small: "Little Army Boots."

Calliope, one of the nine Muses, daughters of Jupiter and Mnemosyne (Memory). Calliope, the Muse of Epic Poetry, was known less reverently as the muse of the whopper.

Century, a military unit of one hundred men presided over by a centurion.

Cerberus, a monster guarding the gates of Hades (hell), portrayed as a dog with three or more heads and a serpentine tail.

Cithera, a stringed instrument; a zither.

Cohort, a military unit of one thousand men (ten centuries or five maniples).

Corselet, a mini-skirt of heavy leather strips that was basic uniform attire for military personnel.

Diana's Stone, a stone that Diana, goddess of the hunt, "sent" to Ephesus; just dropped right in on them. The stone was venerated, a magnificent temple, one of the seven wonders of the ancient world, was built on Diana's behalf. (Paul tangled with its priests in Acts 19:23-41.)

Greaves, metal wrap-around shin protectors worn by soldiers. "Dress" uniform greaves could be quite fancy.

Ides, one of the three units of the monthly calendar by which Rome reckoned her days. Ides fell upon the thirteenth day of most months, but the fifteenth of March, May, July and October. Romans counted days backward from the calendar points; for example, "three before ides, two before ides..." See *Kalends* and *Nones*.

Kalends, the first day of a given month. After ides passed, Romans counted the days before the next month's kalends. Thus March 16, one day after ides, is "17 before kalends."

Jugerum, a land measure of about ⅝ acre, and determined as the squared area a yoke of oxen might reasonably plow in a day.

Lars, the spirits who oversaw smooth operation of the household, from the roof down. They were worshipped daily, albeit briefly, at an altar to that purpose, the lararium.

Legion, a military unit of six thousand men.

Maniple, a military unit of two hundred men; that is, two centuries.

Mulsum, a fermented beverage, the common everyday drink. (In fact, the Romans fermented a lot of things we'd never think of—fish entrails, for instance, to make sauces.)

Nones, nine days before Ides. Considered the fifth day of most months, the seventh day of March, May, July and October. See *Ides* and *Kalends*.

Pauldrons, a soldier's armor protecting his shoulders; of metal, usually iron, and leather.

Plaustrum, plural plaustra. A big, heavy freight wagon.

Quadrans, plural quadrantes; One fourth of an asserion or as. A pittance indeed. (The widow's mite of which Jesus spoke in Mark 12:42 was two lepta, equalling one quadrans.) See Money Equivalents.

Quaestor, the Roman magistrate dealing with state or military finances. His work space was a quaestorium.

Squad, a military unit of six men.

Sestertius, a coin worth 4 asses or asserions; a middle-value piece in the monetary system. See Money Equivalents.

Vesta, the goddess of hearth and home.

Money Equivalents

2 LEPTA = 1 QUADRANS   4 QUADRANTES = 1 AS or AS-SERION
4 ASSES = 1 SESTERTIUS   4 SESTERTII = 1 DENARIUS
25 DENARII (silver) = 1 AUREUS (gold)